On your Side

CW01522179

Microsoft Project 2000

ENI Publishing LTD

500 Chiswick High Road
London W4 5RG

Tel: 020 8956 2320
Fax: 020 8956 2321

e-mail: publishing@ediENI.com
http://www.eni-publishing.com

Editions ENI

BP 32125
44021 NANTES Cedex 1

Tel: (33) 2.51.80.15.15
Fax: (33) 2.51.80.15.16

e-mail: editions@ediENI.com
http://www.editions-eni.com

On Your Side collection directed by Corinne HERVO
Translated from the French by Andrew BLACKBURN

*This is a book for anyone who uses **Microsoft Project 2000**.*

It is designed so that you can look up the task you want to perform and find a clear description of how go about it.

*The screens illustrated throughout these pages add to the efficacy of the explanations, by showing the dialog box corresponding to a particular command, or by giving a precise example. This book is made up of **ten** parts:*

Managing projects
p. 1 to 17

Basic rules for using the software, including how to start the Project 2000 application and how to work with its toolbars.

Documents
p. 18 to 35

Techniques for managing project files that have been created in Project 2000 (such as opening, saving, closing and creating) along with handling template files and workspace files.

Projects
p. 36 to 59

The set of commands that allows you to schedule and to manage the different elements of your project, by linking or consolidating several projects and by sharing resources.

Viewing and printing
p. 60 to 89

The main views of Project 2000 (Gantt Chart, Network Diagram and Calendar views), together with printing and page layout techniques.

Tables
p. 90 to 105

The set of commands that allows you to manage tables, cells and filters.

Task driven projects
p. 106 to 144

How to create, link and manage tasks and milestones.

Resources
p. 145 to 179

The set of commands that allows you to assign and manage work and material resources, along with techniques for modifying and optimizing resource assignments.

Costs and work
p. 180 to 192

Techniques for managing the different costs involved in a project and the workload generated by tasks.

Tracking
p. 193 to 214

Commands for tracking projects, tasks, resources, costs and overall work.

Communications between workgroup members
p. 215 to 255

Setting up the communication methods that allow workgroup members to exchange messages, using two basic techniques: by E-mailing and using Microsoft Project Central.

Microsoft Project 2000

The **appendices** contain a list of the principal fields as well as details of the toolbars and shortcut keys available in Microsoft Project 2000.

The final pages of the book contain an **index** of the topics covered, where you can look up the information you need, and a section on the **menus**.

Typographic conventions

To help you find the information you require quickly and easily, the following conventions have been adopted:

bold indicates the option to take in a menu or dialog box.

italic is used for notes and comments.

 represents a key from the keyboard. When two keys appear side by side, they should be pressed simultaneously.

The following symbols indicate:

♦ an action to carry out (activating an option, clicking with the mouse...).

❏ a general comment on the command in question.

 a useful tip.

 a technique which involves the mouse.

 a keyboard technique.

 a technique which uses options from the menus.

MANAGING PROJECTS

DOCUMENTS

PROJECTS

TABLE OF CONTENTS

VIEWING AND PRINTING

Microsoft Project 2000

TABLE OF CONTENTS

TABLE OF CONTENTS

APPENDICES

Microsoft Project 2000

A definition of project management

♦ A **project** can be defined as: "a unique endeavour that implements human, material, or service resources in order to achieve an objective within a fixed time-limit".

♦ This definition covers most of the questions that you must ask yourself when you are planning a project:

"... achieve an **objective** ...":   What must we do?

"... implements **resources** ...":   With whom and with what must we do it?

"... within a fixed **time-limit** ..."   For when must we complete it?

♦ In addition, there are two other important questions:

– What budget has been allocated for this work?

– What happens if we deliver the project late?

♦ When you have answered these questions, you are ready to manage the project. Managing a project consists of planning, organising, and managing tasks and resources, in order to achieve the defined objective, within defined constraints of time and money.

Techniques of project management

Managing a project involves applying a certain number of techniques.

♦ In 1917, Henry L. Gantt, an American engineer who worked for Frederic Taylor, had to organise the production of a workshop. In order to do this, he developed a graphical system that represents tasks on a time scale. This system became known as the **Gantt Chart**.

Week 1					Week 2				
Mo	Tu	We	Th	Fr	Mo	Tu	We	Th	Fr

Task 1

Task 2

Task 3

♦ In the 1950s, the Dupont Corporation, and Remington Rand Univac were researching techniques of managing large numbers of inter-related tasks. In the course of this program, in 1956/1957, Morgan Walker and James Kelley developed a calculation algorithm that they called **CPM** (**C**ritical **P**ath **M**ethod).

This method allows you to calculate the total duration of a project according to the duration of each task in the project, and the dependencies between them.

♦ In parallel with CPM, the US Navy developed the **PERT** (**P**rogram **E**valuation and **R**eview **T**echnique) for the implementation of its Polaris program. This technique provides a graphical representation of the dependencies between the different tasks of a project.

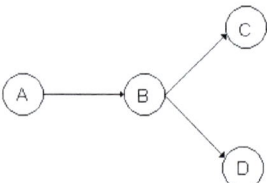

♦ In 1958, the CPM (which was now known simply as the **Critical Path**) was combined with the PERT. According to these calculations, any change in the duration of a task situated on the critical path will result in a change in the finishing date of the project. The US Navy considered that it was the use of these techniques that enabled them to complete the Polaris project in 5 years, instead of the 7 years that were initially planned.

♦ Today, all three of these techniques are combined. A Gantt Chart can show the dependencies between tasks in a **PERT** network, and it can also show the **Critical Path**, which is calculated according to the CPM.

Planning a project

Why plan?

♦ Planning requires time, precision and experience. However, it is a crucial factor in the success of a project.

Planning is carried out before the project is launched, and it shows how the project manager wishes to achieve the objective.

The plan does not show what will happen. It shows what the project manager would like to happen. One of its purposes is to allow all the people who are concerned by the project to see what should happen, and when and how it should happen. As a result, it allows each of the project actors to understand his or her precise role in the project.

♦ Planning is useful only if the plan is updated regularly.

Key planning steps

♦ Step 1: Draw-up the list of tasks and milestones.
Step 2: Determine the dependencies between the tasks.
Step 3: Estimate the length of time that each task will take.
Step 4: Construct the task network diagram.
Step 5: Optimise the task network diagram.

Listing the tasks and the milestones

Defining a task

♦ Defining a task consists of describing the work that must be carried out in order to obtain a precise result.
For example, a task could be: writing the user manual for a piece of equipment.

♦ In order to carry out a task, you must assign it to one or more **resources**.

♦ The more detailed and precise the description of your task, the easier it will be to estimate the **resources** that you will need to carry it out. Consequently, you must not hesitate to break a task down into two or three smaller tasks. On the other hand, you must not introduce more detail than is necessary.

Here is an example of the levels of detail for a task description:

Not detailed enough	Reasonable level of detail	Too detailed
Users manual	Write Set up Proof	Write Introduction Write body of document ...

Defining a milestone

♦ A milestone is an interim goal that indicates the progress that has been made on the project.
For example, a milestone could be an external event that marks the completion of a phase of the project.
A milestone is represented by a task of zero length.

♦ Every project must have a starting milestone in order to identify the start of the project, and a finishing milestone to identify the end of the project.

Dependencies between tasks

Definitions

♦ A **link** is a dependency between two tasks. It indicates when a task must begin, or end, with respect to another task. Generally, a link will have a duration of zero.

♦ Microsoft Project 2000 provides four types of task dependency:

Finish-to-start (FS)

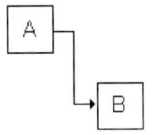

Task B cannot start before task A finishes.

Start-to-start (SS)

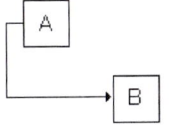

Task B cannot start before task A starts.

Finish-to-finish (FF)

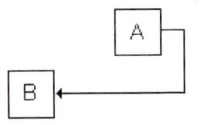

Task B cannot finish before task A finishes.

Start-to-finish (SF)

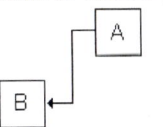

Task B cannot finish before task A starts.

*Task A is called the **predecessor task**, and task B is called the **successor task**. In practice, 90% of links are of the "finish-to-start" type, and the least common link is the "start-to-finish" type.*

Techniques for defining links

♦ Each task is assigned a unique number that corresponds to the number of the row on which it appears in the Gantt chart.

♦ For each task you must ask yourself the following question: in order to start this task, which other task(s) must have started, or have finished?

♦ With the exception of the starting task, and of external tasks, every task must have at least one predecessor task.

Working out the duration of a task

Description of task duration

♦ The **duration** is the length of time between the **start date** and the **finish date** of the task.

♦ The duration of a task will depend on the amount of work involved in the task, and the available capacity of the resources that are assigned in order to carry out the task.

Estimating the task duration

♦ You should base your estimation on personal experience, and on the experience of others, such as experts in the field concerned. In addition, you could apply the **beta law**:

♦ For each task, determine the three following durations: the best-case duration (D_b), the worst-case duration (D_w), and the most probable duration (D_p).
Then, calculate the "average" duration (D_a), as follows:
$D_a = (D_b + D_w + 4*D_p)/6$

♦ Choose a measurement unit that is convenient, and appropriate for the task concerned.

**Constructing
the network
diagram**

Representing your data graphically

♦ You should represent your data graphically in the form of a PERT chart (task diagram). Tasks are presented in boxes and arrows represent the links between them.

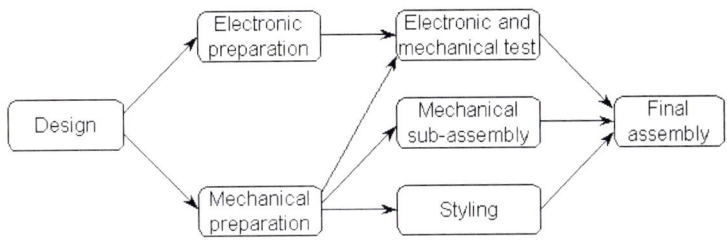

Calculating the total duration of the project

In order to calculate the total duration of the project, you must first take out all milestones, and then you must follow two phases:

♦ Phase 1:
In the first phase you must calculate the earliest start date for each task. In most cases you can calculate these dates using the links alone.
When a task has several predecessors, you must use the predecessor that finishes at the latest date.

Num.	Task	Pred.	Duration	Earliest start date (begining of week)	Earliest finish date (end of week)
1	Design		18 weeks	1	18
2	Electronic preparation	1	30 weeks	19	48
3	Mechanical preparation	1	20 weeks	19	38
4	Electronic and mechanical tests	2;3	50 weeks	$49^{(i)}$	98

5	Mechanical sub-assembly	3	45 weeks	39	83
6	Styling	3	35 weeks	39	73
7	Final assembly	4;5;6	22 weeks	99	120

(i) The tests cannot start until both of the preparation tasks are completed. As one of these preparation tasks finishes at the end of week 38 and the other finishes at the end of week 48, the tests can start only in week 49.

♦ Phase 2:

You must start from the **project finish date** and move backwards in time in order to calculate the **latest** start and finish dates for each task.

♦ This technique allows you to determine the date on which each task must be completed, in order to avoid making the project late. These calculations are easier to carry out if you add a successors column. When a task has several successors, you must use the successor that starts at the earliest date.

Num.	Task	Duration	Succ.	Earliest start date (beginning of week)	Earliest finish date (end of week)
1	Design	18 weeks	2;3	1	18
2	Electronic preparation	30 weeks	4	19	48
3	Mechanical preparation	20 weeks	4;5;6	29	48
4	Electronic and mechanical tests	50 weeks	7	49	98
5	Mechanical sub-assembly	45 weeks	7	54	98
6	Styling	35 weeks	7	64	98
7	Final assembly	22 weeks		99	120

**Balancing
the task network**

*When you balance the task network, you should take into account
an important concept: that of slack time.*

Definition of slack time

*Slack time is the amount of time that a task can slip without
affecting the dates of another task, or the end date of the project.
You must distinguish between two types of slack: **total slack** and
free slack.*

♦ Total slack is the amount of time that a task can slip without
affecting the finishing date of the project.

Num.	Task	Earliest start date	Latest start date	Total slack
1	Design	1	1	0
2	Electronic preparation	19	19	0
3	Mechanical preparation	19	29	10
4	Electronic and mechanical tests	49	49	0
5	Mechanical sub-assembly	39	54	15
6	Styling	39	64	25
7	Final assembly	99	99	0

The total slack for each task is the difference between the earliest
start date of the task, and the latest start date of the task.

♦ Free slack is the amount of time that a task can slip without
affecting other tasks (or in the case of a task that has no successor, without affecting the finishing date of the project).
The free slack for a task is the difference between the earliest
finish date of the task, and the earliest start date of the earliest
successor.

Num.	Task	Earliest finish date	Earliest successor	Earliest start date of earliest successor	Free slack
1	Design	18	2 and 3	18	0
2	Electronic preparation	48	4	48	0
3	Mechanical preparation	38	5 and 6	38	0
4	Electronic and mechanical tests	98	7	98	0
5	Mechanical sub-assembly	83	7	98	15
6	Styling	73	7	98	25
7	Final assembly	120	-	120	0

♦ The sequence of the tasks that have total slack of zero is called the **critical path**. Any change in the duration of one of these tasks will have a direct effect on the finish date of the project. These tasks are called **critical tasks**.

Checking the overlap or the time gap for a link

♦ Tasks can overlap each other, or can have a time gap between them. Task overlap is known as a **lead time**, and a time gap between tasks is known as **lag time**.

♦ An example of **lead time**: you may be able to start the manufacturing phase one week *before* the end of the design phase.

♦ An example of **lag time**: you need to apply the coat of varnish to a set of articles one week *after* they have been painted.

Time management using calendars

♦ In order to plan tasks, taking into account times, resources and groups of resources, Microsoft Project 2000 uses several types of calendar. Each type of calendar is associated with a different element type, such as tasks or resources.

*Microsoft Project knows the number of working hours in the day, which days are working days, and which days are holidays, thanks to **working times calendars**.*

♦ There are two types of working times calendar:

The **base calendar**	specifies working time and non-working time for a project, or for a set of resources. These resources generally carry out similar or related work within the context of the same working team. The default base calendar that Microsoft Project uses is called **Standard**.
The **resource calendar**	specifies working time and non-working time for a specific resource (although it can also contain these details with respect to a set of resources, such as "the Painters", for example). The resource calendar is based on a base calendar and specifies exceptions to this calendar.

Each calendar inherits the working and non-working days and times of the calendar on which it is based. This means that any changes that you make to a base calendar are also implemented in the resource calendars that depend on it. For example, if you change the status of a day in the project calendar (by declaring it a holiday for example) then you will automatically modify the working times of all the resources that are assigned to this calendar. This will change the duration of all the tasks that are assigned to those resources and planned for that day.

Starting Microsoft Project 2000

♦ On the Windows taskbar, click the **Start** button.

♦ Drag the mouse pointer up to the **Programs** option and then click the **Microsoft Project** option.

The application window appears.

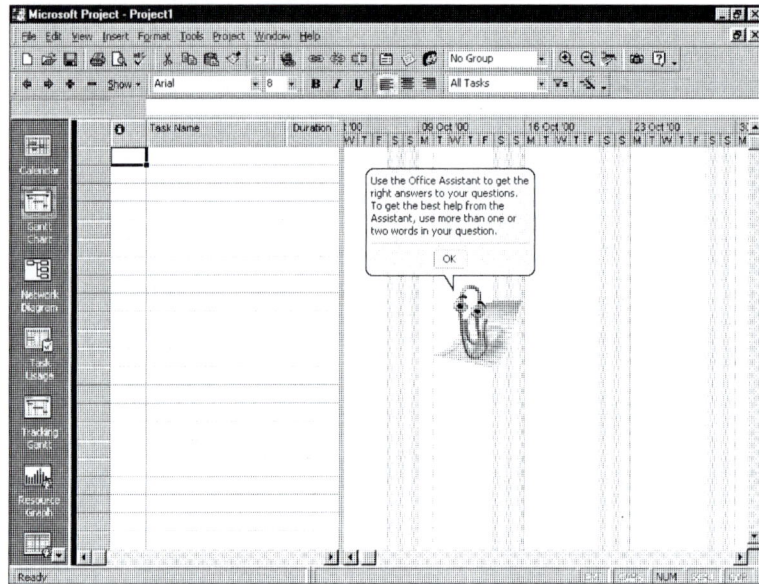

The Office Assistant may display the Tip of the Day.

♦ In addition to the Office Assistant, Microsoft Project provides a **Help** window. This window is started up automatically when you start up **Microsoft Project**. If it is not visible on your screen when you start up **Microsoft Project**, then you can display it by clicking the **Microsoft Project Help** button on your taskbar (this depends on your version of Windows).

♦ The **Welcome** screen of the **Microsoft Project Help** window:

– tells you **What's New** with **Microsoft Project 2000**,

– provides a **Quick Preview** of the application's features,

– allows you to follow a **Tutorial** in order to learn about **Microsoft Project**,

– provides a **Project Map** that describes the different phases of project management,

– allows you to seek information using the **Office Assistant**,

– provides a **Reference** section that contains more detailed information on **Microsoft Project**,

– can be closed by clicking the ☒ button in its top right corner.

♦ When you start up Microsoft Project 2000 you generally go into the **Gantt Chart** view. The information in this view is presented in two ways. The left hand side shows the information in the form of a **sheet**, and the right hand side displays the information in the form of a **chart**. The sheet frame comprises seven columns (the first one being the **Task Name** column) and each task occupies a separate row on the sheet. The chart frame includes the current date and displays each task graphically as a horizontal bar.

♦ The vertical bar on the far left of the screen is called the **View Bar**. You can display or hide the View Bar by opening the **View** menu and clicking the **View Bar** option.

❏ *To stop the help window appearing each time you start up Project, use* **Tools - Options - General** *tab and deactivate the* **Display Help at startup** *option.*

If you want Microsoft Project 2000 to open the last file that you used when it starts up, select ***Tools - Options***, *click the* ***General*** *tab and activate the* ***Open last file on startup*** *check box.*

Leaving Project 2000

♦ **File**
   Exit

Click the ☒ button in the application window

♦ Alt F4

♦ If you have not yet saved your latest modifications, then you can choose to save, or not to save, these changes before closing **Project**.

Undoing your last action

♦ **Edit**
   Undo

♦ Ctrl **Z**

*The **Undo** option changes according to the last action that you carried out.*

❏ *After you undo an action, the **Redo** option replaces the **Undo** option, and the ⟲ tool button becomes the ⟳ tool button. You can use either of these techniques in order to redo your action.*

**Managing
the toolbars**

♦ **View
Toolbars**

*This menu option lists all the toolbars, and provides access to
the **Customize** option.*

Displaying/hiding a toolbar

*In the toolbar list, a tick indicates each toolbar that Project 2000
is currently displaying.*

♦ Click a toolbar in the list to display or to hide it.

Creating a toolbar

♦ If necessary, select **View - Toolbars** then click **Customize**.

♦ Under the **Toolbars** tab, click the **New** button.

♦ Enter the **Toolbar name** for your new toolbar.

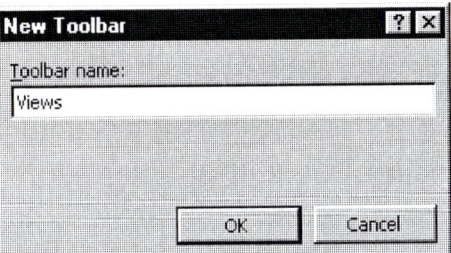

♦ Create your new toolbar by clicking **OK**.

*Microsoft Project displays a small floating toolbar and updates the **Toolbars** list in the **Customize** dialog box.*

♦ You can now add tool buttons to your new toolbar.

Adding/deleting tool buttons

♦ If necessary, go into **View - Toolbars** and click **Customize**.

♦ To add a tool button:

- Click the **Commands** tab.

- Choose one of the **Categories**.

- Choose one of the **Commands**.

- If necessary, consult the **Description** of your selected command.

- Drag the command that you selected onto the destination toolbar.

*The **Modify Selection** button provides a number of options, including the means of modifying the contents of the ScreenTip.*

♦ To remove a tool button, drag it off the toolbar.

♦ When you have finished, click the **Close** button.

❑ *Your toolbar customisations are stored in the GLOBAL.MPT file. Microsoft Project will apply them to all your projects.*

Docking/floating a toolbar

♦ You can dock a floating toolbar by double-clicking its title bar.

♦ To float a docked toolbar, point to the move handle, which is situated on the far left of the toolbar, and then drag it onto the work area.

Opening
a project file

♦ **File**
Open

♦ Ctrl **O**

*The **Open** dialog box appears, in which you can indicate the location and the name of your project file. The **Look in** list box contains the **My Documents** folder, by default. When you point to a tool button, its name appears in a ScreenTip.*

♦ Open the **Look in** list and select the drive that contains your document.

♦ Open the folder that contains your document by double-clicking its icon.

The  tool button allows you to return to the folder above.

♦ If necessary, you can change the view of the document list by opening the list on the [⊞▾] tool button:

[⊞] displays only the names of the documents.

[⊞] displays details of the documents.

[⊞] allows you to display the properties of a selected document.

[⊞] allows you to display a preview of a selected document. A preview will be available only if you previously activated the **Save preview picture** check box for the document concerned (**File - Properties - Summary** page).

♦ Select the project that you want to open.

Open				? ✕
Look in:	☐ ENI Project 2000	▾	⇦ ⬆ 🔍 ✕ 📁 ▦ ▾ Tools ▾	
Name		**Size**	**Type**	**Modified**
📄 Book Project.mpp		93 KB	Microsoft Projec...	12/10/00 19:25
📄 Building Project 1.mpp		89 KB	Microsoft Projec...	02/11/00 11:37
📄 Central building project.mpp		83 KB	Microsoft Projec...	02/11/00 11:38
📄 Galahad.mpp		105 KB	Microsoft Projec...	22/11/00 19:12
📄 Lancelot.mpp		93 KB	Microsoft Projec...	24/11/00 10:43
📄 Manuals.mpp		114 KB	Microsoft Projec...	27/10/00 10:35
📄 Marketing.mpp		77 KB	Microsoft Projec...	31/10/00 14:46
📄 Merlin.mpp		89 KB	Microsoft Projec...	22/11/00 15:56
📄 Order 512.mpp		118 KB	Microsoft Projec...	14/11/00 14:38
📄 Pottery.mpp		144 KB	Microsoft Projec...	14/11/00 09:26
📄 Prototype 525.mpp		156 KB	Microsoft Projec...	27/07/00 15:33
📄 Sales of new video cassette.mpp		74 KB	Microsoft Projec...	07/11/00 10:52
📄 Video Cassette Project.mpp		220 KB	Microsoft Projec...	08/08/00 18:49
📄 Video.mpp		142 KB	Microsoft Projec...	18/10/00 17:02
File name:		▾	ODBC...	📂 Open ▾
Files of type:	Microsoft Project Files	▾		Cancel

♦ Click the **Open** button.

*If you want only to consult the project, then click the down-arrow on the **Open** button and choose the **Open Read-Only** option.*

❏ You can also open a project by double-clicking its name.

You can open one of the last files you used by clicking its name at the bottom of the *File* menu. You can alter the number of files proposed in this menu by using *Tools - Options - General* tab and modifying the *entries* in the *Recently used file list* option.

Viewing several projects simultaneously

♦ Open all the projects that you want to view simultaneously, and no others.

♦ **Window**
Arrange All

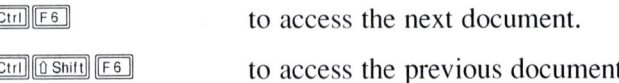

This option divides the work area up into a number of windows. Each of these windows displays one of the projects that you have opened. The active project window is the one with maximize, minimize and close buttons on its title bar.

♦ You can activate another project either by clicking in its window or by using one of the following shortcut keys:

Ctrl F6   to access the next document.

Ctrl ⇧ Shift F6   to access the previous document.

♦ To display only the active project again over the whole work area, click the maximize button ▢ on its title bar.

**Activating
a file which
is open in the
background**

♦ Open the **Window** menu.

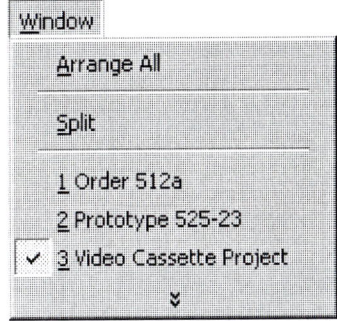

The lower part of the menu lists all the open files in alphabetical order. A tick indicates the active file.

♦ Click the name of the file that you would like to activate.

The file immediately appears in the foreground.

❑ *You can also activate other open files from the keyboard. The* Ctrl F6 *shortcut key activates the next project, and the* Ctrl ⇧ Shift F6 *shortcut key activates the previous project.*

In addition, you can activate an open document by clicking the corresponding button on the taskbar, although this is only possible with later versions of Windows.

**Closing
a project file**

♦ **File
Close**

Click the  button
in the document window

♦ Ctrl F4

♦ If you have not yet saved your latest changes to the project, then you can choose to save, or not to save these changes before closing your file.

Microsoft Project 2000

Saving a project file

Saving a new project

♦ **File**
Save

♦ Ctrl **S**

♦ Enter a name for your project file.

*You must enter this name in the **File name** box.*

♦ Select the disk drive on which you want to save your project using the **Save in** list.

♦ Access the folder in which you want to save your project by double-clicking its icon.

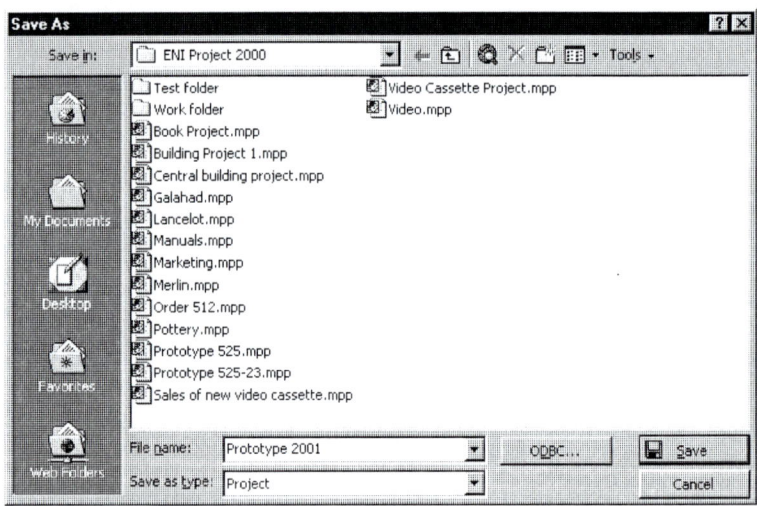

♦ Click the **Save** button.

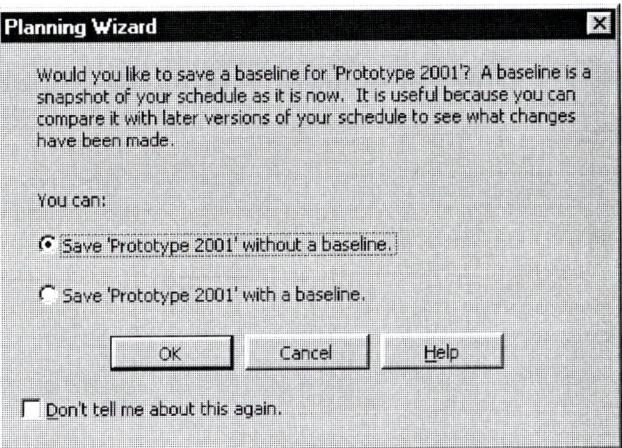

*The **Planning Wizard** then offers its services.*

♦ If your project is not yet in its realisation phase then you should leave the default option: **Save... without a baseline.**

♦ Click the **OK** button.

*The project name appears in the title bar, followed by the **.mpp** extension.*

Saving an existing project

♦ **File**      ♦ Ctrl **S**
   Save

♦ The **Planning Wizard** appears. If your project is not yet in its realisation phase then you should leave the default option: **Save... without a baseline**.

♦ Click the **OK** button.

Restricting access to a project

♦ In the **Save As** dialog box, click the **Tools** button and choose **General Options**.

♦ According to the level of restriction that you require you can choose one or more of the following options:

- – enter a **Protection password** to ensure that any user who does not know this password will not be able to open the project file,

- – enter a **Write reservation password** to ensure that any user who does not know this password will be able to open the project file only in read-only mode,

- – if you activate **Read-only recommended**, Project 2000 will display a message when a user tries to open a file, to recommend opening the file as read-only.

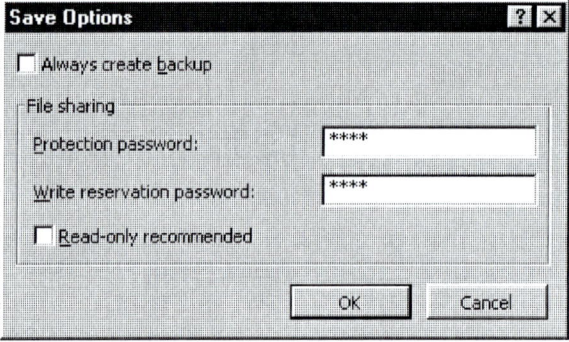

When you enter passwords, the characters that you type appear on the screen as asterisks.

♦ Click the **OK** button.

♦ If you entered any passwords, you must re-enter them at this stage, to confirm them.

Passwords are case-sensitive: you must always respect the case of the individual characters in your passwords.

Creating a new project

♦ **File**
New

♦ Ctrl **N**

♦ If you use the **File - New** menu option, the **New** dialog box opens: choose one of the **Project Templates**.

♦ If you are prompted to, enter **Project Information** for your project.

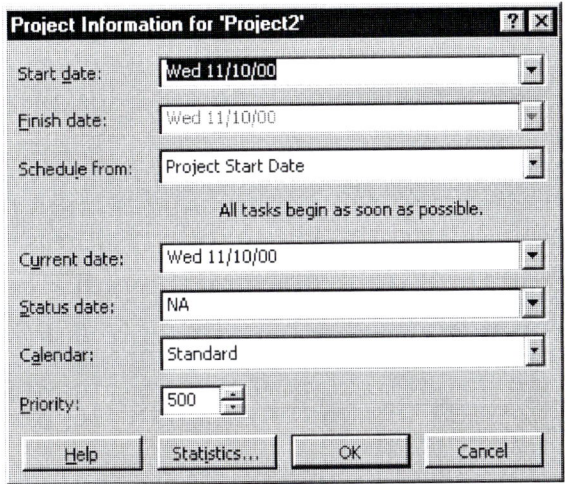

♦ Click the **OK** button.

❏ If you never enter specific **Project Information** data when you create a new project, you may want to deactivate the display of this dialog box. To do this, select **Tools - Options**, click the **General** tab, and deactivate the **Prompt for project info for new projects** check box.

Defining your preferences for file saving

♦ **Tools**
Options
Save tab

♦ Open the **Save Microsoft Project files as** list and choose the default file type that Microsoft Project must use when you save your projects (this file type is **Project (*.mpp)** by default).

♦ Under **File Locations**, use the **Modify** button to define the default opening or saving locations when you use **File - Open** or **Save As**.

♦ Under **Auto Save**, you can activate the **Save every** check box and specify, as a number of **minutes**, the frequency with which Project 2000 must automatically save your work.

According to your requirements, you can choose to **Save Active Project Only**, or to **Save all open project files**. Finally, you can activate the **Prompt Before Saving** check box, if you want Project 2000 to ask your permission before it carries out the auto save.

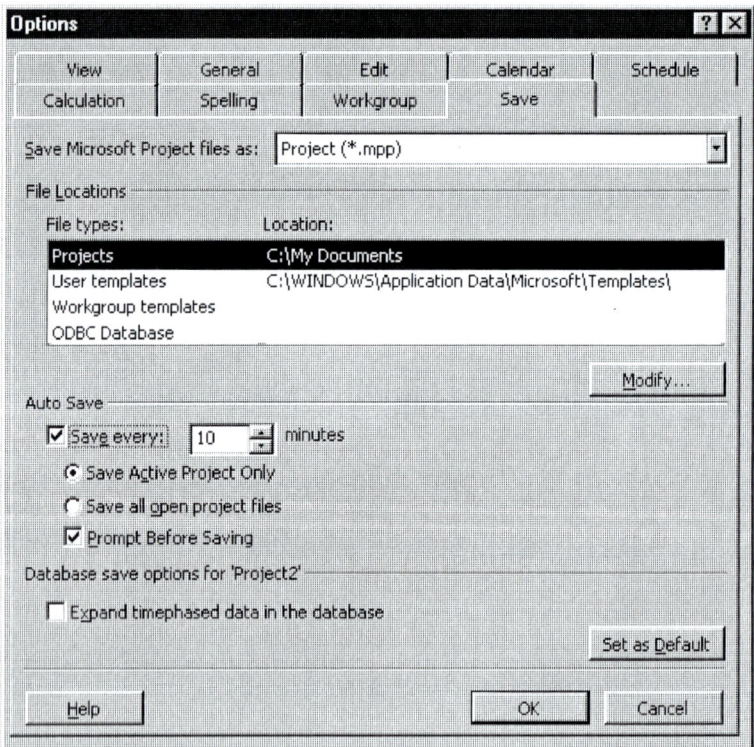

♦ Click the **OK** button.

Saving information in HTML format

Microsoft Project 2000 allows you to save elements from your project in HTML format, so that you can publish them on the World Wide Web.

♦ **File**
Save As Web Page

♦ Modify the **File name**, as necessary.

♦ Check that the **Save as type** is **Web Page (*.html; *.htm)**.

♦ In the **Save in** list box, specify the folder in which you want to save the file.

♦ Click the **Save** button.

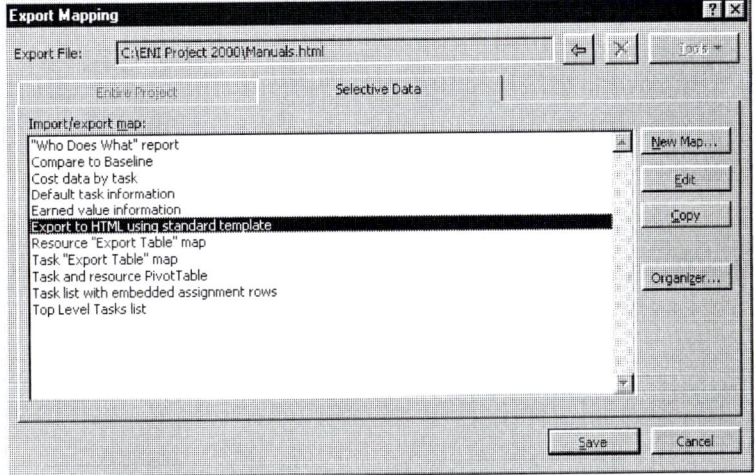

♦ On the **Selective Data** page of the **Export Mapping** dialog box, choose an **Import/export map** according to the information that Microsoft Project must display in the **HTML** file.

By default, Microsoft Project offers 11 different import/export maps.

♦ Click the **Save** button.

♦ You can then open the HTML file in a browser to view the result.

Exporting Project data to Excel using a predefined map

To export a Microsoft Project 2000 file you must first save the file in the format concerned (in this case Excel format) then use an import/export map. An import/export map is a set of instructions enabling Project 2000 to identify the types of data you want it to import or export. It specifies such information as the order of the data and the field names in the destination format. Microsoft Project provides a number of predefined maps, which you can modify. You can also create your own maps.

♦ Open the project whose data you want to export, either totally or partially.

♦ **File**
Save As

♦ Open the **Save as type** list, and choose one of the following formats:

Microsoft Excel Workbook   to export data to a worksheet.

Microsoft Excel PivotTable   to export data to a pivot table.

♦ Enter the name of your export file in the **File name** box.

♦ In the **Save in** box, specify the folder in which you want to save your export file.

♦ Click the **Save** button.

*The **Export Mapping** dialog box opens.*

*By default, Microsoft Project 2000 offers 11 different maps in the **Import/export map** frame.*

Import/export map	To import and export
"Who Does What" report	resources and assignments, start and finish dates and the associated work.
Compare to Baseline	tasks with their numbers, their names and their durations (actual, planned and variances), start and finish dates (actual and scheduled), work and cost (actual, scheduled and variances).
Cost data by task	tasks with their numbers, their names and their costs: total, fixed, real, remaining, scheduled and variances.
Default task information	tasks with their numbers, names, durations, start and finish dates, predecessors and resource names.
Earned value information	tasks with their numbers, their names, their earned value fields (BCWS, BCWP, ACWP, SV, CV) cost, scheduled cost and cost variances.
Export to HTML using standard template	tasks (names, durations, dates etc...), resources (names, % completion, etc...), and assignments (names, durations, dates etc...), in HTML format.
Resource "Export Table" map	resources and all associated data
Task "Export Table" map	tasks and all associated data
Task and resource PivotTable	tasks (names, resources and dates) and resources (durations, dates, names and costs) in Excel PivotTable format.
Task list with embedded assignment rows	tasks (names, durations, dates etc...), in Excel and HTML formats
Top Level Tasks list	tasks (names, durations, dates, % completion, costs etc...).

♦ To use an existing map, select it in the **Import/export map** list then click the **Save** button.

You create an export file that you can open directly in Microsoft Excel.

**Publishing
a project
in a new
Web folder**

*Microsoft Project 2000 allows you to publish a project. Publishing
a project consists of making a copy of the project on a Web server,
so that everyone who has access to the server can consult it.*

♦ Prepare your project as it should appear on the Web server.

♦ **File
Save As**

♦ Click the  button on the **Places Bar**.

♦ To create a new Web folder, click the **Create New Folder**
tool button. This starts the **Add Web Folder** wizard.

♦ First, enter the address where you want to add your Web folder
under **Type the location to add**, or alternatively click the
Browse button to find an address using your Internet browser.

♦ Click the **Next** button.

♦ In the following screen, you can **Enter the name for this Web
Folder**, then click the **Finish** button.

By default, Microsoft Project suggests a URL address as a name for this folder. Microsoft Project then creates the Web folder and its supporting files.

♦ In the **Save As** dialog box, change the **File name** that you want to publish on the Web, then click the **Save** button.

Now that you have published your project, you can use a browser to consult it at the URL address defined previously.

. . . . *Personal notes* . . . .

Creating a project template

You should use a template when several projects have one of more of the following:

– a similar task structure,

– similar elements (such as calendars or reports),

– a similar set of resources.

♦ Open a new project and create the common elements (such as common tasks, resources and calendars).

♦ **File**
  Save As

♦ Enter the name of your template in the **File name** box.

♦ Open the **Save as type** list and choose the **Template(*.mpt)** option.

Once you have chosen a file type, the file list displays only files of this type.

♦ By default, Microsoft Project will save your template in the **Templates** folder. Although you can choose a different location if you wish, it is not normally recommended.

♦ Confirm your action by clicking the **Save** button.

*The **Save As Template** dialog box opens.*

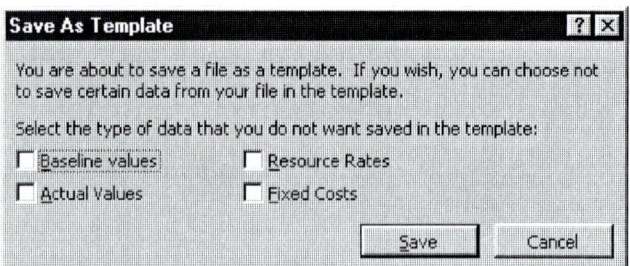

♦ Activate the necessary options to omit the appropriate data from your project template.

♦ Click the **Save** button.

❏ *When you are working <u>in</u> a template, Microsoft Project displays the template name extension .mpt in the title bar.*

❏ *By default, Microsoft Project saves templates in the **Templates** folder, for which the full path is c:\Windows\Application Data\Microsoft\Templates.*

Using a project template

♦ **File**
   New

♦ Click the tab that contains the template you want to use.

♦ Select your template.

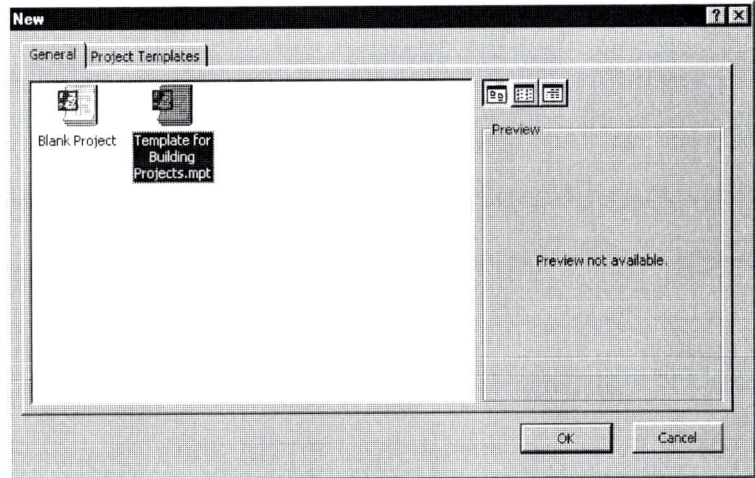

♦ Click the **OK** button.

A new project appears. The extension .mpt does not appear on the title bar. This shows that you are not working <u>in</u> the template, but in a new project that is <u>based on</u> it.

♦ Work on your project.

♦ Save using the 🖫 tool button.

Microsoft Project invites you to enter the **File name** *and suggests that you save your file in* **Project** *format.*

♦ Enter the **File name** and click the **Save** button.

❏ *Microsoft Project 2000 provides 12 different templates. You can access these templates with* **File - New** *and choosing the* **Project Templates** *tab.*

❏ *If you chose to save the template in a folder other than the default* **Templates** *folder, you will need to use the* **File - Open** *command to open the template file, followed by the* **File - Save As** *command to create your* **Project (*.mpp)** *file.*

Customising your future projects

You can define the elements that you will need for all your new projects.

♦ Select the **Tools - Organizer** menu option. Copy into the **GLOBAL.MPT** file all the elements that will be common to all your new projects (cf. "Copying elements from one project to another").

♦ When you have finished copying the elements, click **Close**.

Creating
a workspace

A workspace file defines a set of projects which open at the same time, the way the windows are arranged on the screen, the views which are active etc...

♦ Open all the projects that you want to include in your workspace. Arrange your windows and views as you want them to appear when you open your workspace.

♦ **File**
Save Workspace

♦ Enter the **File name** of your workspace.

♦ In the **Save in** box, indicate the folder in which you want save your workspace.

♦ Confirm your workspace by clicking the **Save** button.

❑ *You can open a workspace in the same way as you would open a project. However, you should note that workspace files have an* ***.mpw*** *name extension.*

Adding comments to a project

♦ **File Properties**

♦ If necessary, activate the **Summary** tab.

*Microsoft project proposes the name of the file as the **Title** of the project.*

♦ Click in the **Comments** box and enter your remarks.

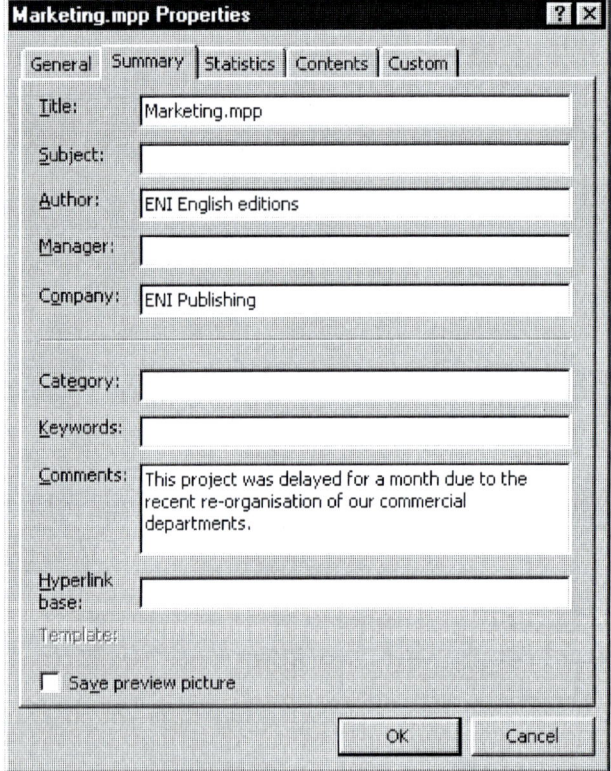

♦ Click the **OK** button.

**Entering
the project
start date**

♦ **Project
Project Information**

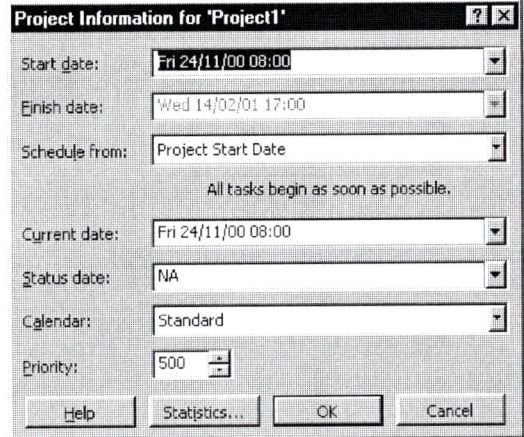

*Unless you specify otherwise, Microsoft Project will calculate
with respect to the start date of the project and the tasks will
begin as early as possible.*

♦ Check that the **Schedule from** box contains **Project Start Date**.

♦ To open the calendar, click the down-arrow to the right of the
Start date box.

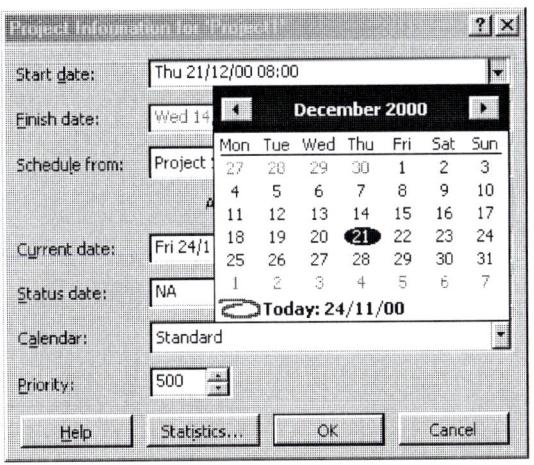

Microsoft Project 2000

You can view other months by clicking the *and* ▶ *buttons.*

♦ Click to select the required date.

♦ Click the **OK** button.

❑ *Microsoft Project calculates the **Finish date** according to the start date and according to the links between the tasks, the constraints etc...*

You can also enter a date directly in the text box concerned.

Scheduling from the finish date

♦ **Project**
Project Information

♦ Open the **Schedule from** list and select **Project Finish Date**.

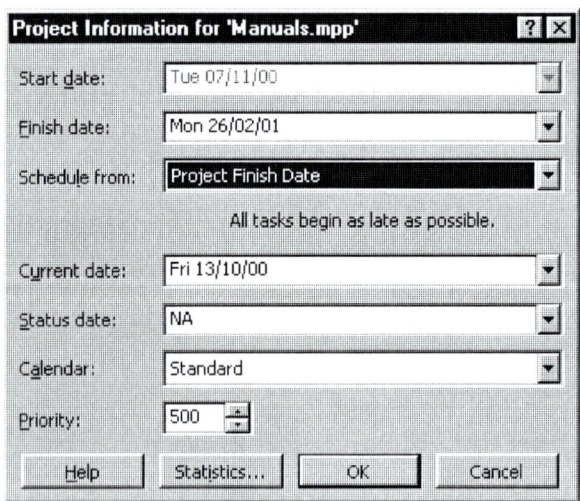

*When you choose this option Microsoft Project indicates that **All tasks begin as late as possible** and no longer allows you to access the **Start date** box.*

♦ Modify the **Finish date**, as necessary.

♦ Click the **OK** button.

Consulting the overall statistics of a project

Project 2000 always carries out an overall analysis of project files.

Displaying the statistics

♦ **Project**
  Project Information

♦ Click the **Statistics** button.

Project 2000 displays the following information:

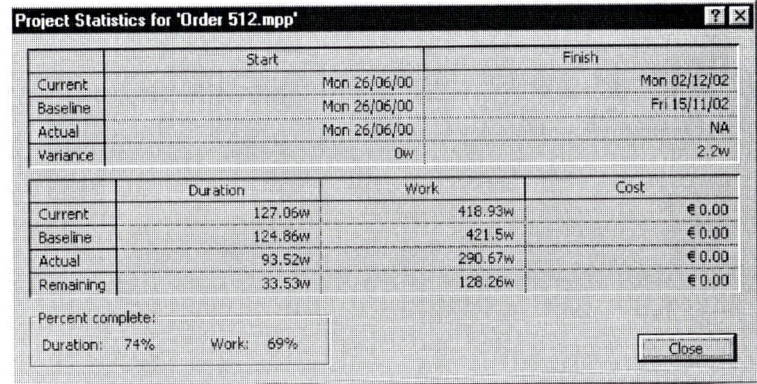

♦ To leave these statistics, click the **Close** button.

❏ When the **Tracking** toolbar is displayed, you can consult these statistics using the **Project Statistics** tool button.

Printing the statistics

♦ **View**
  Reports

♦ Double-click **Overview**, followed by **Project Summary**.

♦ Click the **Print** button, followed by the **OK** button.

Any comments that you entered for the project will be printed at the end of the report.

♦ Click the **Close** button to close the **Reports** dialog box.

Customising the project calendar

The basic elements of the project calendar

♦ The project calendar by default is the Standard calendar of Project 2000, which shows all weekdays (from Mondays to Fridays) as workdays.

♦ The working hours for each weekday are as follows:
From 08:00 to 12:00, and from 13:00 to 17:00, which corresponds to 40 hours per week.

♦ The Standard calendar does not include any holidays.

♦ All calendars begin on 1st January 1984 and end on 31st December 2049.

Accessing the project calendar

♦ **Tools**
Change Working Time

♦ Check that this dialog box is set up **For:** the **Standard (Project Calendar)**.

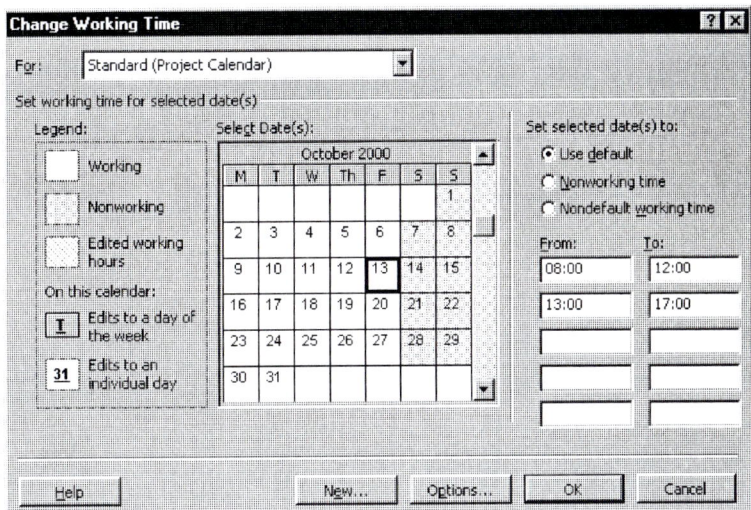

This dialog box shows the current month in the form of a calendar. Nonworking days are shown with a grey background.

❏ You can display other months, and other years using the vertical scroll bar to the right of the calendar.

Defining nonworking days

♦ Select the day that you want to define as a nonworking day.

If you want to define several consecutive days as nonworking days, then select them using Shift *-clicks. If you want to define several non-consecutive days, then select them using* Ctrl *-clicks (you can use these two techniques only within the same month).*

♦ Under **Set selected date(s) to**, activate the **Nonworking time** option.

*As soon as you select this option, the **From** and **To** fields are no longer accessible, and the selected date(s) in the calendar are underlined and have a grey background.*

❏ It is advisable to define your working calendars over a longer period of time than that initially scheduled, as projects are often late!

Defining working hours

♦ Select the days for which the working hours are different from the default values.

If you click a day-of-the-week column header, you select that day for all the weeks of all the months of all the years.

♦ Indicate the new working hours in the **From** and **To** fields.

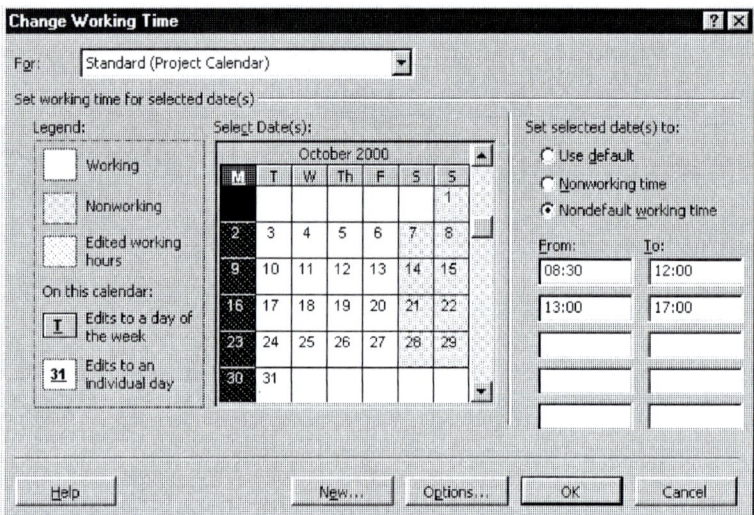

♦ Click another day box in the calendar to remove the selection.

*When you change the working time for a day it appears with a light grey background. When you click one or more of them, the **Nondefault working time** option is selected under **Set selected date(s) to**. Take care when you are defining half working days: you must delete the times that do not apply (do not replace them by spaces, for example). Also, the first line must not be empty (if the working time is only in the afternoon, for example, then you must write the afternoon working hours in the top **From** and **To** fields, and delete the times in the second row). Companies that work three round-the-clock shifts would also use the third row.*

Closing the calendar

♦ Once you have adapted the calendar to suit your company and the project period, confirm your changes either by clicking **OK**, or by pressing Enter .

❏ *The changes that you make will affect the start and finish dates of each task and they will also generally affect the finish date of the project.*

Printing the calendar

♦ **View**
  Reports

♦ Double-click **Overview**, followed by **Working Days**.

♦ On the **Print Preview** screen that appears, click the **Print** button and confirm with **OK**.

♦ Close the **Reports** dialog box by clicking the **Close** button.

Project 2000 lists the days of the week and their working hours for the base calendar of your project and for its exceptions.

Modifying the general calendar options

♦ **Tools**
  Options

♦ Double-click the **Calendar** tab.

♦ Update the calendar options as necessary.

Notice that you can specify the month in which the **Fiscal year starts**, in order to adapt the reference time scale to suit your company.

♦ Click the **OK** button.

❑ It is preferable to set the general calendar options before you create the project tasks (especially before you specify task durations).

Changing the global calendar by replacing it with a project calendar

♦ **Tools**
Organizer

♦ Click the **Calendars** tab.

♦ In the right-hand frame, select the project calendar that you want to copy.

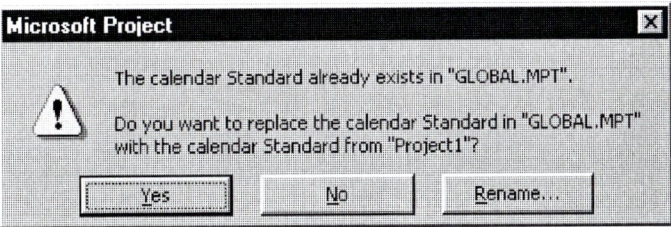

♦ Click the **Copy** button.

♦ Click the **Yes** button to replace the **Standard** calendar in **GLO-BAL.MPT**.

♦ To close the **Organizer** dialog box, click **Close**.

Copying elements from one project to another

♦ Open the project that contains the element that you want to copy, along with the project to which you want to copy it.

♦ If the resources for the project are shared with other projects, then you can choose to open the resource pool in one of three ways:

1st option   in read-only mode: this technique allows other users to work on other projects that are connected to the pool.

2nd option   in read-write mode: this technique allows you to modify the resource information.
However, whilst your project is open in this mode, other projects cannot modify this resource information.

3rd option   this option allows you to consolidate the resource pool and all the files which share it into a new master project file.

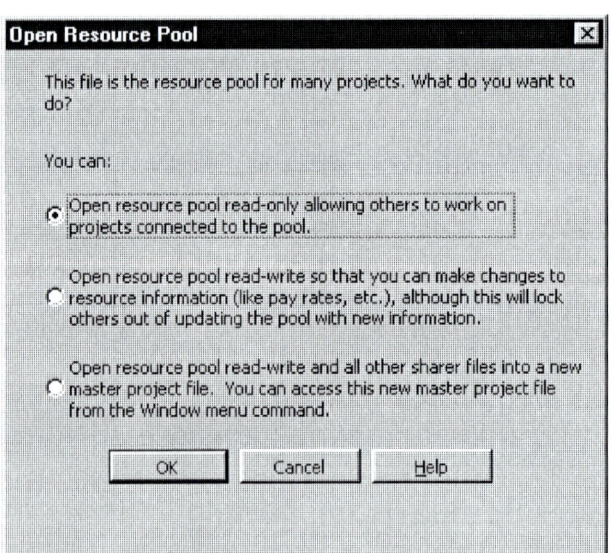

♦ **Tools**
Organizer

This dialog box contains a tab for each type of element that you can copy between projects.

♦ Choose the tab that corresponds to the element you want to copy.

Each page contains two lists: one for the source project and one for the destination project.

♦ You can choose the source and destination project from the **... available in** lists.

Only those elements that a particular project uses will be included in the corresponding list. The list contents vary according to the tab concerned.

♦ To copy an element, select it in the source list.

♦ Click the **Copy** button.

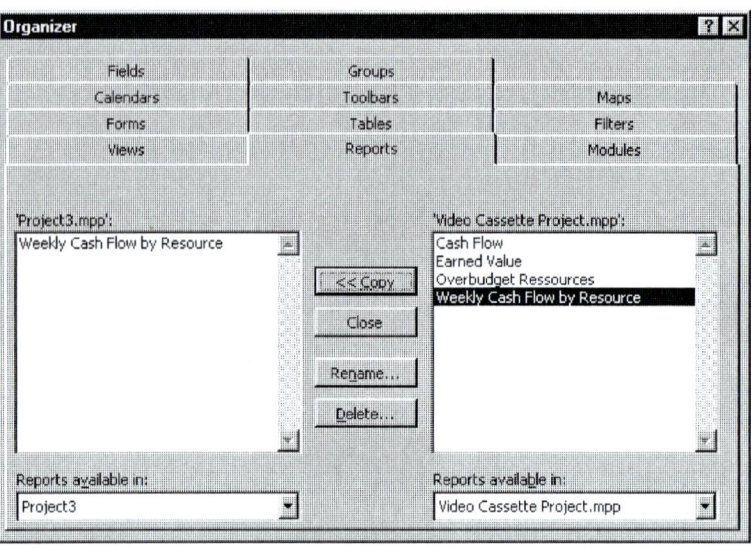

Project 2000 copies the element immediately.

♦ When you have finished copying, click the **Close** button.

Renaming/ deleting a project element

♦ **Tools**
Organizer

♦ Click the tab corresponding to the element type then select the element on which you want to work.

♦ To modify the name of the element, click the **Rename** button, enter the new name, and confirm with Enter.

♦ To delete the element from the project, click the **Delete** button, and confirm by clicking **Yes**.

♦ Confirm your changes by clicking the **Close** button.

Customising the elements of a project

You can customise the elements of Microsoft Project 2000 to suit your working habits. First, you must decide how you want to customise your project elements.

How do you want to customise your project elements?

♦ Do you want to **create** a completely new element?

♦ Do you want to **create** a new element **from** an existing element?

♦ Do you want to **modify** an existing element?

Customisation techniques

♦ The technique used depends on the type of element:

Element type	Technique
Task table or resource table	-Display the tasks or the resources **-View - Table - More Tables** -To create a table, click the **New** button -To copy a table, select the table and click **Copy**
Task filter or resource filter	-Display the tasks or the resources **-Project - Filtered for - More Filters** -To create a filter, click the **New** button -To copy a filter, select it and click **Copy**
Report	**-View - Reports - Custom** -To create a report, click the **New** button -To copy a report, select it and click **Copy**
View	**-View - More Views** -To create a view, click the **New** button -To copy a view, select it and click **Copy**

♦ The techniques required to modify an element vary according to whether you want to modify the contents or the presentation.

♦ You can modify the contents of an element by choosing the menu options listed above, selecting the element concerned, then clicking the **Edit** button. There are numerous ways to change the look of the various project elements. Some of the more useful techniques are described at different points in this book.

Working on a complex project

♦ Suppose that you must manage a large project that comprises several distinct phases.

♦ One way of managing this type of project is to break it down into a number of smaller projects, with a distinct project for each main phase of your big project. You can then refer to this set of subprojects from another project called the master project.

♦ Isolating the tasks from a subproject in a separate file from the main project lets you concentrate on either the subproject or on main project summary tasks, as this limits the number of lines displayed.

♦ In addition, this approach makes it easier to delegate distinct parts of a big project to other project managers.

♦ Finally, this technique allows you to use your computer memory more efficiently, as you do not need to open all your sub-projects when you are working on the main project.

Creating a subproject task

♦ In the main project, create your list of tasks without the sub-project tasks.

♦ Select the task that appears just after the point where you want your subproject to appear.

♦ **Insert
Project**

♦ Select the folder that contains your subproject.

♦ Select your subproject file.

♦ If your subproject must not be modified from your main file, open the list on the **Insert** button and choose the **Insert Read-Only** option.

♦ If you do not want any modifications that you make to your master project to affect your subproject and vice-versa, deactivate the **Link to project** option.

♦ Click the **Insert** button.

The duration of the subproject task is the total duration of your subproject. This task appears on the Gantt chart as a summary task for the project. The name of the task is that of the project file you inserted.

♦ Update the links between the tasks, as necessary.

❏*In the* 🛈 *column, the* 🗐 *icon indicates a task that contains a subproject and the* 🗐 *icon indicates a task that contains a subproject in read-only mode. Project 2000 considers a task containing a subproject that is not linked to the main project as an ordinary task and not as a subproject task.*

Consolidating several individual projects

While you can create a complex project using subprojects, consolidation techniques can also be used to oversee several separate projects at once.

♦ Consolidating a set of projects makes it easier to review them all together and to produce reports on them.

♦ You can change the format of the consolidated information, without affecting the format of the project source files.

♦ This technique also allows you to consolidate schedules and resources.

Consolidating schedules and resources

♦ Open the projects that you want to consolidate.

♦ **Window**
New Window

♦ Use Ctrl-clicks to select all the projects that you want to consolidate.

New Window

Projects:
Order 512.mpp
Pottery.mpp
Video cassette.mpp

View: Gantt Chart

OK   Cancel

◆ Click the **OK** button.

Microsoft Project 2000 displays the results of the consolidation in a new project.

❑ *Unless you specify otherwise, the project summary tasks are linked to their source files and you can modify these tasks from the consolidated project.*

❑ *You can set up links between the tasks of the different projects.*

**Exploring
a consolidated
project**

In the Gantt sheet

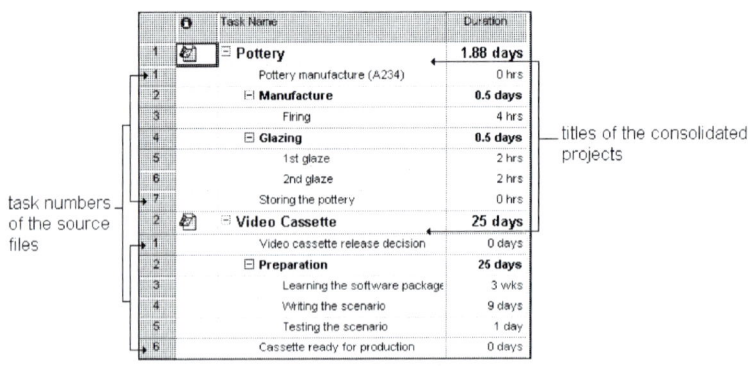

task numbers of the source files

titles of the consolidated projects

The "Pottery" and "Video Cassette" titles have reference numbers of 1 and 2 respectively. These are the task numbers of the consolidated project. These tasks are called "project summaries".

In the Gantt chart

♦ Project summary bars look like other task summary bars, except that they are grey instead of being black.

Saving a consolidated project

♦ Save a consolidated file as you would save any other file.

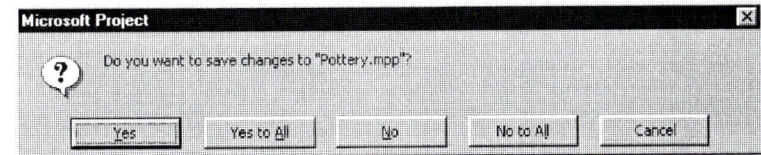

Microsoft Project 2000 asks you if you want to save the changes to each of the source files.

♦ Accept or refuse to save the changes to each source file.

♦ If Microsoft Project asks you, specify whether you want to save the projects with or without a baseline.

Modifying the links between a project and a source file

♦ Double-click the project summary task.

♦ Activate the **Advanced** tab.

♦ If the source file has been moved or has changed, click the **Browse** button to update its name (or access path).

♦ If you no longer want to link the project summary task to the source file, deactivate the **Link to project** check box.

♦ If you do not want the source file to be modifiable from the master (or consolidated) document, activate the **Read only** check box.

♦ Click the **OK** button.

Displaying the names of subproject files in the Gantt Chart

♦ Display the Gantt chart concerned.

♦ **Format**
Bar Styles

♦ Select the **Project Summary** bar style.

♦ Activate the **Text** tab.

♦ Choose where you want the file names to appear with respect to the bar (**Left, Right, Top, Bottom**, or **Inside**).

♦ Open the list and select **Subproject File**.

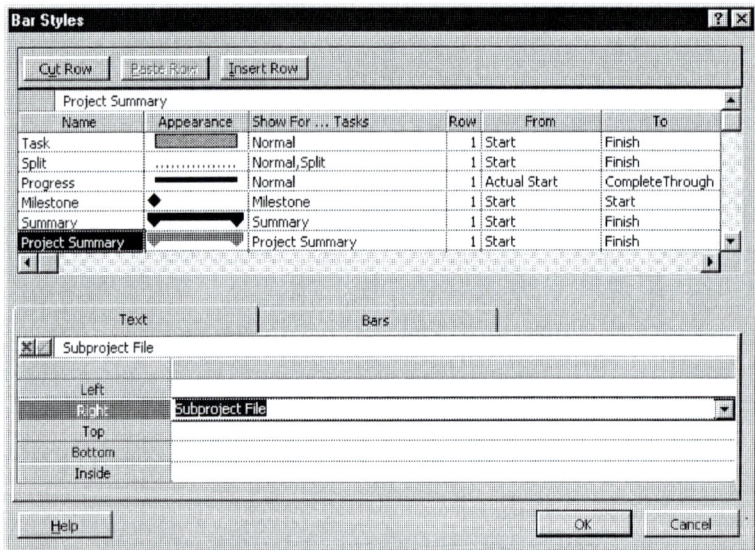

♦ Click the **OK** button.

The subproject file names appear on the Gantt Chart, with their access paths.

Microsoft Project 2000

Displaying the subproject statistics

♦ Double-click the subproject task concerned.

♦ Click the **Project Info** button.

*If the **Project Info** button is unavailable, then close the **Inserted Project Information** dialog box, expand the subproject details by clicking the corresponding + sign, then collapse the subproject details by clicking the - sign and double-click the subproject task once again.*

♦ Click the **Statistics** button.

♦ To leave the statistics, click the **Close** button then click **Cancel**.

. . . . *Personal notes* . . . .

Sharing resources between projects

♦ Open the file that contains the resources that you want to share (this file is called the **resource pool**), and one of the files that need to share the resources (a **sharer file**).

♦ Activate the sharer file.

♦ **Tools**
Resources

♦ Choose the **Share Resources** option.

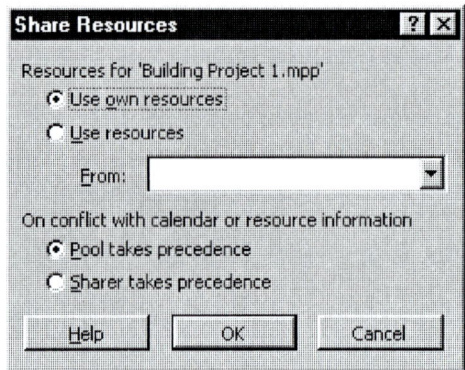

♦ Activate the **Use resources** option.

♦ Open the **From** list and select the resource pool file.

This list contains only open, non-active files.

♦ Indicate whether the **Pool takes precedence**, or whether the **Sharer takes precedence**.

If you choose the first option, then the resource pool will take priority in the case of a resource conflict, or a calendar conflict. Alternatively, if you choose the second option, then the sharer (the active file) will take priority in such cases.

♦ Click the **OK** button.

❑ You can access shared resources from all projects. The **Resource Usage** view lists all the tasks to which the resources have been assigned.

❏ *When you save projects that share resources, Project 2000 asks how you want to save your changes:*

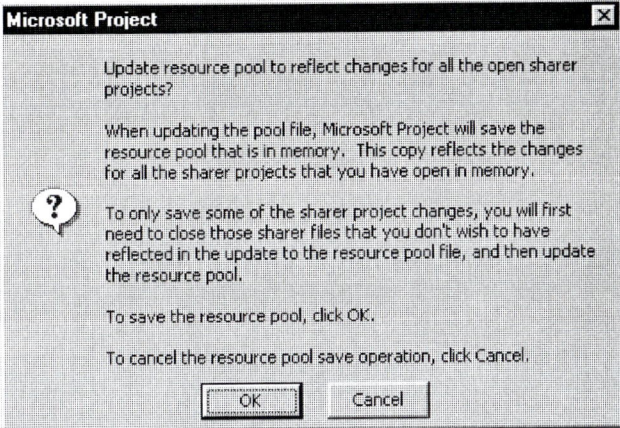

Managing shared resources

Opening the resource pool

♦ You can open a resource pool as you would open any other project.

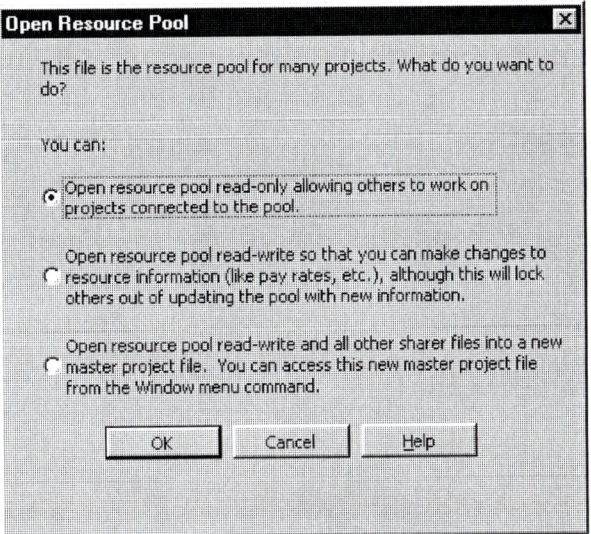

♦ To open the resource pool in read-only mode, choose the first option.

♦ To open the resource pool in read/write mode, choose the second option.

♦ To open the resource pool, along with all the sharer files, choose the third option.

♦ Click the **OK** button.

Opening a sharer project

♦ Open the sharer project as you would any other project.

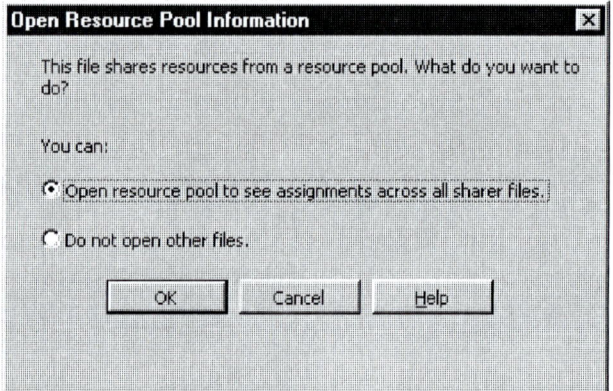

♦ To open the resource pool, along with all sharer files, choose the first option. If you want to open only the sharer file, choose the second option.

Modifying shared resources

♦ Open the resource pool and the sharer projects.

♦ Modify the resources as necessary from any of the projects.

**Grouping
tasks or resources**

With Microsoft Project 2000, you can group tasks or resources in a project according to your requirements, without modifying the underlying structure of your project.

♦ To group tasks or resources you must first display them. To display tasks you can view the **Task Sheet** (by selecting **View - More Views - Task Sheet - Apply**). Alternatively you can view the **Gantt Chart** (**View - Gantt Chart**).

♦ To display resources you can view the **Resource Sheet** (by selecting **View - Resource Sheet**). Alternatively you can view the **Resource Usage** (**View - More Views - Resource Usage - Apply**).

♦ **Project
Group by**

♦ Choose a grouping criterion from the list in the menu or click the **More Groups** option to choose from the full list of groups.

♦ In the **More Groups** dialog box, activate **Task** or **Resource**, select the required group then click the **Apply** button.

❏ *To cancel your task or resource grouping and restore the normal view, use* **Project - Group by - No Group**.

Using the Gantt Chart

Displaying the Gantt Chart

♦ **View**
Gantt Chart

*The **View Bar** contains this icon.*

*The left part of the chart shows the task sheet (the **Entry Table** by default), and the right part shows the Gantt Chart in graphic format.*

Moving around in the Gantt Chart

♦ You can move around in the task sheet using the following shortcut keys:

Ctrl Home	to move to the first column of the first row (first task).
Ctrl End	to move to the last column of the last row (last task).
Home	to move to the first column of the current row.
End	to move to the last column of the current row.
Ctrl Pg Up	to display the screen page to the left.
Ctrl Pg Dn	to display the screen page to the right.
Pg Dn	to display the screen page above.
Pg Up	to display the screen page below.

♦ In the graphical part of the Gantt Chart, you can view the required period by dragging the horizontal scroll cursor.

♦ To view a specific task bar, select the task concerned in the task sheet, and then click the **Go To Selected Task** tool button ( ).

This technique displays the start of the task bar concerned.

♦ When you are working with large projects, you can locate a specific task very easily, using:

Edit   ♦ Ctrl **G**
Go To

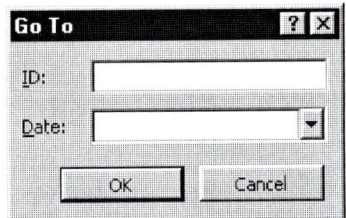

♦ Enter the task's **ID** number, or its **Date** and confirm with Enter .

With this technique you move to the required place in both the task sheet and in the graphical part of the Gantt Chart.

Changing the magnification used to display the Gantt Chart

♦ Use the **Zoom In** (⊕) and the **Zoom Out** (⊖) tool buttons.

♦ **View**
Zoom

♦ Choose the level of zoom detail that you require.

*The **Entire Project** zoom option is often used for short and medium term projects.*

♦ Click the **OK** button.

Changing the timescale of the Gantt Chart

♦ **Format**
Timescale

GANTT CHART

*In Project 2000, a **Timescale** comprises a **Major scale** and an optional **Minor scale**.*

◆ On the **Timescale** page, specify the required timescale using the following options:

Units	to specify the time unit you want to use (**Years, Half Years, Quarters, Months, Thirds of Months, Weeks, Days, Hours, Minutes**). The **Minor scale**'s units should be smaller than or equal to those in the **Major scale**.
Count	to specify the display frequency for the specified unit.
Label	to specify the format of the unit label.
Align	to indicate whether the unit must be centre, left or right aligned.
Tick lines	to indicate whether you want separation lines to appear between the unit labels.

♦ If you wish, click the **Non-working Time** tab and change the formatting options.

♦ Click the **OK** button.

❏ *When you change the **Units** and **Counts** settings, you automatically alter the zoom settings and vice-versa.*

Printing the Gantt Chart

♦ Display the **Print Preview** by clicking the 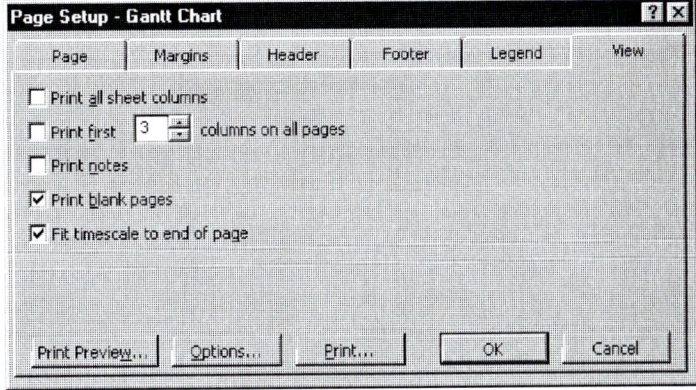 tool button.

By default, Project 2000 prints the columns displayed on the screen. If only one column of the task sheet is displayed, then only that column is printed.

♦ To print all the columns from the task sheet, click the **Page Setup** button and activate the **View** tab.

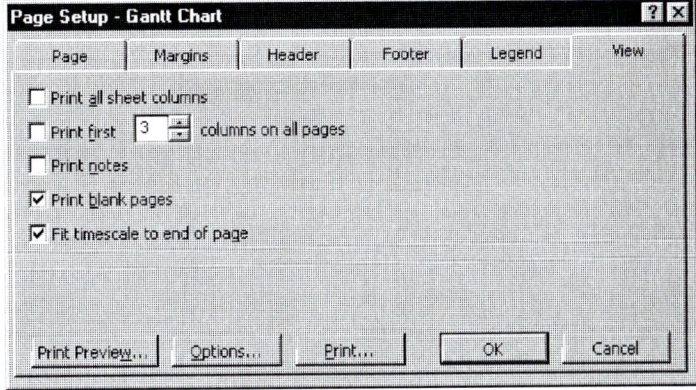

♦ Activate the **Print all sheet columns** check box.

♦ Check that the **Fit timescale to end of page** option is activated.

♦ Click the **OK** button to confirm your settings.

♦ Start the printing by clicking the **Print** button, then **OK**.

Displaying only the task sheet

♦ **View**
  More Views

♦ Double-click the **Task Sheet** option.

The graphical portion of the Gantt Chart is no longer visible. You can adjust the view of the task sheet to suit your requirements.

Changing the look of the current date line

♦ **Format**
  Gridlines

♦ Under **Line to change**, choose **Current Date**.

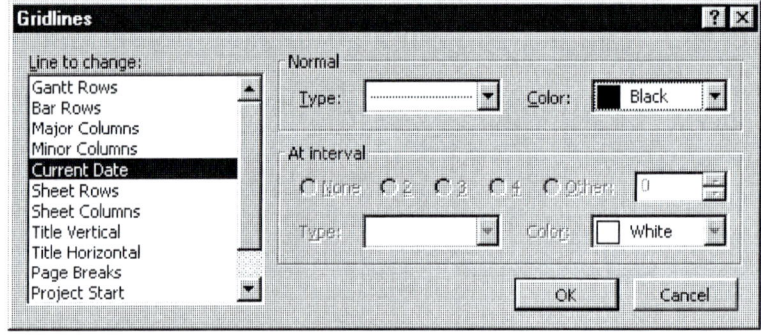

♦ In the **Normal** frame, adjust the settings as required.

♦ Click the **OK** button.

Changing the date format for the Gantt Bars

♦ Display the Gantt chart for the project concerned.

♦ **Format**
  Layout

♦ Open the **Date format** list.

♦ Choose the format that you require.

♦ Click the **OK** button.

| Customising the look of your Gantt Chart | Changing the timescale |

♦ **Format**
Timescale

♦ Under the **Timescale** tab, change the settings to customise the timescale.

♦ Modify the **Nonworking Time** options as required:

   – specify the **Calendar** that Microsoft Project must use to identi-fy nonworking time.

   – choose the **Color** and the **Pattern** for the nonworking time.

   – use the **Draw** options to place these periods **Behind task bars** on **In front of task bars,** or **Do not draw** not to draw them.

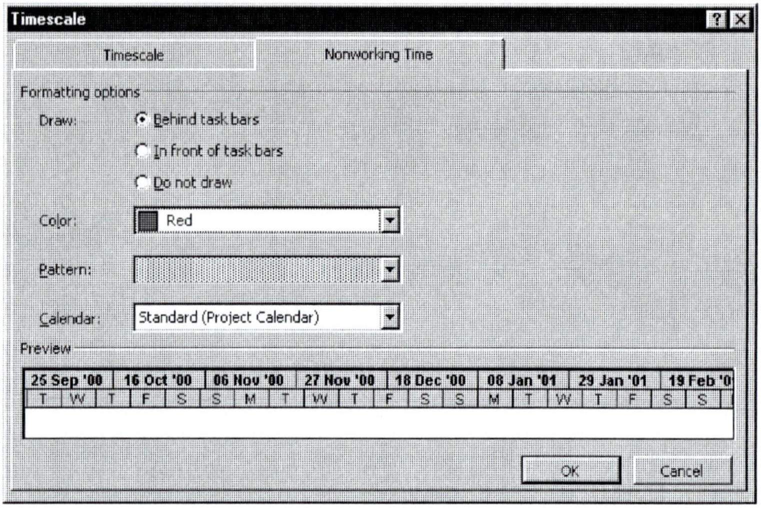

♦ Click the **OK** button.

Changing the text format

♦ **Format**
Text Styles

♦ Choose the **Item to change**.

♦ Change the **Font**, the **Font style**, the **Size** and the **Color** to suit your requirements. Adjust these settings until you are satisfied with the result.

♦ Click the **OK** button.

Changing the gridlines

♦ **Format**
Gridlines

♦ Select the **Line to change**.

♦ Change the look of the gridline in the **Normal** frame and specify how often you want that type of gridline to appear in the **At interval** frame.

♦ Repeat this for each line you wish to change.

♦ Click **OK**.

Changing the look of the Gantt bars

♦ **Format**

♦ To change the look of a specific selected bar, choose **Bar**. To change the look of a category of task bar, choose **Bar Styles**.

*The **Bar Styles** dialog box lists the different categories of task bar (such as **Task**, **Milestone** and **Summary**) and indicates how the Gantt Chart represents them.*

♦ To modify a category of task bar, click that category's row. Specify the appearance of the bar category under the **Bars** tab and the position and content of the displayed text under the **Text** tab.

♦ You can specify your own bar categories as follows:

– click the **Name** column in the first empty row.

– enter a name for the future task bar category (this name is important, as it will appear when you print your Gantt Chart).

– select the **Show For... Tasks** cell for this row and open the list.

– select the type of task that you want the bar category to represent. If it represents several types of task, specify these types as a list, with a comma separating each element.

*Yes/No type fields are the only customised fields that you can represent differently on the Gantt Chart. By default, Microsoft Project will represent the tasks differently only when their **Indicator** fields are set to **Yes**.*

*If you want negations to appear, use the **Not** keyword.*

♦ Specify the look of the bar category and its contents.

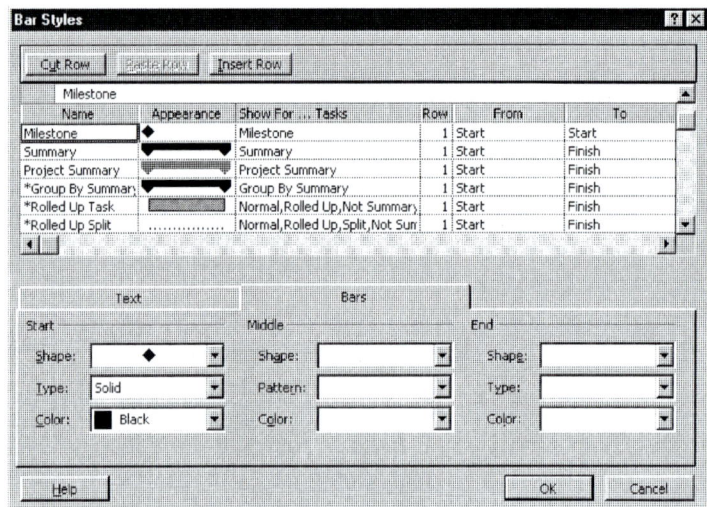

♦ Click the **OK** button.

Changing other aspects of a Gantt Chart

♦ **Format**
  Layout

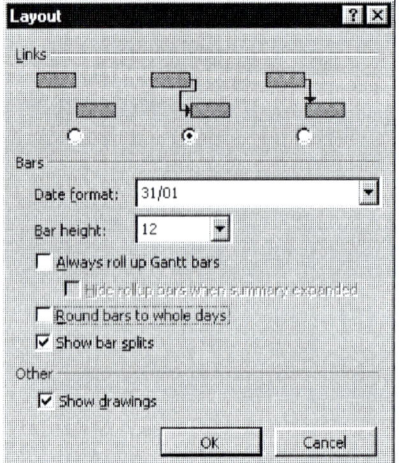

This menu option allows you to modify a number of different aspects.

♦ You can specify the following items:

Links	this frame allows you to specify how you want the links to appear between tasks.
Date format	use this list to define the date format for your Gantt bars.
Bar height	this list allows you to define the height of your Gantt bars, in points.
Always roll up Gantt bars	when this is active, the details of the Gantt bars are rolled up to the summary task, for all the tasks in the project.
Round bars to whole days	when this is active, the bar durations are wrounded up to the next unit on the minor timescale. This does not affect the actual duration, only its representation.
Show bar splits	when this is active, the Gantt Chart can show split task bars.
Show drawings	when this is active, the Gantt Chart shows any drawings that you have created or included.

♦ Click the **OK** button.

Using the Network Diagram

Viewing and understanding the Network Diagram

♦ **View**
Network Diagram

*The **View Bar** contains this icon.*

*If Project 2000 was installed on your computer as an update of a previous version, the **PERT Chart** option may appear instead of the **Network Diagram** option in both the **View Bar** and the **View** menu (the **Network Diagram** was formerly called the **PERT Chart**).*

*Even if your Microsoft Project 2000 is not an update, but you are working with Project files that were created with a previous version, then the **PERT Chart** option may appear in both the **View Bar** and the **View** menu.*

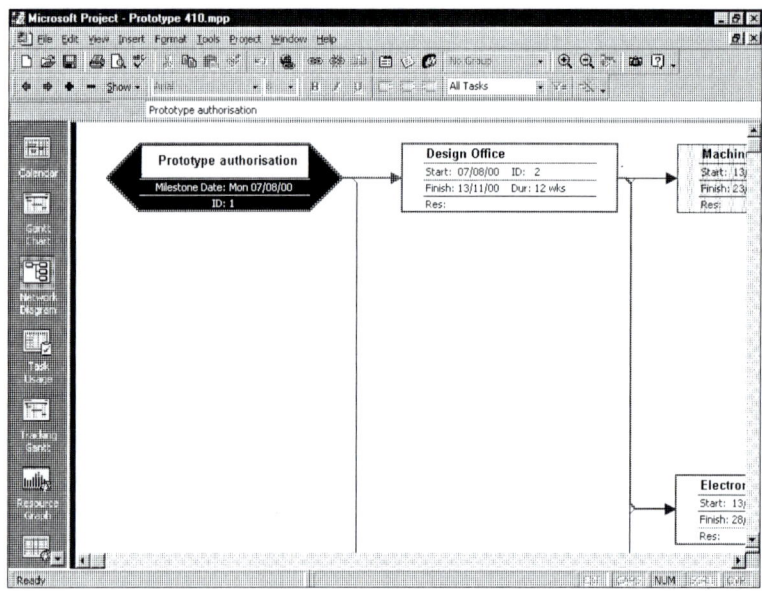

♦ The Network Diagram (or PERT chart) shows each task in a box, which is also called a node.

♦ The box contains the name of the task, its duration, its start and finish dates, and the resources that have been assigned to the task.

♦ By default, tasks appear in rectangular boxes, and milestones appear in hexagonal boxes.

♦ The boxes on the critical path are outlined in red.

Remember that if you change the execution dates of any of the tasks on the critical path, then you will directly affect the finish date of the project.

♦ The Network Diagram also shows the dependency between two tasks, by a line linking the two boxes. By defaut, a single diagonal line represents a tasks in progress and two crossed diagonal lines a completed task.

♦ Using the Network Diagram ensures that no link has been left out: each task must have at least one predecessor and one successor (except the first and last tasks).

Changing the magnification used to display the Network Diagram

 ♦ Use the **Zoom In** (🔍) and the **Zoom Out** (🔍) tool buttons.

 ♦ **View**
Zoom

♦ Choose the level of zoom detail that you require.

*The **Entire project** zoom option is often used for short and medium term projects.*

♦ Click the **OK** button.

The dotted lines indicate page breaks that will occur during printing.

Moving the boxes

♦ **Format**
  Layout

♦ Under **Layout Mode**, activate the **Allow manual box positioning** option.

♦ Click the **OK** button.

♦ Point at the border of the box that you want to move.

♦ Check that the mouse pointer now appears as a black four-headed arrow.

♦ Drag the box to the required position.

The task links remain attached to the box.

Defining a Finish-to-Start link

♦ Click in the predecessor task box.

♦ Check that the mouse pointer now appears as a white cross.

♦ Drag to the successor task box.

As you drag, a line appears with a chain-link at the end.

♦ When the border of the successor box changes colour, release the mouse button.

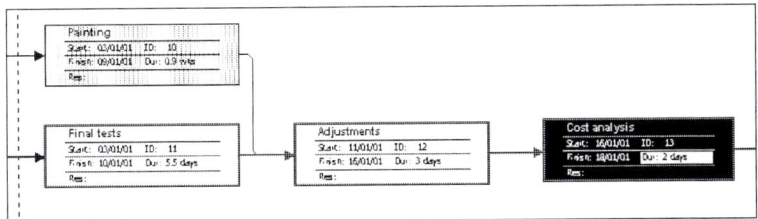

Microsoft Project creates the Finish-to-Start link.

Moving around using the keyboard

♦ Return to viewing the first tasks in the Network Diagram using Ctrl Home. Conversely, Ctrl End allows you to view the final tasks.

♦ You can select other adjacent boxes using the arrow keys.

Changing the look of the Network Diagram

♦ You can change the **Link style** by selecting the **Format - Layout** menu option.

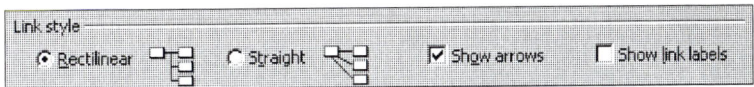

♦ Under **Link style**, choose either the **Rectilinear** option, or the **Straight** option.

♦ Activate the **Show link labels** check box if you want your **Network Diagram** to display the link types (such as FS for a Finish-to-Start link, and FF for a Finish-to-Finish link).

♦ Click **OK** to confirm your settings.

♦ To align the task boxes horizontally, in chronological order, select the **Format - Layout now** menu option.

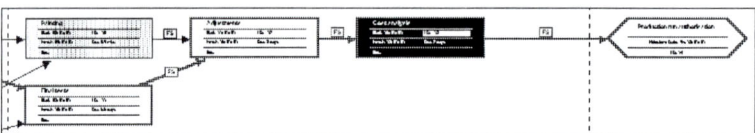

♦ To change the look of the boxes, use **Format - Box Styles**. Indicate how you want your boxes to appear and click **OK** to confirm your settings.

. . . . *Personal notes* . . . .

**Showing
a Calendar
of the project**

Displaying the Calendar

◆ **View
Calendar**

*The **View Bar** contains this icon.*

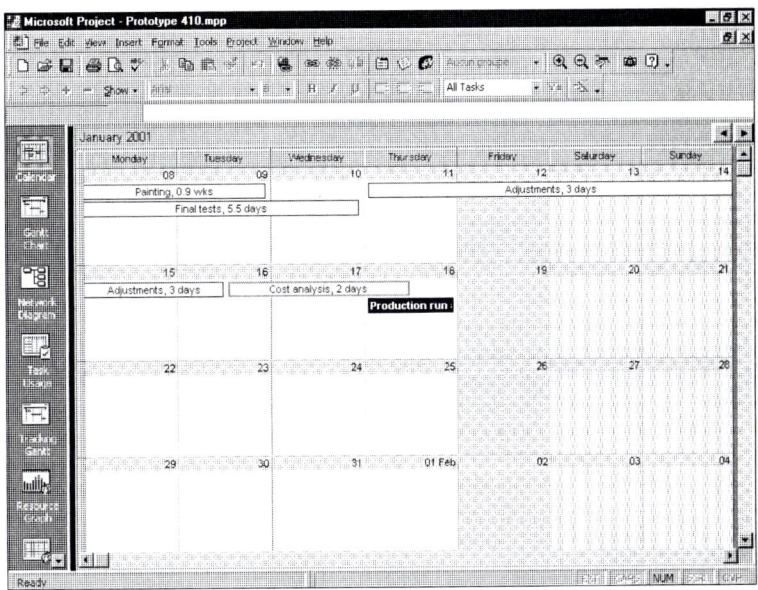

The calendar displays the days of the month whose name appears at the top. It shows one week per row.

Nonworking days are shown in light grey, and days that have special working hours are shown in a darker grey.

◆ The calendar view shows each task as a bar that extends across the days over which it has been scheduled.
These bars have blue borders and contain the name and the duration of the tasks concerned.

◆ Milestones appear on black bars with the name of the task in white characters.

Microsoft Project 2000

♦ You can view more information on the tasks that are scheduled on a specific day by double-clicking the date title bar of the day concerned.

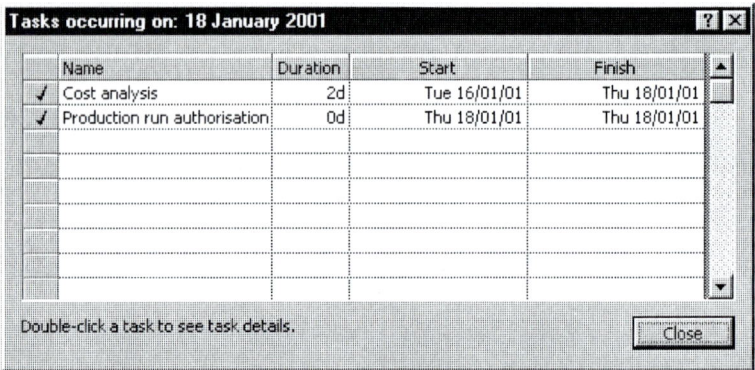

This table shows that day's scheduled tasks, with each task's **Name**, *its* **Duration** *and its* **Start** *and* **Finish** *dates.*

Choosing the month

♦ Move from month to month using the ◄ and ► tool buttons.

♦ You can display different ranges of dates by dragging the vertical scroll cursor.

Changing the magnification used for displaying the Calendar

♦ As with the Gantt Chart and the Network Diagram, you can zoom the Calendar using the 🔍 and 🔍 tool buttons or using **View - Zoom**.

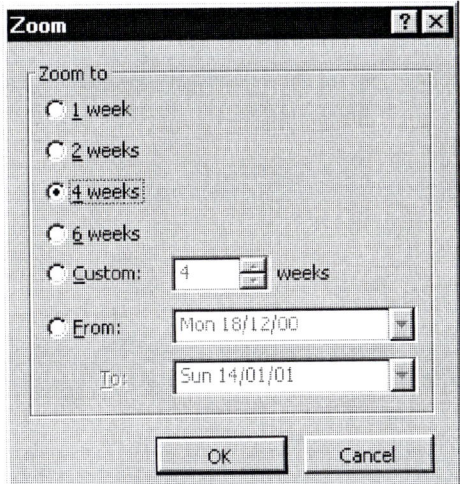

*The **Zoom to** options are different from those of the Gantt Chart or the Network Diagram, as they are based on time periods.*

♦ Choose the level of zoom detail that you require.

♦ Click the **OK** button.

Changing the timescale of the Calendar

♦ **Format**
  Timescale

*The **Headings** page of this dialog box concerns the contents of the calendar, and the format of the Calendar titles.*

♦ In the **Display** frame under the **Week Headings** tab, choose the number of days that you would like to appear in a week.

*The **Sample** frame provides a useful preview when you are changing these settings.*

♦ In the **Weekly titles** box, choose the format for the row titles that appear in your Calendar.

♦ Click the **OK** button.

Printing the Calendar

♦ Display the **Print Preview** using the tool button.

By default, Microsoft Project prints a page for every month of your project.

♦ To reduce the number of pages, click the **Page Setup** button and activate the **View** tab.
Under **Print** specify what you want to print on each page (the **Week height as on screen** option prints the weeks with the same height as you see them on your screen).

Page Setup - Calendar

Page	Margins	Header	Footer	Legend	View

Print
- ● Months per page: ○ 1   ● 2
    - ☑ Only show days in month
    - ☑ Only show weeks in month
- ○ Weeks per page: [   ]
- ○ Week height as on screen

Details
- ☑ Print calendar title
- ☐ Print previous/next month calendars
- ☑ Show additional tasks
    - ● After every page
    - ○ After the last page
    - ☐ Group by day
- ☐ Print notes

[Text Styles...]

[Print Preview...] [Options...] [Print...] [OK] [Cancel]

◆ Under **Details**, indicate how you want to print other items.

◆ Click the **OK** button.

◆ To start printing, click the **Print** button and confirm with **OK**.

If you choose to print two months per page, Project 2000 may print a month that does not concern your project.

Changing the displayed date format

♦ **Tools**
Options

♦ If necessary, activate the **View** tab.

*The second option on this page allows you to choose the **Date format**.*

♦ Open the **Date format** list and choose one of the formats.

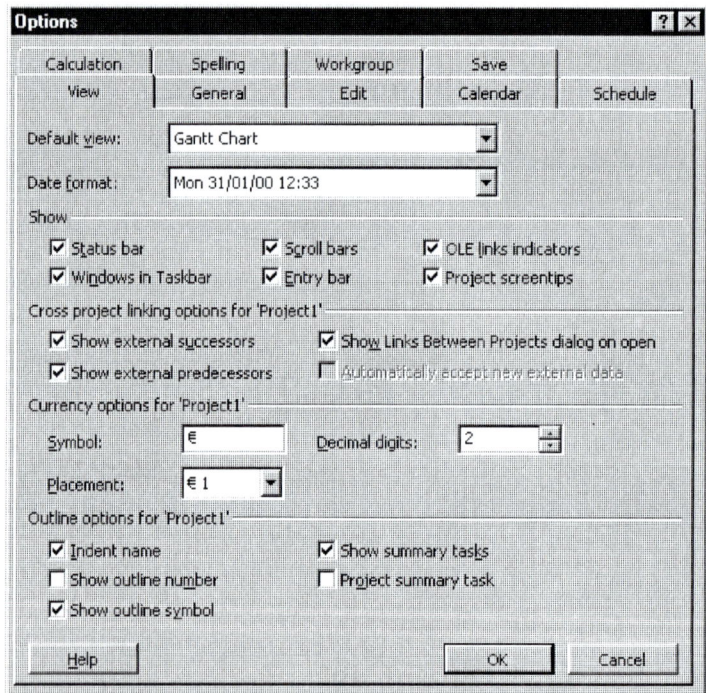

♦ Click the **OK** button to confirm your settings.

**Creating
a new view**

♦ **View
More Views
New**

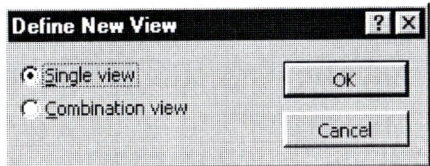

*A **Combination view** refers to a split window.*

Creating a single view

♦ In the **Define New View** dialog box, select the **Single view** option, then click the **OK** button.

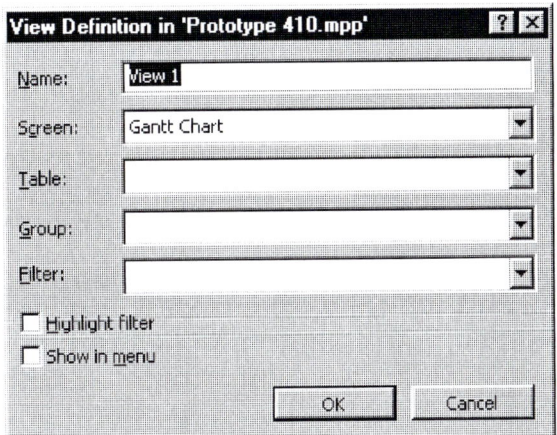

♦ Give a **Name** to your new view.

♦ Indicate the type of **Screen**.

According to the type of screen that you choose, the other options may not be available.

♦ If Microsoft Project allows you to, specify the **Table** that you want to associate with your view.

Microsoft Project 2000

♦ Indicate the **Group** concerned by your view.

♦ Indicate the **Filter** that you want to apply to your view.

♦ Choose, as required, the **Highlight filter** and the **Show in menu** options.

♦ Click the **OK** button.

♦ Click the **Apply** button, or the **Close** button.

Creating a combination view

♦ In the **Define New View** dialog box, select the **Combination view** option, and click **OK**.

♦ Give a **Name** to your view.

♦ In the **Top** box, indicate what you want to appear in the top part of the screen.

♦ In the **Bottom** box, indicate what you want to appear in the bottom part of the screen.

♦ Specify if the view should **Show in menu**.

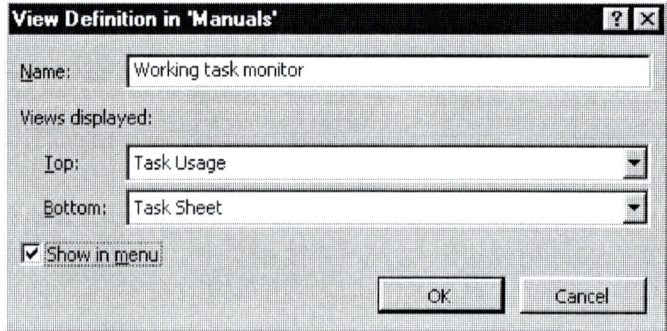

♦ Click the **OK** button.

♦ Click the **Apply** button, or the **Close** button.

Using the Print Preview

♦ Before you print, check the result with the **Print Preview**:

**File
Print Preview**

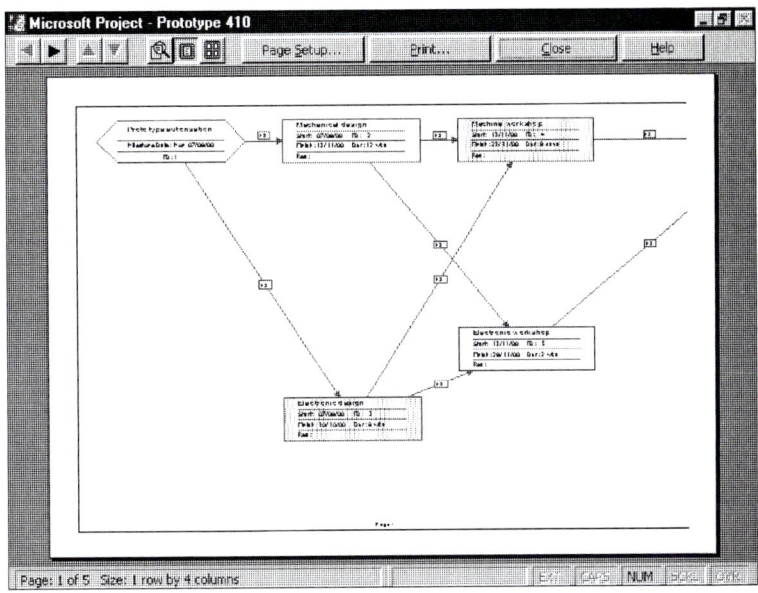

*The status bar of the **Print Preview** shows the number of pages that Microsoft Project will print.*

♦ You can zoom in on the print preview by clicking the part that you want to see in detail.

♦ To zoom back out to the original view, click again.

♦ To view other pages, click the [▶] and [◀] tool buttons.

♦ To start printing, click the **Print** button and confirm with **OK**.

Changing the page setup

You can change the print orientation, the margins, the page borders, the header and footer and the legend.

◆ **File**	**Page Setup** button
Print Preview	in the Print Preview

The number of tabs available depends on what you are printing: some pages contain further tabs.

Changing the page orientation and scaling

◆ Activate the **Page** tab of the **Page Setup** dialog box.

◆ Under **Orientation**, choose either **Portrait** for a vertical orientation, or **Landscape** for a horizontal orientation.

◆ Change the scaling, if necessary, by choosing to enter or select a percentage of **normal size** (**Adjust to**) or with **Fit to**, to make all the data appear on a set number of pages.

Changing the margins

◆ Activate the **Margins** tab of the **Page Setup** dialog box.

◆ Specify the sizes of the **Top, Bottom, Left** or **Right** margins.

Changing the borders

◆ Activate the **Margins** tab of the **Page Setup** dialog box.

◆ Choose one of the options under **Borders around**.

Modifying the header and the footer

◆ Activate the **Header** tab, or the **Footer** tab, of the **Page Setup** dialog box.

◆ Activate the required **Alignment**.

♦ Enter the text for the header or footer.

♦ To insert special items, select them from the **General** list, or from the **Project fields** list, or click the following buttons:

A	Text Font (format)
#	Page Number
	Total Page Count
	Current Date
	Current Time
	File Name
	Picture

Modifying the legend

♦ Activate the **Legend** tab of the **Page Setup** dialog box.

♦ Define the general legend setup as for a header or footer.

♦ Define where you want the legend to appear using the **Legend on** options.

Modifying the print contents

♦ Activate the **View** tab of the **Page Setup** dialog box.

♦ Specify the print contents using the options under this tab.

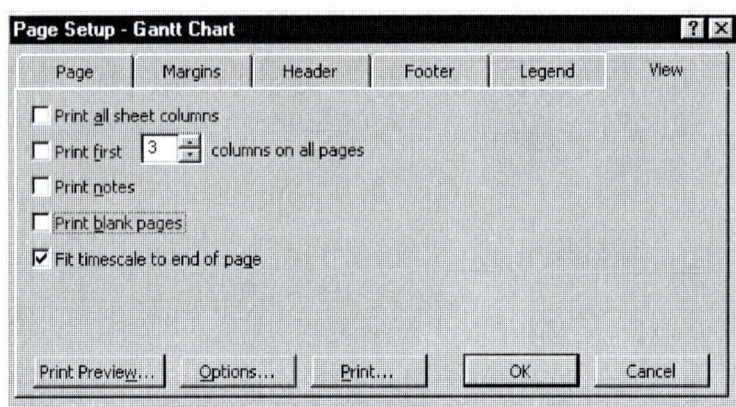

Some of these options may not be available, depending on what you are printing.

Customising reports

You can customize the contents and appearance of your reports.

♦ **View**
  Reports

♦ Double-click the **Custom** button.

♦ Select the **Report** concerned and click to **Edit** or **Copy** it. You can also create a **New** report.

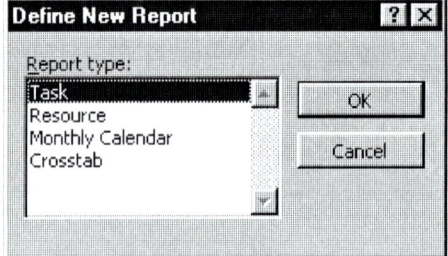

*There are two main types of report: simple reports (**Task** or **Resource**) and **Crosstab** reports.*

*Project 2000 offers the **Monthly Calendar** option only to be compatible with previous versions.*

Creating a simple report

♦ In the **Define New Report** dialog box, select **Task** or **Resource** according to the data used for the report, then click **OK**.

♦ Under the **Definition** tab, specify the name and the contents of the report.

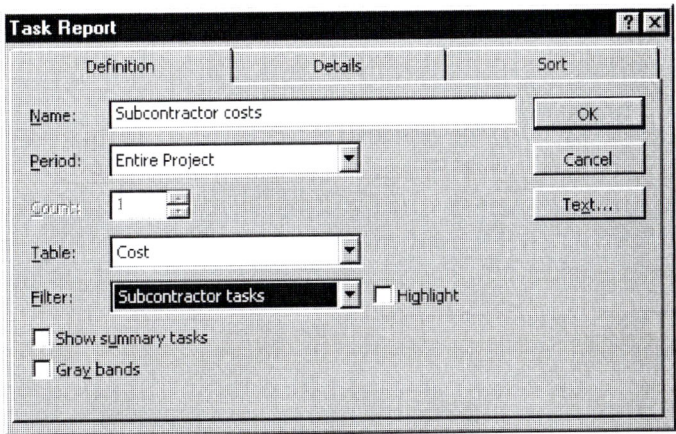

♦ Under the **Details** tab, you can specify more information relating to the contents of the report.

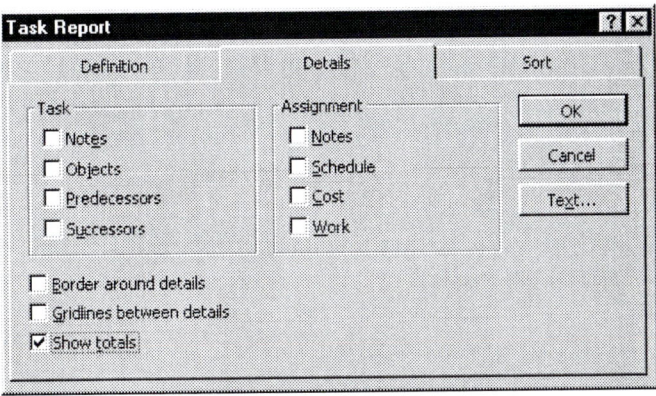

*According to the choices that you make under the **Definition** tab, some of these options may not be available.*

♦ If necessary, request a **Sort**, using the **Sort** page.

♦ To change the character format, click the **Text** button that is available under all the tabs of this dialog box.

*A dialog box appears, similar to that obtained with **Format - Text Styles**.*

♦ Specify the formatting that you require and confirm.

♦ Confirm your report definition by clicking **OK**.

♦ Display a **Preview**, or choose to **Print** directly.

Creating a "Crosstab" report

♦ In the **Define New Report** dialog box, double-click **Crosstab**.

♦ Under the **Definition** tab:

– enter the **Name** of the report,

– specify the type of data that must appear in each **Row** (**Tasks** or **Resources**),

– specify the analysis time period in **Column**,

– in the next list, specify the field to be analysed,

– if required, apply a **Filter** to your report data,

– if required, specify the **Highlight** option.

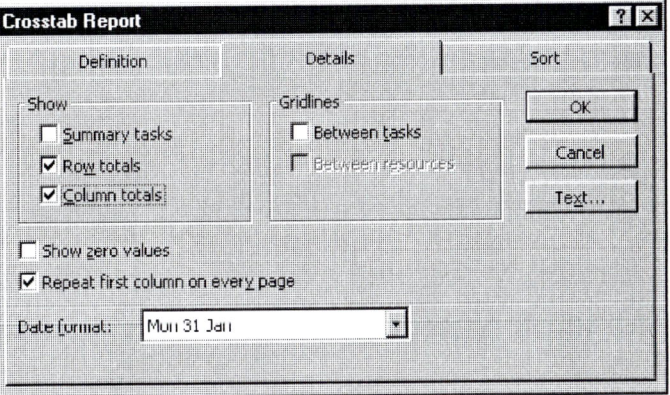

♦ To change the character format, click the **Text** button.

♦ Click the **Details** tab to specify further information.

♦ If necessary, activate a **Sort** under the corresponding tab.

♦ Click the **OK** button.

♦ Display a **Preview** or choose to **Print** directly.

Creating a table   Defining the contents of the table

♦ **View**
 Table
 More Tables

♦ To define the contents of a task table, activate **Task**.
 To define the contents of a resource table, activate **Resource**.

♦ Click **Copy** or click **New**.

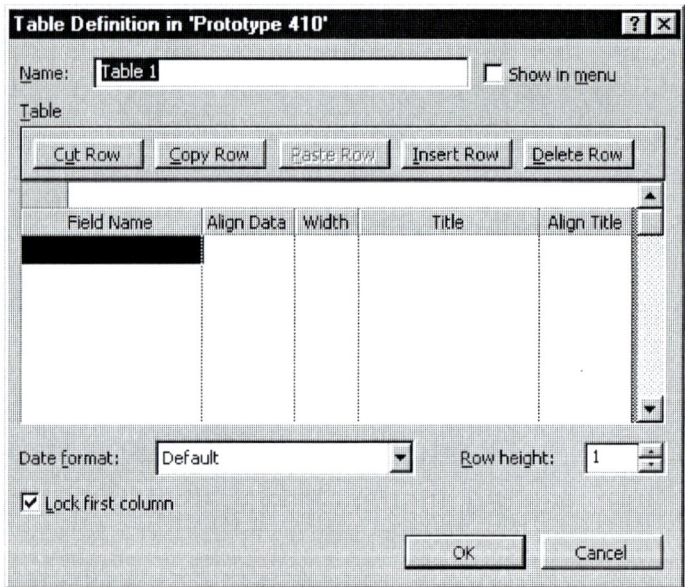

♦ Give a **Name** to your new table.

♦ If you wish, activate the **Show in menu** check box.

 *If this option is active, you can access your table with **View -
 Table**. Otherwise, you will have to use the **More Tables** option.*

♦ For each column in your new table:

 – select the **Field Name**.

 – select the alignment under **Align Data**.

Microsoft Project 2000

*For numerical and date fields, **Right** alignment is generally used.*

*For the **Name** type field, avoid **Right** and **Center** alignments, as they prevent you from seeing indents when viewing the outline.*

♦ Specify the default column **Width**.

♦ Under **Title** you can specify a header for the column.

*If you leave the **Title** cell empty, then Microsoft Project will use the **Field Name** as the column header.*

*Entering your own **Title** allows you to personalise the column header. However, it can cause problems. For example, when you request a sort, Project 2000 will propose field names as criteria, and not column headers.*

♦ If required, open the **Align Title** list and choose the alignment you want for the column header.

♦ If you want your date type fields to have a particular format, specify it using the **Date Format** list.

♦ If you wish, you can adjust the **Row height**.

♦ If you want the first column to remain visible when you scroll the table horizontally, then activate the **Lock first column** check box.

♦ Click the **OK** button. Then click **Apply** or **Close**.

Using specific task fields

♦ Project 2000 reserves a certain number of its task fields for the personal use of each user.

Here are some of these fields:

Field type	Field Name	Comments
Numerical	Number1 to Number20	for storing numbers.
Cost	Cost1 to Cost10	for storing numbers in monetary format. Important note: this data is not taken into account in the total cost.
Yes/No	Flag1 to Flag20	for entering only "Yes" or "No" values ("No" by default).
Text	Text1 to Text30	for entering text.
Duration	Duration1 to Duration10	for storing duration or work values.
Date	Date1 to Date10 Finish1 to Finish10 Start1 to Start10	For storing dates. For storing finish dates or other dates. For storing start dates or other dates.
Code	Outline Code1 to Outline Code10	For storing outline code information.

Using specific resource fields

♦ The resource fields that you can personalise are the same as those for the task fields.

Field type	Field Name
Text	Text1 to Text30
Numerical	Number1 to Number20
Cost	Cost1 to Cost10
Date	Date1 to Date10 Finish1 to Finish10 Start1 to Start10
Duration	Duration1 to Duration10
Code	Outline Code1 to Outline Code10
Yes/No	Flag1 to Flag20

Modifying the contents of a table

Changing the contents of a column

♦ Double-click the header of the column whose contents you wish to modify.

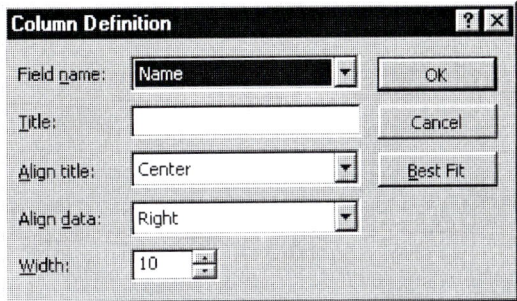

♦ You can modify the **Field name**, the **Title**, the **Align title**, the **Align data** and/or the **Width**.

♦ Click the **OK** button.

Inserting a column

♦ Click the header of the column before which you want your new column to appear.

♦ **Insert Column**   ♦

*The **Column Definition** dialog box appears.*

♦ Specify the characteristics of the new column.

♦ Click the **OK** button.

<u>Removing a column</u>

♦ Click the header of the column you want to delete.

♦ **Edit**   ♦
  Hide Column

Project 2000 removes the column, but it does not remove the field from your project.

<u>Moving a column</u>

♦ **View**
  Table
  More Tables

♦ Select the name of the table concerned.

♦ Click the **Edit** button.

♦ Click a cell in the column that you want to move.

♦ Click the **Cut Row** button.

The column row disappears.

♦ Click the destination column.

♦ Click the **Paste Row** button.

♦ Click the **OK** button. Then click **Apply** or **Close**.

Resizing columns and panes

<u>Resizing columns</u>

♦ Point to the vertical line to the right of the header of the column that you want to resize.

♦ Check that the pointer changes into a double-headed arrow.

♦ Drag the line to its required position, or double-click it.

When you double-click this line, Project 2000 automatically adjusts the column to fit its widest contents.

Resizing panes

♦ Point at the appropriate split bar.

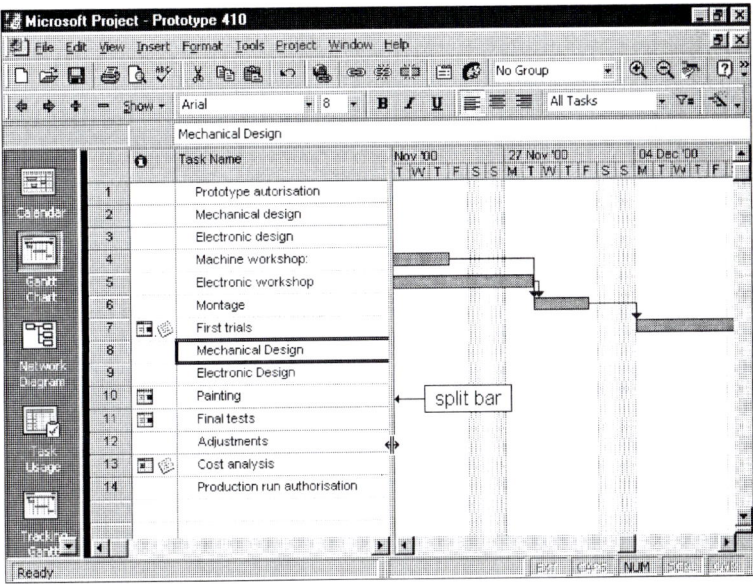

The mouse pointer changes into a double-headed arrow.

♦ Drag the split bar to the required position.

♦ When you have released the mouse button, you can double-click the vertical split bar to align it with the nearest column border.

❏ *Double-clicking a horizontal split bar removes the window split.*

Changing the look of a table

Modifying the gridlines

♦ **Format**
Gridlines

♦ Under **Line to change** choose one of the following options: **Sheet Rows**, **Sheet Columns**, **Title Vertical**, **Title Horizontal**, or **Page Breaks**.

♦ Define the format of the line that you selected.

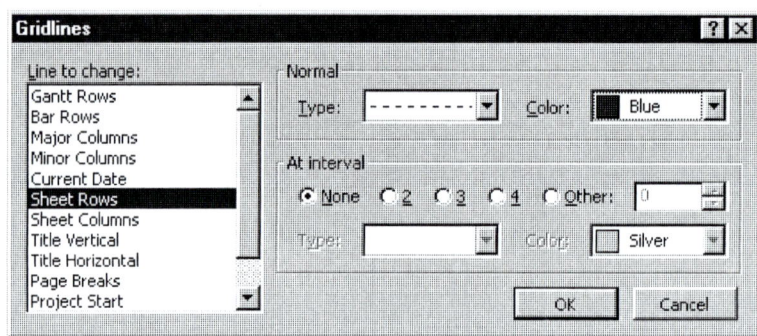

♦ Click the **OK** button.

Modifying text formats

♦ To modify the text in a specific row in a table, select that row and choose **Format - Font**.

To modify the text of specific items, select **Format - Text Styles**.

♦ If you have chosen the **Format - Text Styles** menu option, indicate the **Item to Change**.

*The **Item to Change** list differs, according to whether you are working with a task table or with a resource table.*

♦ Indicate the **Font**, the **Font style**, the **Size**, the **Color**, and whether or not it should have an **Underline**.

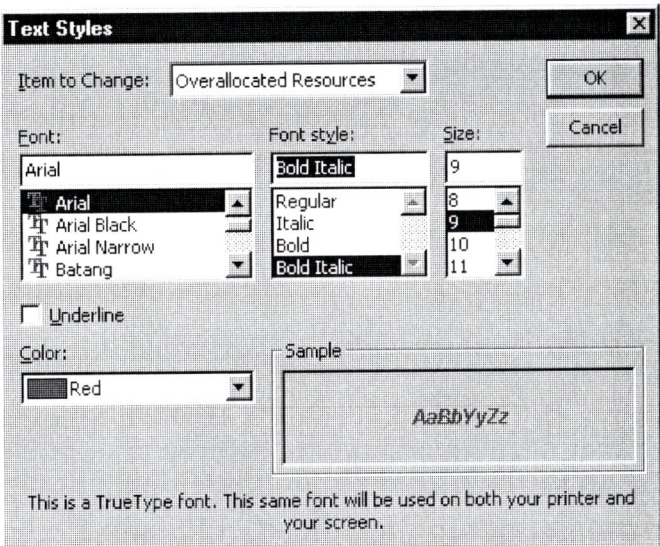

♦ Click the **OK** button.

When you change the look of a table, you change the look of all the tables of the current category (tasks or resources) and not only that of the current table.

Modifying the contents of a cell

When you are entering data into a cell

♦ To delete preceding characters, press the ⬅ key on the alphanumerical keyboard.

♦ Complete your entry.

♦ Press the Enter key.

After you have entered data into a cell

♦ Select the cell whose contents you want to modify.

♦ Click in the entry bar at the place where you want to make your modification.

The inserting point flashes at the point that you indicated: the ✖ *and* ✔ *buttons appear.*

♦ Make your modifications.

The new characters that you type are added to the existing characters. By default, the entry mode is Insert mode.

You can replace characters by activating overwrite mode: when you are in this mode, the letters OVR appear on the task bar, and the characters that you type replace the existing characters. You can toggle between these modes by pressing Ins *.*

♦ Press the Enter key.

You can also start modifying a cell by clicking it and then pressing the F2 *key. Then, use the arrow keys to move the insertion point.*

Deleting the contents of a cell

♦ Click the cell whose contents you want to delete.

♦ Press the ⬅ key or use [Ctrl][Del].

The cell contents disappear.

♦ Move to another cell, either by pressing the [Enter] key, or by pressing an arrow key.

❏ *Be careful not to press [Del] alone, as this will delete the contents of the current row.*

Copying the contents of a cell to adjacent cells

♦ Select the cell you want to copy and the destination cells.

❶	Resource Name	Type	Material Label	Initials	Group	Max. Units
	Sales Force	Work		SF	SF	1,400%
	Tele-marketing	Work		TM		500%
	Sales Executives	Work		SE		500%
	Commercial Agents	Work		CA		400%

The destination cells must be contiguous and adjacent to the source cell.

♦ **Edit**
  File

♦ Choose the copy direction.

❏ *To copy downwards, use the [Ctrl] **D** shortcut key.*

Highlighting filtered tasks or resources

Filters are used to view a subset of tasks or resources and also to present filtered rows differently while still showing the other rows.

♦ **Project**
Filtered for
More Filters

♦ Select the name of the filter that you want to apply.

♦ Apply the filter by clicking the **Highlight** button.

By default, filtered rows appear highlighted in blue.

 You can change the highlight colour with: ***Format - Text Styles -
Item to Change: Highlighted Tasks*** (or ***Highlighted Resources***).

Customising a filter

♦ **Project**
Filtered for
More Filters

♦ Specify whether you are interested in **Task** or **Resource** filters.

♦ Click **Edit**, **Copy** or **New** to modify, copy or create a new filter.

♦ Give a **Name** to the filter, if necessary, and specify whether or not you want the filter to **Show in menu**.

♦ Set up your filter as required.

♦ Click the **OK** button then click **Apply** or **Close**.

Setting a sort criterion

♦ Choose to create or modify a filter.

♦ Click in the first **Field Name** cell, open the list and choose the field to which you want to apply your criterion.

♦ Open the **Test** list and choose the operator that you want to use.

♦ Click in the **Value(s)** column and enter the comparison value(s).

*When you specify **is within** and **is not within** tests, you must specify a pair of values. Enter the lower value, a comma or a semi-colon, then the higher value. You can use the * and ? wildcards. To compare your field with another field, open the list. The field names appear in square brackets.*

Setting several sort criteria

♦ Choose to create or modify a filter.

♦ Set one test per row.

*Even if you apply several tests to the same field, you must repeat the **Field Name** on each row.*

♦ Activate the **And/Or** cell for each row, except for the first row. Choose **And** to indicate that all the test criteria must be satisfied or **Or** if only one of the test criteria needs to be satisfied.

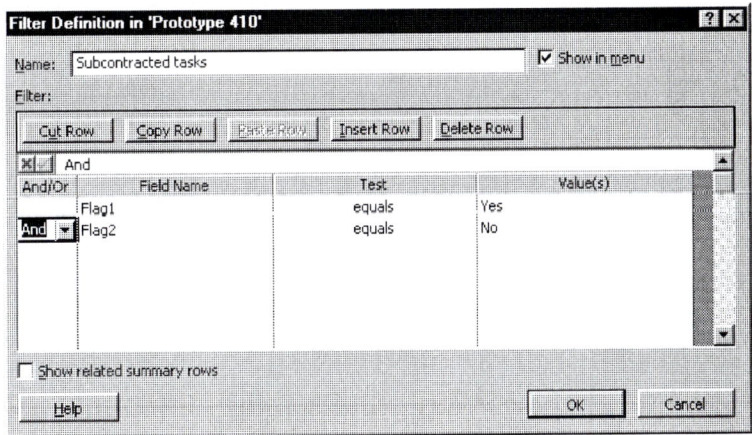

Creating an interactive filter

An interactive filter allows users to specify their own criteria.

♦ Choose to create or modify a filter.

♦ Define the test rows, and access the **Value(s)** cell for the row whose test you want to make interactive.

♦ Enter the user message prompt between quotation marks.

♦ Enter a question mark after the closing quotation marks (without inserting a space).

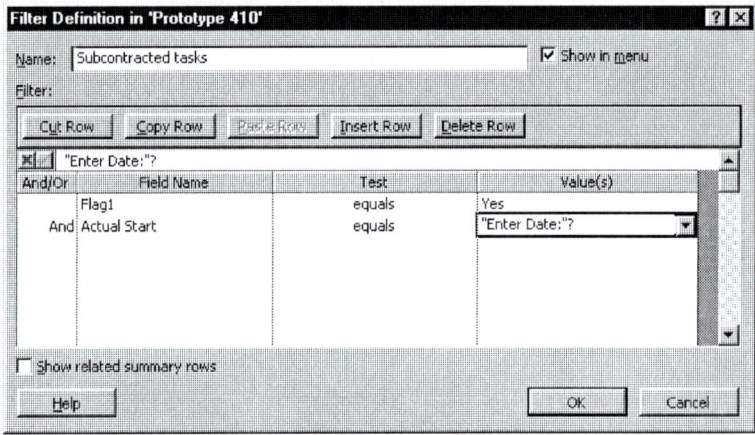

If you applied this filter, the following dialog box would appear:

Using AutoFilters

AutoFilters can rapidly display subsets of tasks and resources.

Activating/deactivating AutoFilters

♦ Click the 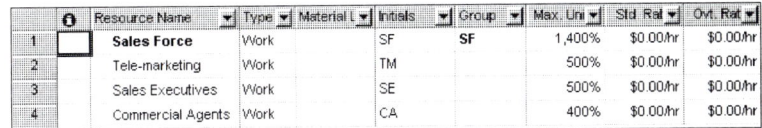 tool button.

	❶	Resource Name	Type ▼	Material L ▼	Initials ▼	Group ▼	Max. Uni ▼	Std. Rat ▼	Ovt. Rat ▼
1		**Sales Force**	Work		SF	SF	1,400%	$0.00/hr	$0.00/hr
2		Tele-marketing	Work		TM		500%	$0.00/hr	$0.00/hr
3		Sales Executives	Work		SE		500%	$0.00/hr	$0.00/hr
4		Commercial Agents	Work		CA		400%	$0.00/hr	$0.00/hr

When you activate the AutoFilters, Project 2000 displays arrow buttons to the right of each column header.

Filtering according to a column value

♦ Click the arrow button for the column concerned.

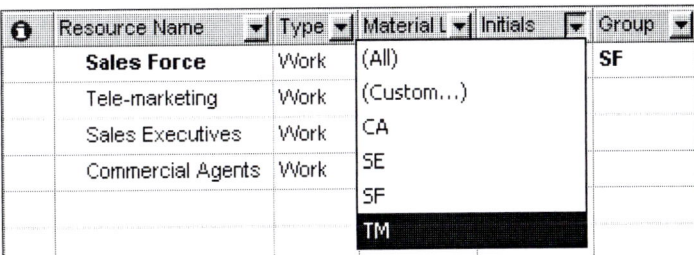

Project 2000 lists the different values that the column contains.

♦ Click the criterion value for the rows that you want to filter.

When an AutoFilter has been applied, the column header and the arrow appear in blue.

Combining criteria on different fields with an "And"

♦ Specify your test criterion in each of the columns concerned.

Setting two criteria on the same field

♦ Click the arrow button for the column concerned, and choose **(Custom...)**.

♦ Specify your first test criterion.

♦ Indicate how you want to combine your criteria (by activating either the **And** option or the **Or** option).

♦ Specify your second test criterion.

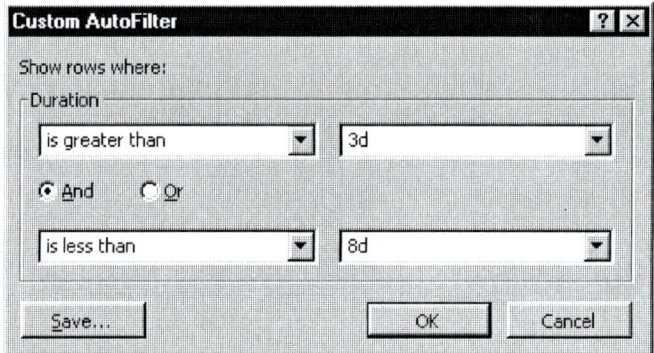

♦ Confirm with **OK**.

Removing a filter from a column

♦ Click the arrow button in the column header.

♦ Choose the **(All)** option.

The column header and button return to their original colour.

**Saving
an AutoFilter**

You can create a new filter from an AutoFilter.

♦ Access the **Custom AutoFilter** dialog box.

♦ Set your test criteria.

♦ Click the **Save** button.

♦ Give a **Name** to your new filter.

♦ Choose to **Show in menu**, if required.

♦ Click **OK** to create the new filter.

♦ Apply the AutoFilter by clicking the **OK** button.

. . . . *Personal notes* . . . .

Microsoft Project 2000

Entering the task names for a project

♦ In the **Entry Table** of the **Gantt Chart**, activate the first cell in the **Task Name** column.

♦ Enter the **Task Name**.

As soon as you start entering the first characters, the tool bars grey out. The text appears in the cell and in the entry bar, where the ⊠ *and* ✓ *buttons also appear.*

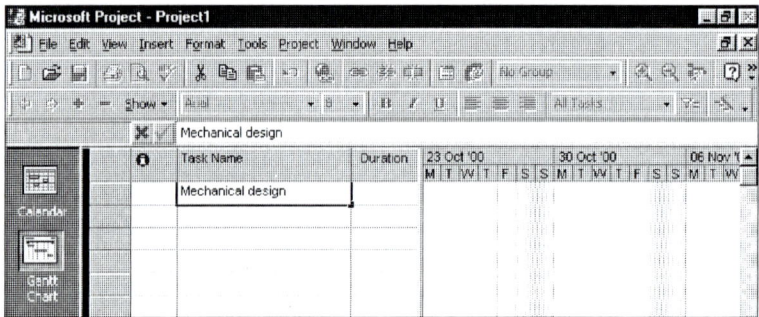

If the entry bar does not appear, use ***Tools - Options****, click the* ***View*** *tab and activate the* ***Entry bar*** *option.*

♦ Confirm your entry by pressing the Enter key or the ⏎ key.

The next cell is activated immediately. The duration of the confirmed task becomes 1 day, followed by a question mark, indicating the Project has assigned this duration by default. A bar appears in the ***Gantt Chart****.*

You can also confirm or cancel your entries by clicking *or* ⊠.

♦ Enter the different tasks of your project in this way.

❏ *If Project does not activate the next cell down when you press* Enter *, select* ***Tools - Options - Edit*** *tab and activate the* ***Move selection after enter*** *option.*

Microsoft Project 2000

Defining milestones in a project

Creating a milestone

♦ A milestone is a special task, as it has zero duration. You can define a milestone, simply by entering zero as the task duration.

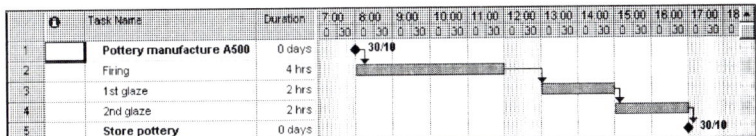

By default Microsoft Project represents a milestone in a Gantt Chart as a diamond shape followed by the date of the task.

Transforming a task into a milestone

You should consider as milestones certain tasks of short duration.

♦ Double-click the task concerned.

♦ Click the **Advanced** tab.

♦ Click the **Mark task as milestone** check box.

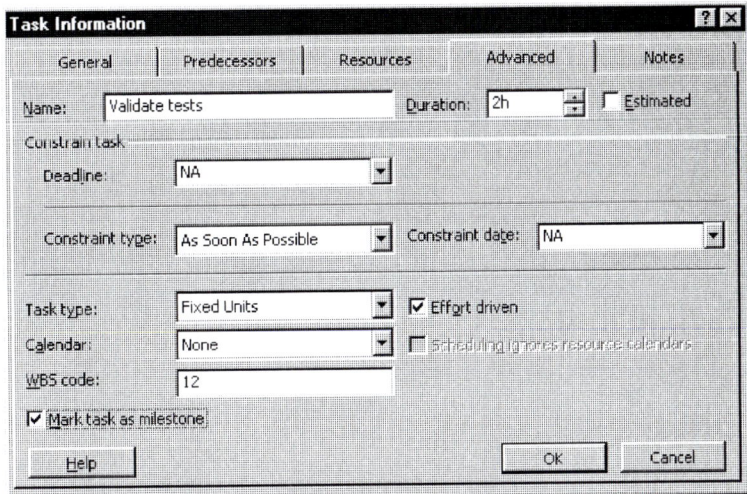

♦ Click the **OK** button.

Microsoft Project indicates that it has accepted the request by displaying the task in the Gantt Chart, as a diamond shape. Of course, the task still keeps the same duration.

Managing milestones

Printing milestones

♦ **View**
  Reports

♦ Double-click the **Overview** button.

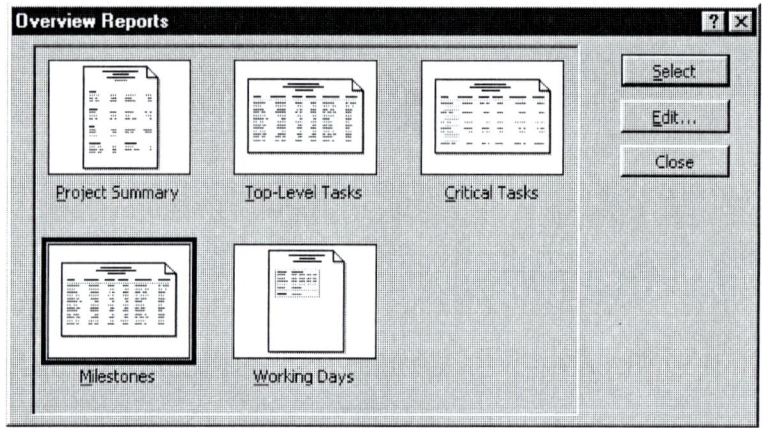

♦ Double-click **Milestones**.

A preview of the report appears.

♦ Click the **Print** button then click **OK**.

♦ Click the **Close** button to close the **Reports** dialog box.

Filtering milestones

♦ Open the **Filter** list.

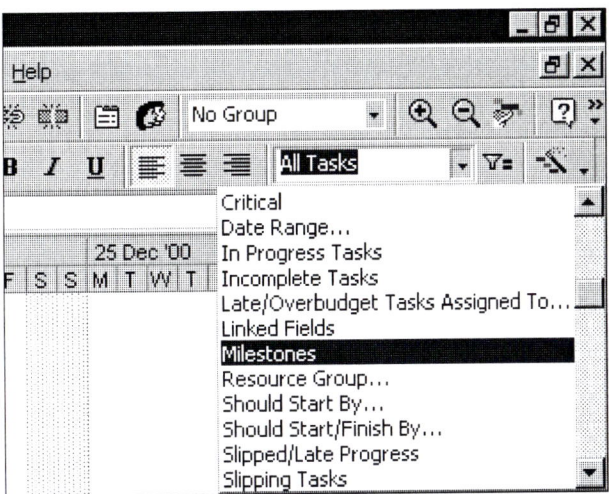

♦ Choose **Milestones**.

Assigning durations to tasks

Entering the duration

♦ Activate the **Duration** cell.

♦ If the duration is already in the units that you want, enter only the number.
Otherwise, enter the number followed by: "m" for minutes, "h" for hours, "d" for days, "w" for weeks, or "mo" for months.

You can specify the units in either lowercase or uppercase letters.

♦ Enter.

Microsoft Project 2000

	❶	Task Name	Duration			
1		Prototype authorisation	0 days	◆ 27/10		
2		Mechanical design	12 wks			
3		Electronic design	8 wks			
4		Mechanical workshop	8 days			
5		Electronic workshop	2 wks			
6		Assembly	3 days			
7		First trials	3 wks			
8		Mechanical design	3 days			
9		Electronic design	2 days			
10		Painting	1 wk			
11		Final trials	3 days			
12		Adjustments	3 days			
13		Cost analysis	2 days			
14		Production run authorisation	0 days	◆ 27/10		

Microsoft Project sizes the bars in the Gantt Chart according to the durations that you enter.

Changing the default duration units

♦ **Tools**
  Options

♦ Activate the **Schedule** tab.

*By default, **Duration is entered in: Days**.*

♦ Open the **Duration is entered in** list and choose the new units.

♦ Click the **OK** button.

Working in elapsed time, rather than working time

♦ To specify elapsed duration, prefix the duration units by the letter "e". For example, instead of typing "m" (minutes), "h" (hours), "d" (days), "w" (weeks), or "mo" (months), type "em" (elapsed minutes), "eh" (elapsed hours), "ed" (elapsed days), "ew" (elapsed weeks), or "emo" (elapsed months).

You can use these codes whenever you enter a duration.

Choosing the duration display format

♦ **Tools**
  Options

♦ Activate the **Edit** tab.

♦ Choose your required view options:

  Minutes using the format: **m**, **min** or **minute**
  Hours using the format: **h**, **hr** or **hour**
  Days using the format: **d**, **dy** or **day**
  Weeks using the format: **w**, **wk** or **week**
  Months using the format: **mo**, **mon** or **month**
  Years using the format: **y**, **yr** or **year**.

♦ If you do not want a space to appear between the numbers and the unit labels, deactivate the **Add space before label** option.

♦ Click the **OK** button.

Allowing Project 2000 to calculate the duration of a task

To do this, Project 2000 uses a technique called "PERT Analysis".

Displaying the PERT Analysis toolbar

♦ **View**
  Toolbars
  PERT Analysis

Entering the duration data for the PERT analysis

♦ Click the [PERT Entry Form icon] tool button (**PERT Entry Form**) or the [PERT Entry Sheet icon] tool button (**PERT Entry Sheet**).

*The first of these tools displays the **PERT Entry** dialog box, and the second displays a table called the **PA_PERT Entry Sheet**.*

♦ For each task being reviewed, enter its **Optimistic Duration**, its **Expected Duration** and its **Pessimistic Duration**.

Starting the PERT analysis

♦ Click the ▦ tool button (**Calculate PERT**).

*Project 2000 calculates a weighted average and displays the result in the **Duration** column.*

❏ *To modify the weightings that Project 2000 uses for this calculation, click the ⚖ tool button, set the new PERT weights (the sum of these weights must be 6), then click **OK**.*

Displaying the Gantt Chart with the different durations

♦ Use the following tool buttons: ▦ (**Optimistic Gantt**), ▦ (**Expected Gantt**) or ▦ (**Pessimistic Gantt**).

Setting up links between tasks

*A **Predecessor** is a task that must start or finish before another task can start or finish. A **Successor** is a task that depends on the start date or the finish date of a previous task.*

Setting up a finish-to-start link between two tasks

♦ In the **Gantt Sheet**, select the tasks that you want to link.

♦ Click the ⊕ tool button or use Ctrl F2.

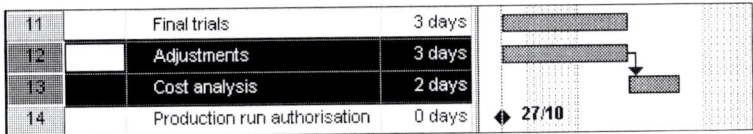

11		Final trials	3 days	
12		Adjustments	3 days	
13		Cost analysis	2 days	
14		Production run authorisation	0 days	♦ 27/10

*The link appears in the **Gantt Chart** as an arrow.*

Setting up other types of link between tasks

♦ Double-click the **Successor** task row in the **Gantt Sheet**.

♦ Click the **Predecessors** tab.

♦ If you know the number of the predecessor task, click in the **ID** cell of the first empty line in the **Predecessors** table, enter the number of this task and press the ⏎ key.

If you do not know this number, click the first empty **Task Name** cell, open its drop-down list, choose the name of the predecessor task and click ✔.

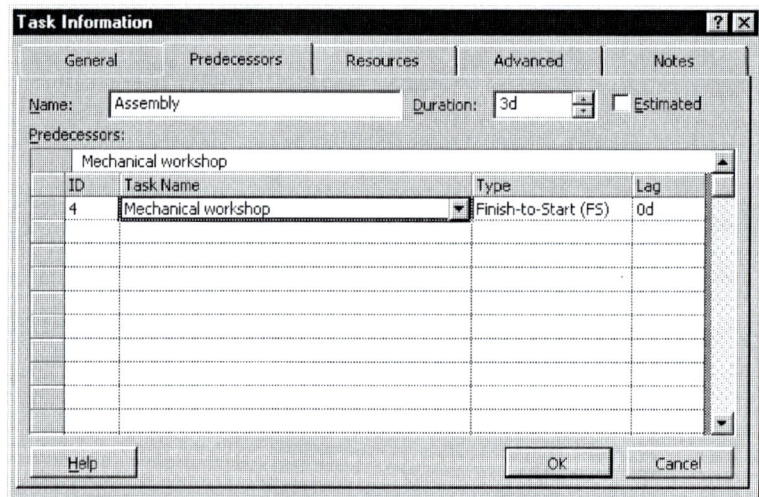

*Microsoft Project displays the **ID**, the **Task Name**. In addition, it displays the **Type** of the link as **Finish-to-Start (FS)**.*

♦ To assign another type of link, click in the **Type** cell, open the list in this cell, and choose the type of link required.

♦ Set up all the other links between this task and its predecessors in this way.

♦ Click the **OK** button.

Setting up other types of link (alternative method)

♦ In the **Gantt Sheet**, click in the **Predecessors** cell of the successor task row.

♦ Enter the predecessor task numbers, using the following rules:

– Predecessor number(s):
  Only one predecessor   enter a single task number
  Several predecessors   enter the numbers as a list separated by commas

– Type of link:
  Finish-to-Start link   enter only the number
  Start-to-Start link   suffix the number by the letters SS
  Finish-to-Finish link   suffix the number by the letters FF
  Start-to-Finish link   suffix the number by the letters SF

♦ Press Enter.

To unlink a successor from all its predecessors, select the successor task and click the *tool button or use* Ctrl 1 Shift F2 .

Specifying lag times and lead times for links

Using the Task Information dialog box

♦ Double-click the successor task.

♦ Activate the **Predecessors** tab.

♦ Click in the **Lag** cell for the link concerned.

♦ Enter the lag time or the lead time using the following rules:

To specify a:	Enter a:
Lag time	positive value
Lead time	negative value
You can specify lag times and lead times in working time units, in elapsed time units (minutes, hours, days, weeks or months) or as percentages.	

♦ Click **OK**.

*The **Gantt Chart** takes into account the link durations that you specify.*

Using the Entry Table

♦ Activate the **Predecessors** cell of the successor task.

♦ Follow the rules outlined

♦ above. Remember that for Finish-to-Start links, the letters FS **must** be entered when you specify these lag or lead times.

♦ Enter + (plus) to specify a lag time or - (minus) to specify a lead time.

♦ Enter the duration of the lag time or the lead time.

♦ Enter.

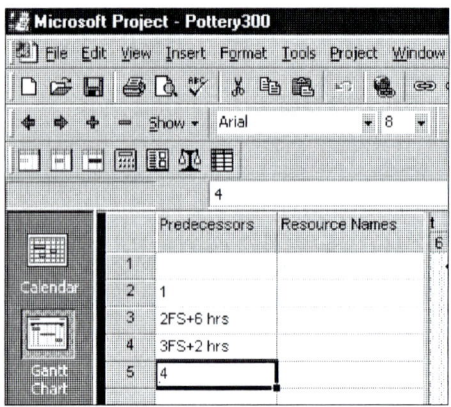

**Viewing the start
and finish dates
for a task**

♦ Scroll the **Gantt Sheet** horizontally.

♦ By default, you will view successively: the **Indicators** column, the **Task Name** column, the **Duration** column, the **Start** column and the **Finish** column (you can also scroll using the ⬛➡ key).

*Although it is possible to enter dates directly into the **Start** column and the **Finish** column, you are not advised to do so. It is wiser to let Project calculate these dates. If something must occur on a certain date, use the module that Project 2000 provides for this purpose.*

♦ Microsoft Project carries out its calculations taking into account a number of factors, including the links between the different tasks and the project calendar.

. . . . *Personal notes* . . . .

Modifying the task list

Deleting a task

◆ Click one of the cells on the row of the task you want to delete.

◆ **Edit**
Delete Task

◆

Project 2000 removes the task from the table and renumbers the other tasks.

Inserting a new task

◆ Click in one of the cells of the task that must appear just after your new task.

◆ **Insert**
New Task

◆

Microsoft Project inserts an empty row into the table and renumbers the other tasks.

◆ Enter the details of your new task and confirm.

Copying a task

◆ Select the task that you want to copy by clicking its number.

The whole row appears in inverse-video.

◆ **Edit**
Copy Task

◆ **C**

Project 2000 copies the task into the clipboard.

◆ Select the row where you want the copy to appear.

◆ **Edit**
Paste

◆  **V**

Microsoft Project inserts the task on the row that you indicated and renumbers the other tasks.

Moving a task

♦ Select the task row that you want to move.

♦ Point to a border of the row, until the pointer appears as an arrow pointing upwards and to the left.

♦ Drag the row to its new position using the horizontal bar that appears as a guide.

♦ Release the mouse button when you reach the correct location.

❏ *If you are unable to use this technique, use* ***Tools - Options - Edit*** *tab and activate the* ***Allow cell drag and drop*** *option.*

When you carry out these different modifications, Project 2000 will normally attempt to update the links. If it does not do so, select ***Tools - Options - Schedule*** *tab and activate the* ***Autolink inserted or moved tasks*** *check box. If you want to manage the links yourself, deactivate this option.*

Sorting the task list

Using a standard criterion

♦ **Project**
   Sort

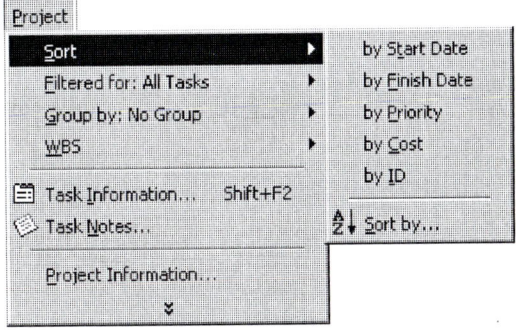

By default, Project offers five standard sort criteria.

♦ Choose the criterion that you want to use.

Project sorts all the tasks in the task list. However, it will not renumber the tasks, unless you request this before you start the sort.

Using other criteria

♦ **Project**
  Sort

♦ Choose the **Sort by** option.

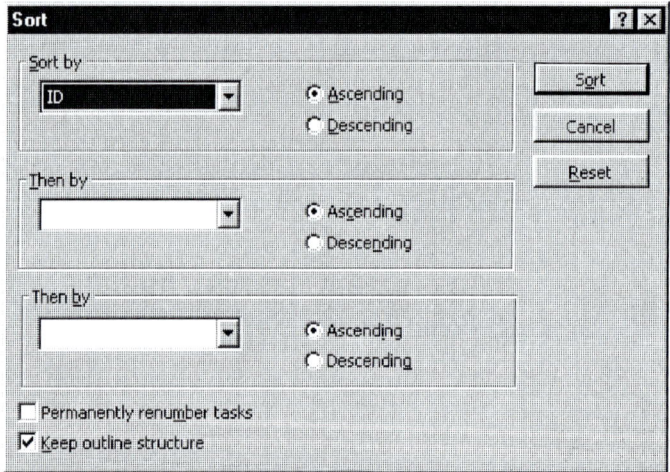

The Sort dialog box allows you to specify up to three sort criteria (Sort by, Then by, and Then by again). You can specify either Ascending or Descending for each of these criteria.

♦ For each sort criteria, select a field name from the list and give a sort order.

♦ If the tasks must keep their original numbers, deactivate the **Permanently renumber tasks** option. If this option is active you will not be able to undo the sort.

♦ To start the sort, click the **Sort** button.

Project sorts the tasks as specified.

> *If you did not ask Project to renumber the tasks, you can restore the tasks to their original order with **Projet - Sort - by ID**, or* ⇧ Shift F3 .

Outlining the task list

*You can simplify your work in Project by summarising sets of tasks (called **subtasks**) as more general tasks (**summary tasks**). This technique is called outlining.*

Setting up an outline

♦ Create the summary task immediately above the subtasks that it must summarise.

♦ Drag to select the subtasks concerned.

♦ Click the **Indent** tool button ( ), or use Alt ⇧ Shift → .

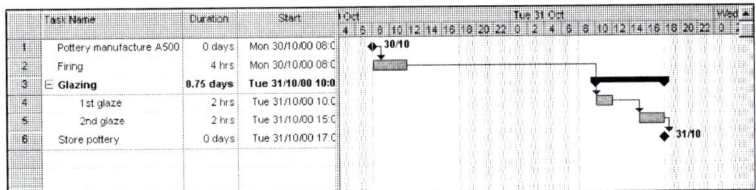

*The subtasks appear indented in the **Task Name** column.*

*The summary task appears in bold characters. Project 2000 calculates its start and finish dates automatically and represents this task as a new bar in the **Gantt Chart**.*

❏ *You can modify only the name of the summary task. Microsoft Project calculates all the other details.*

❏ *With Project 2000, you can include a summary task within another summary task, as long as you do not exceed 10 levels.*

Moving a task up one outline level

♦ Click the task that you want to move up one level.

♦ Click the **Outdent** tool button ( ) or use Alt ⇧ Shift ←.

Hiding/showing subtasks

♦ To hide subtasks, select the summary task concerned then click the tool button. You can click also the minus sign (-) that precedes the name of the summary task.

Project 2000 immediately hides the subtasks.

♦ To show the subtasks again, select the summary task concerned and click the tool button. Alternatively, you can click the plus sign (+) that precedes the name of the summary task.

Accessing a specific outline level

♦ On the **Formatting** toolbar, open the **Show** drop-down list and choose the outline level that you require.

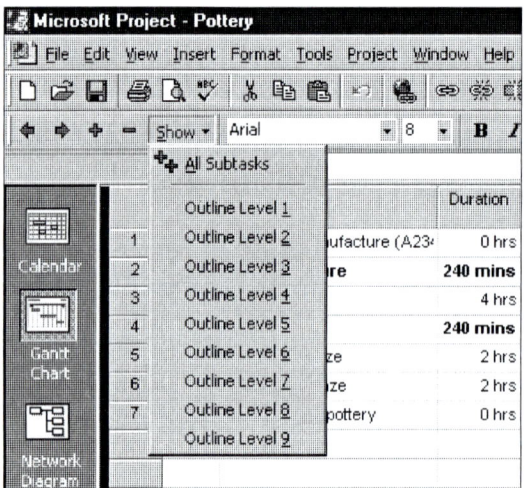

♦ To display all the subtasks, whatever their outline level, open the **Show** drop-down list and choose the **All Subtasks** option.

Moving an outline set of tasks

♦ Collapse the summary task that covers the subtasks you want to move.

♦ Move the summary task.

Changing the outline display

Rolling up the Gantt bar into the summary

♦ Display the Gantt Chart.

♦ Double-click the subtask you want to roll up into its summary (so that the summary bar will also represent this subtask).

♦ Activate the **General** tab, if necessary.

♦ Activate the **Roll up Gantt bar to summary** check box.

♦ Click the **OK** button.

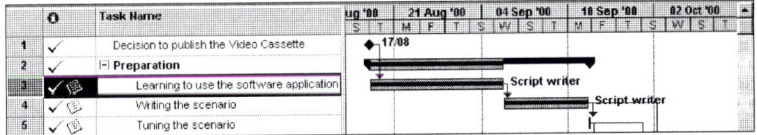

In the example above, the bar for task number 3 has been rolled up to its summary bar.

Setting display options

♦ **Tools**
Options

♦ Click the **View** tab, if necessary.

♦ Under **Outline options for**, activate the required options:

Indent name	If you activate this option, Project 2000 will indent the subtasks.
Show outline number	If you activate this option, Project 2000 will show the outline number to the left of the **Task Name**. The outline number is assigned to each task according to its level in the task list hierarchy. You cannot modify this number.
Show outline symbol	If you deactivate this option, outline symbols appear next to each summary task name.
Show summary tasks	If you deactivate this option, Project 2000 hides the subtasks and you will not be able to use any of the outlining commands.
Project summary task	If you activate this option, Project 2000 will show a project-level summary task. This will have an ID of 0.

♦ Click the **OK** button.

Managing the tasks in an outline

Printing the tasks in an outline

♦ **View
Reports**

♦ Double-click the **Overview** option, then double-click the **Top-Level Tasks** option.

♦ Click the **Print** button and confirm with **OK**.

Filtering the tasks in an outline

♦ To hide all the subtasks, open the **Filter** list and choose the **Top Level Tasks** option.

♦ To display only the summary tasks, open the **Filter** list and choose the **Summary Tasks** option.

♦ To display all the subtasks once again, open the **Filter** list and choose the **All Tasks** option.

Setting a constraint date

Setting a time constraint for a task

If you do not set constraints, tasks begin As soon as possible in projects scheduled from a start date and As late as possible in projects scheduled from a finish date.

♦ Double-click the task concerned.

♦ Activate the **Advanced** tab.

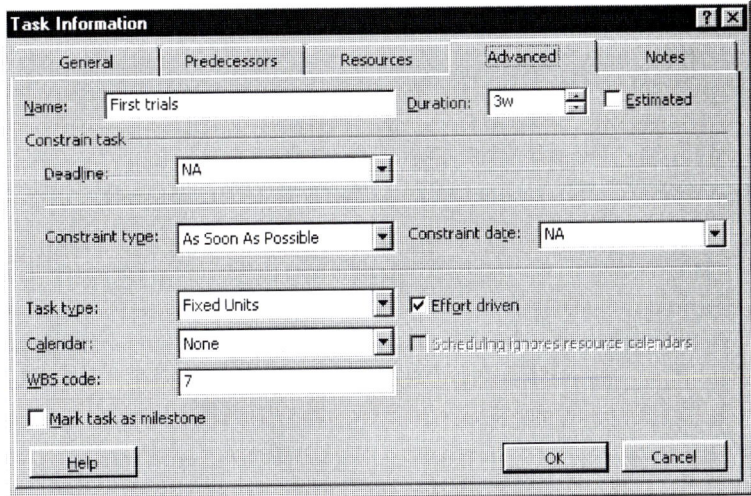

*Use the options under **Constrain task**.*

♦ Open the **Constraint type** list and choose from the following options:

As Late As Possible	The task must finish as late as possible according to the other constraints and links.
As Soon As Possible	This option is the equivalent of applying no constraint at all. The task will start as soon as possible according to the other constraints and links.
Finish No Earlier Than	The task must finish on the date you specify, at the earliest. Use this option if you want to ensure that a task will not finish before a specific date.
Finish No Later Than	The task must finish on the date you specify, at the latest. Use this option if you want to ensure that a task will not finish after a specific date.
Must Finish On [1]	The task must finish on a specific date.
Must Start On [1]	The task must start on a specific date.
Start No Earlier Than	The task must start on the date you specify, at the earliest. Use this option if you want to ensure that a task will not start before a specific date.
Start No Later Than	The task must start on the date you specify, at the latest. Use this option if you want to ensure that a task will not start after a specific date.

*(1) These two constraints are called **inflexible** constraints as they leave no flexibility in the timing of the tasks to which you apply them.*

♦ Select the **Constraint date**, if applicable.

In addition to the date, you can specify the time, after you have inserted a space (for example: 21/12/00 17:00).

♦ Click the **OK** button.

Understanding constraint indicators

	Finish No Earlier Than	for projects that are scheduled from the start date.
	Finish No Later Than	for projects that are scheduled from the finish date.
	Start No Earlier Than	for projects that are scheduled from the start date.
	Start No Later Than	for projects that are scheduled from the finish date.
	Finish No Earlier Than	for projects that are scheduled from the finish date.
	Finish No Later Than	for projects that are scheduled from the start date.
	Start No Earlier Than	for projects that are scheduled from the finish date.
	Start No Later Than	for projects that are scheduled from the start date.
	Must Finish On	for all projects.
	Must Start On	for all projects.

Entering notes

♦ Select the task for which you want to enter notes.

♦ Click the tool button or use **Project - Task Notes**.

♦ Click in the **Notes** frame and enter your notes. To start a new paragraph, press `Enter` and to insert a line break, use `⇧ Shift` `Enter`.

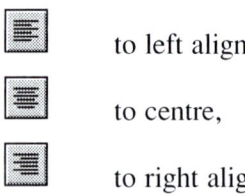

♦ You can format your text as follows:

– select the text that you want to format,

– click the **A** button,

– specify the formatting that you require,

– click **OK**.

♦ To format your paragraphs, select them and use the following tool buttons, as required:

to left align,

to centre,

to right align,

to present the text as a bulleted list.

♦ Use the tool button to insert an OLE object in your notes.

♦ Click the **OK** button.

❏ *When you have entered notes for a task, a small notes icon appears in the indicator column.*

Managing tasks with notes

Consulting task notes

♦ Select the task concerned.

♦ Click the tool button.

*The **Notes** page of the **Task Information** dialog box appears.*

♦ Consult the notes and click **Cancel** to close.

> *To view the notes associated with a task in a ScreenTip, point to the notes icon in the task sheet's indicator column (Gantt).*

Viewing the Notes form

♦ Display the Gantt Chart.

♦ **Window**
Split

The Gantt Chart remains visible in the top part of the screen, and a form appears in the bottom part of the screen.
This form concerns the task selected in the Gantt Chart.

♦ Right-click the form.

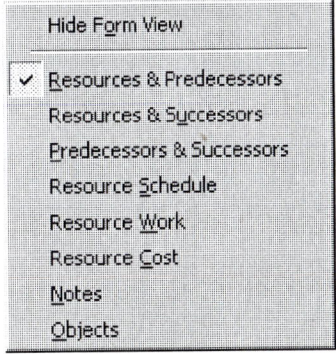

A list of forms appears for the task selected in the Gantt Sheet. A tick indicates the active form.

♦ Choose the **Notes** form.

♦ Click the required task(s) to consult the associated notes.

❏ *To return to the original view, use **Window - Remove Split**.*

Filtering tasks with notes

♦ On the **Formatting** toolbar, open the **Filter** list.

♦ Choose the **Tasks With Attachments** option.

Splitting tasks   *Work on a task may be interrupted. In this case, you can split the task to indicate the period(s) when no work will be carried out.*

♦ Display the Gantt Chart.

♦ On the **Standard** toolbar, click the [⬚] tool button.

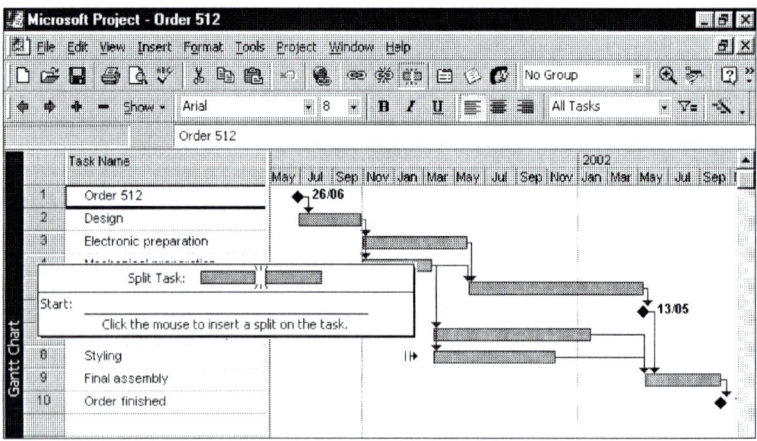

The pointer changes form and is accompanied by a ScreenTip.

♦ On the task bar, point to where you wish to split it. Drag the split section to the right.

❏ *When you drag the split, Project 2000 proposes dates according to the minor timescale defined with* **Format - Timescale**.

Creating recurring tasks

A recurring task is a task that is repeated at regular intervals.

♦ Go to the position where the recurring task should appear.

♦ **Insert**
   Recurring Task

♦ Enter the **Task Name**.

♦ Press the ⬅➡ key to enter the **Duration** of the task.

♦ Specify the **Recurrence pattern** of the event by choosing one of the following options: **Daily**, **Weekly**, **Monthly** or **Yearly**.

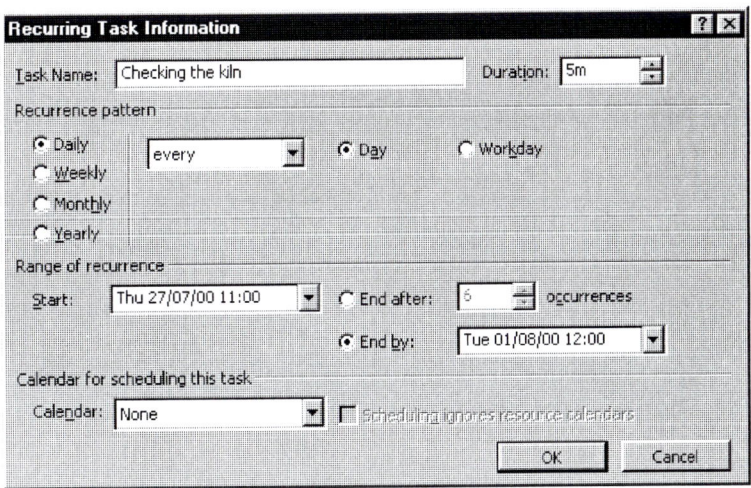

♦ Specify all the details concerning the frequency of the task.

The frequency information depends on the type of **Event**.

♦ If the recurrence is limited, either in time or in the number of its occurrences, use the options under **Range of recurrence**.

    – to limit the time range, give a **Start** date and an **End by** date.

    – to limit the number of occurrences, enter a number in the **End after ... occurrences** box.

♦ Click the **OK** button.

The task appears in the entry table as a summary task. It has the following indicator: ↻ .

Project creates one subtask for each occurrence of the task. Each subtask takes the name of the summary task, followed by a number.

❏ *Project creates these tasks at specific times. Recurring tasks do not take into account changes in a project's duration.*

❏ *All of these tasks have a constraint date.*

Filtering tasks on a date range

♦ Open the **Filter** list.

♦ Choose the **Date Range** option.

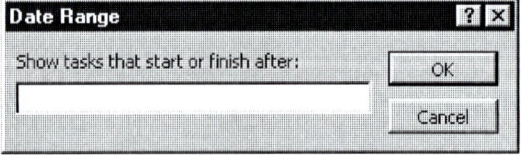

♦ Enter the earlier date in the range and click **OK**.

♦ Enter the later date in the range and click **OK**.

**Creating
a task category**

♦ Display the Gantt Chart.

♦ **Format
Bar Styles**

♦ Click the first empty cell in the **Name** column.

♦ Assign a **Name** to your task category. This name is important, as it will appear in the legend when you print.

♦ Activate the **Show For... Tasks** cell in the current row and open the list.

♦ Select the type of the tasks for the group that you are creating.

*Yes/No type fields are the only customised fields that you can represent differently on the Gantt Chart. Project will represent the tasks differently only when their **Indicator** fields are set to **Yes**. If you want negations to appear, then use the **Not** keyword. If the category represents several tasks, then separate each one with a comma.*

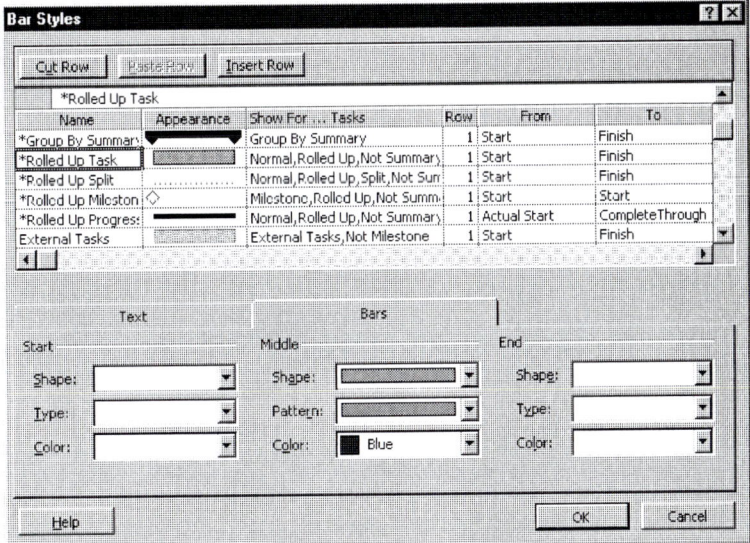

♦ Specify the appearance and contents of the bar.

♦ Click the **OK** button.

**Creating a new
task group
or resource group**

♦ Display either tasks (**Task Sheet - Gantt Chart**) or resources (**Resource Sheet - Resource Usage**).

♦ **Project
Group by
More Groups**

♦ Click the **New** button.

♦ Activate the **Task** or **Resource** option, as required.

♦ In the **Group Definition** dialog box, enter the **Name** of your group. Activate the **Show in menu** check box, if you want your group to appear in the **Group By** list.

♦ Define your group using the **Field Name** list, and the **Order** list.

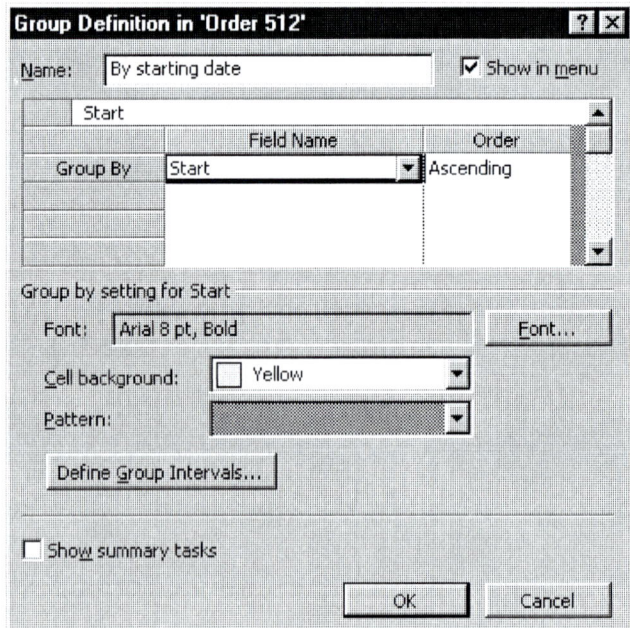

♦ Click **OK**.

Optimising your project

♦ At this design stage, you will have entered the project tasks that you consider to be essential.

♦ Adjusting your project's critical path ensures that you meet project deadlines and optimise task durations while maintaining quality standards.

♦ You can never optimise a project perfectly: changing circumstances inevitably interfere with your plans! However it is a good idea to fine-tune the critical path before the project starts.

Adjusting the critical path

Why adjust the critical path?

♦ The project finish date is directly related to the durations of the tasks that are on the critical path. This is why these tasks are called **critical tasks**.

♦ To optimise the overall project duration, you must first optimise the critical tasks.

Viewing the critical path

♦ Display the Gantt Chart, using **View - Gantt Chart** or by clicking the ▭ button.

♦ Customise your Gantt Chart view using the ▨ tool button.

♦ Click the **Next** button to go to the second step.

GanttChartWizard - Step 2 [?] [X]

What kind of information do you want to display in your Gantt Chart?

(•) Standard

( ) Critical path

( ) Baseline

( ) Other: [▼]

( ) Custom Gantt Chart

[Cancel] [< Back] [Next >] [Finish]

♦ Choose the **Critical path** option and click **Finish**.

♦ Click the **Format It** button, then click **Exit Wizard**.

In the Gantt Chart, the critical task bars now appear in red, as do the links between them.

To display the critical path as a Network Diagram (or PERT chart), use the **View - Network Diagram** (or **PERT Chart**) command or the tool button. Critical tasks are shown in red boxes.

Managing critical tasks

Printing critical tasks

♦ In the Gantt Chart, filter the critical tasks, display the required columns and start printing
or
show the **Network Diagram** and print it
or
use **View - Reports**: double-click the **Overview** button then the **Critical Tasks** button, click **Print** then **OK**.

This print-out provides detailed information on the critical tasks, which helps you to identify the tasks that need adjusting.

Filtering critical tasks

♦ Open the **Filter** list.

♦ Select the **Critical** option.

Setting the critical task definition threshold

By default, tasks are critical when they have zero slack.

♦ **Tools**
  Options

♦ Activate the **Calculation** tab.

♦ Enter the critical task definition threshold in the **Tasks are critical if slack is less than or equal to** box.

♦ Click the **OK** button.

Displaying several critical paths

By default, Project 2000 displays only one critical path. However, you can choose to display a critical path for each independent task network.

♦ **Tools**
  Options

♦ Activate the **Calculation** tab.

♦ Activate the **Calculate multiple critical paths** check box.

♦ Click the **OK** button.

Checking the date constraints

Using a filter

♦ Open the **Filter** list.

♦ Select the **Tasks With Fixed Dates** option.

*Project 2000 lists those tasks that have a constraint different from **As soon as possible**. However, you cannot view these constraint dates directly in the task table.*
As your project tracking progresses, this filter will also show tasks that have a real start date.

Using the Constraint Dates table

♦ Open the **View** menu and choose the **Table** option.

♦ Choose the **More Tables** option.

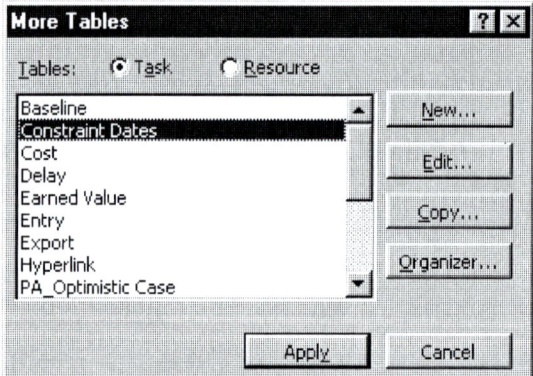

♦ Double-click the **Constraint Dates** option.

	Duration	Constraint Type	Constraint Date
1	0 days	As Soon As Possible	NA
2	**25 days**	**As Soon As Possible**	**NA**
3	3 wks	As Soon As Possible	NA
4	9.5 days	As Soon As Possible	NA
5	0.5 days	As Soon As Possible	NA
6	0 days	As Soon As Possible	NA
7	**1.94 days**	**As Soon As Possible**	**NA**
8	5 hrs	Must Start On	Fri 29/09/00 13:00
9	12 hrs	As Soon As Possible	NA
10	12 hrs	Must Start On	Sun 01/10/00 08:00
11	5 hrs	As Soon As Possible	NA

*For each task, this table lists the **Task Number**, the **Task Name**, the **Duration**, the **Constraint Type** and the **Constraint Date**.*

Optimising the links

Displaying the Predecessors & Successors form

♦ Display the Gantt Chart with **View - Gantt Chart** or 🖵 (on the **View** bar).

♦ **Window**
  Split

The Gantt Chart remains visible in the top part of the screen and a form appears in the bottom part of the screen.

♦ Right-click the form.

A list of forms appears for the task selected in the Gantt Sheet. A tick indicates the active form.

♦ Choose the **Predecessors & Successors** form.

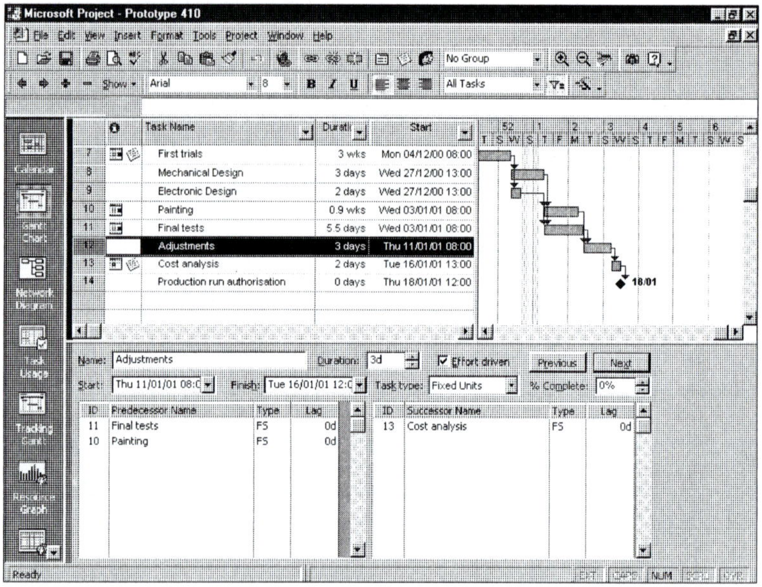

For the task selected in the Gantt Sheet, this form shows the predecessors on the left and the successors on the right.

♦ Select the task for which you want to view the predecessor and successor details.

♦ To close the form and return to the original view, select **Window - Remove Split**.

Displaying the Relationship Diagram

♦ Display the Gantt Chart.

♦ **Window**
Split

The last form displayed appears once again.

♦ Click the form to activate this part of the screen.

♦ **View**
More Views

*The **View** bar contains this button.*

♦ Double-click the **Relationship Diagram** option.

The Relationship Diagram appears for the task selected in the Gantt Sheet.

♦ Select the task whose Relationship diagram you wish to see.

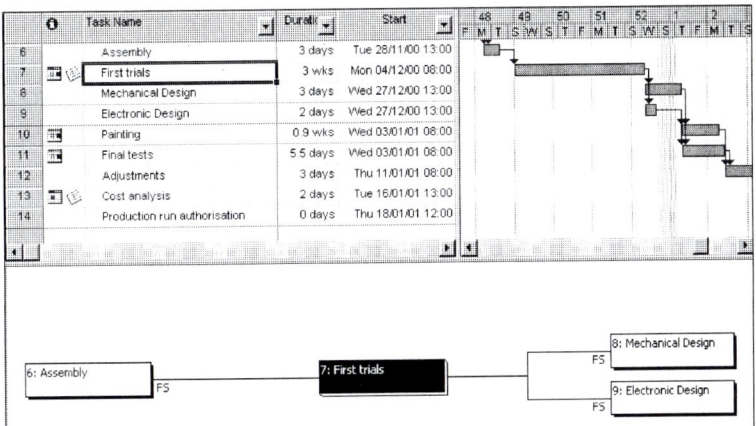

♦ To close the form and return to the original view, select **Window - Remove Split**.

Creating a links table

♦ **View
Table
More Tables**

♦ Click the **New** button.

♦ Enter the **Name** for the table.

♦ If you wish, click the **Show in menu** option to find your table easily.

♦ Using the lists in each column, insert at least these fields:

Table Definition in 'Prototype 410'

Name: Links   ☑ Show in menu

Table

| Cut Row | Copy Row | Paste Row | Insert Row | Delete Row |

Field Name	Align Data	Width	Title	Align Title
ID	Right	4		Center
Name	Left	33		Center
Predecessors	Center	16		Center
Successors	Center	13		Center

Date format: Default   Row height: 1

☑ Lock first column

OK   Cancel

♦ Click the **OK** button.

♦ Click the **Apply** button.

Your new table replaces the Gantt Sheet and can be used as any other standard Project table. The main difference is that this table exists only in the current project.

A few optimisation techniques

♦ Try to find tasks that can run simultaneously. In practice, you can often convert Finish-to-Start links to Start-to-Start links with a lag or leave them as Finish-to-Start types, but with a lead.

♦ See if you can break long tasks down into smaller tasks with their own links. This technique can considerably shorten the critical path, and the overall duration of your project.

Microsoft Project 2000

Checking the slack

Before you start your project, it is advisable to check the slack.

Using the Schedule table

♦ **View**
  Table
  Schedule

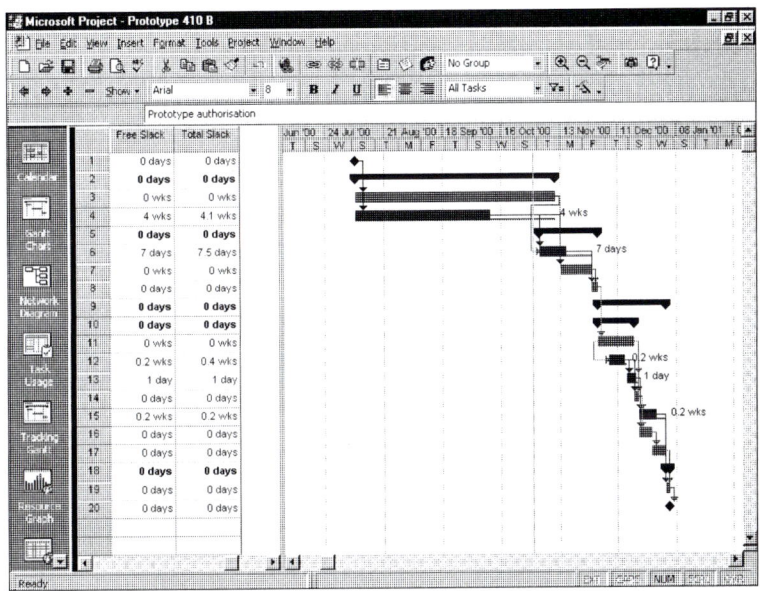

*The two last columns of this table show **Free Slack** and **Total Slack**.*

Using the Detail Gantt

♦ **View**
  More Views

*The **View** bar contains this button.*

♦ Double-click the **Detail Gantt** option.

*The critical task bars appear in red. The non-critical tasks appear in blue. Green lines represent the total slack of these tasks, and their free slack durations are displayed in figures. The **Delay** table appears in this view.*

♦ If you cannot see the Gantt Chart, then select **View - Zoom - Entire project - OK**.

. . . . *Personal notes* . . . .

Introduction to resources

♦ The tasks in a project are carried out using resources. There are two types of resource: **Work Resources** and **Material Resources**. You can assign a resource to one or more tasks.

♦ Work resources are resources that do work, such as people and equipment. These resources devote time to the tasks that they carry out. On the other hand, material resources do no work. They are consumable stocks used to carry out tasks.

♦ Work resources and material resources have some characteristics in common: they have limited availability, you can share them between different projects, they have their own production capacities and they have costs associated with them.

♦ However, material resources differ from work resources in several respects. For example, material resources do not use resource calendars and you cannot level material resources. In addition, for material resources, you cannot specify the number of available units, and the usage cost is not managed in the same way as for work resources.

♦ Before you create any resources, determine for each task the skills and the material items that you will need. This will allow you to determine the resources needed to meet your deadline dates. You can then specify the resource list.

Creating the resource list

Creating a work resource

♦ **View**
Resource Sheet

*The **View** bar contains this button.*

♦ For each work resource, specify the **Resource Name**, the **Type**, the **Initials**, the **Group** and the **Max. Units**.

	❶	Resource Name	Type	Material Label	Initials	Group	Max. Units	Std. Rate	Ovt. Rate
34		Terry GORDON	Work		TG	DPE	100%	€ 0.00/hr	€ 0.00/hr
35		Oscilloscope	Work		OS	TO	100%	€ 0.00/hr	€ 0.00/hr
36		Printed circuit board	Material		PCB	EH		€ 0.00	
37		R2 component	Material		CR2	EC		€ 0.00	
38		Glue	Material	Tube	GL	CH		€ 0.00	
39		Epoxy resin	Material	Pot	ER	CH		€ 0.00	

The **Resource Name** indicates whether the resource is a person, a piece of equipment or a service. When you enter your resources, notice that the default value of the **Type** cell is **Work**.

The **Material Label** concerns resources with a **Material Type**.

The **Initials** field is often used instead of the **Resource Name**. It allows you to designate a resource by its initials, rather than using its full name. When you enter your resources, notice that Microsoft Project 2000 proposes the first letter of the **Resource Name** as the **Initials** field.

The **Group** field allows you to group together resources of a common category.

The **Max. Units** cell allows you to specify the maximum number of units available for that resource, as a percentage or a number. Its default value is 100%.

Creating a material resource

♦ Display the **Resource Sheet**.

♦ For each material resource specify the **Resource Name**.

♦ Choose **Material** as the **Type**.

♦ In the **Material Label** cell, indicate, if necessary, the name of the measurement unit that the material resource uses.

This label will be used to qualify the units that you assign to the resource, for example: 5 pots. You can specify any measurement unit in this way, for example: ton, m (for metre), or box.

♦ Enter the **Initials** and the **Group** fields.

*There is no need to enter information in the **Max. Units** cell for a material resource.*

❏ To insert a resource into the list, click the row on which you want your new resource to appear and press the ⌶Ins⌶ key (or use the **Insert - New Resource** command).

❏ To delete a resource, click it and press the ⌶Del⌶ key (or use **Edit - Delete Resource**).

Defining the maximum number of units for a work resource

Remember that you must always define a work resource in terms of time.

♦ Display the **Resource Sheet**.

♦ Click in the **Max. Units** field of the resource concerned.

♦ Indicate how much time the resource must devote to the project. For example: 100% for full time, 50% for half time, or 300% for "multiple time" (for instance, the resource could correspond to three people who will work full time on the project).

The time specified at this level concerns time that is available for the project as a whole. Do not confuse it with the time that you indicate when you assign a resource to a task. In the latter case, you indicate the amount of time that the resource can devote to a specific task.

Note that you must define the maximum number of units for each resource or for each set of consolidated resources. Project 2000 does not carry out any tests or checks at this level. On the other hand, Project does compare the maximum number of units with the number of units that you assign to task(s) to determine whether or not the resource is overallocated.

❏ To present the maximum number of units as a percentage or as a decimal number, use the **Tools - Options** command and activate the **Schedule** tab. Then, in the **Show assignment units as a** box, choose either **Percentage** or **Decimal**.

**Sorting
the resource list**

♦ **Project**
  Sort

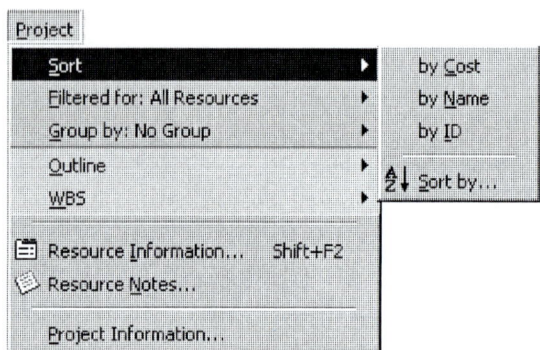

♦ Choose one of the criteria that Project offers (**by Cost**, **by Name**, or **by ID**), or choose the **Sort by** option.

♦ If you choose the **Sort by** option, you can specify up to three sort criteria, their sort order (**Ascending** or **Descending**) and whether the resources must be renumbered or not.

♦ To start the sort, click the **Sort** button.

> As with task sorts, you can cancel sort orders using ⌀ Shift F3 (provided that you did not ask Project to renumber the resources).

**Adapting
the calendar
to a resource**

♦ **Tools**
  Change Working Time

♦ Open the **For** list.

*In addition to the base (**Standard**) calendar, and the calendars that you specify yourself, Microsoft Project 2000 allows you to specify a calendar for each resource that you create.*

♦ Select the name of the resource concerned.

♦ Adapt the calendar to suit the needs of the resource.

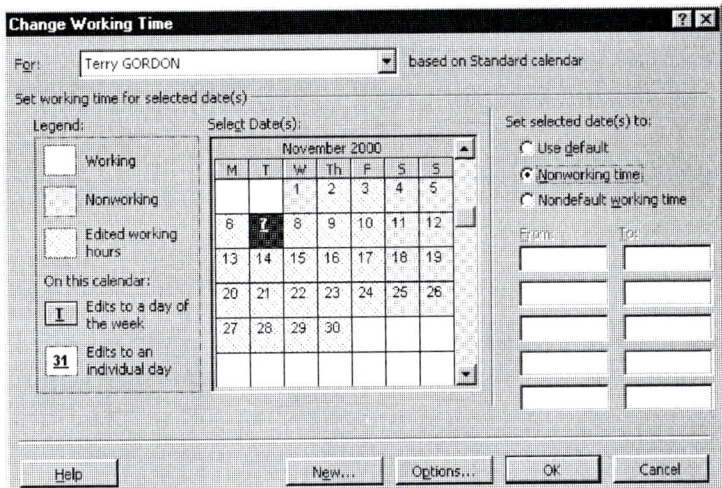

♦ Click the **OK** button.

 If you want a hard copy of the calendars created, proceed as if you were printing the project calendar.

Managing a calendar for several resources

Creating a new calendar

♦ **Tools**
 Change Working Time

♦ Click the **New** button.

♦ Give a **Name** for the new calendar.

♦ Choose to **Create** a **new base calendar** or to **Make a copy of** a **calendar** from the corresponding list.

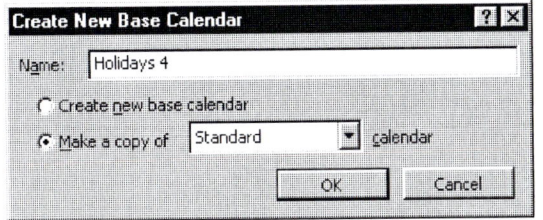

♦ Click the **OK** button.

♦ Adapt the calendar to suit your needs.

♦ Confirm your new calendar by clicking **OK**.

Applying the calendar to the resources concerned

In this step you must associate the new calendar with the re-sources concerned.

♦ Activate the **Base Calendar** cell for the resource concerned (this is the penultimate cell in the row).

♦ Open the list on this cell.

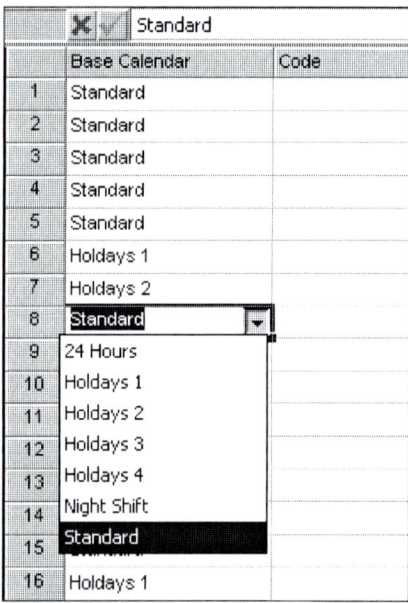

♦ Click the calendar that you want to assign to the resource.

♦ Confirm by pressing [Enter] or click the ☑ tool button on the entry bar.

Managing notes for resources

Entering notes

♦ Select the resource for which you want to enter notes.

♦ On the **Standard** toolbar, click the 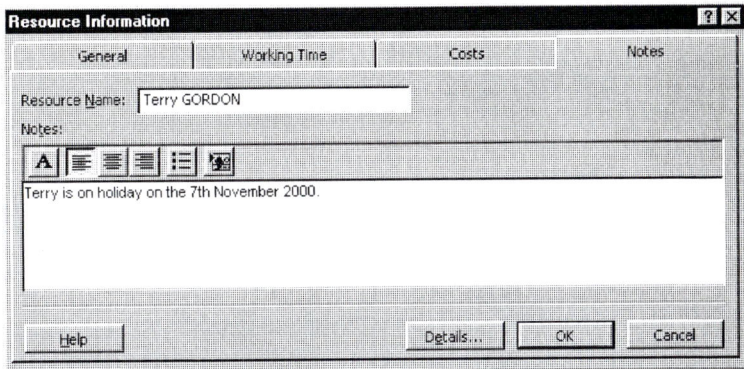 tool button.

♦ Enter your comments in the **Notes** frame.

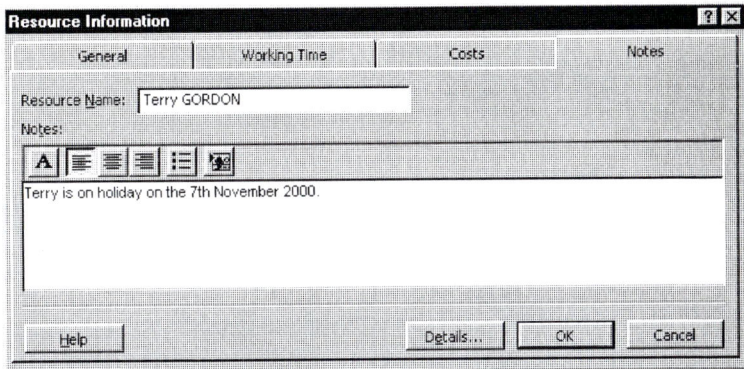

♦ Format your notes as required.

♦ Click the **OK** button.

As with task notes, a small notes icon appears in the indicator column for the resource concerned.

❏ *To modify the notes for a resource, double click the* icon in *the indicator column, make your changes and confirm with **OK**.*

Consulting resource notes

♦ If there is only one note to consult, select the task concerned and click the tool button on the **Standard** toolbar or point to the icon in the **Indicators** column.

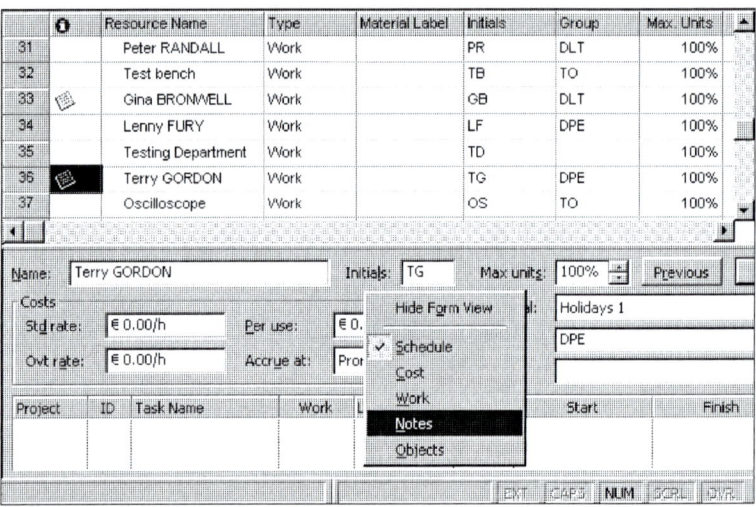

34	Lenny FURY	Work	LF	
35	Testing Department	Work	TD	
36	Terry GORDON	Work	TG	DPE
37	Notes: 'Terry is on holiday on the 7th November 2000.'		OS	TO
38	Printed circuit board	Material	PCB	EH
39	R2 component	Material	CR2	EC

The notes appear in a ScreenTip.

♦ To read the notes of several resources, use **Window - Split**.

As with the task views, a form appears in the bottom part of the screen.

♦ Right-click the form in the lower part of the screen.

❶		Resource Name	Type	Material Label	Initials	Group	Max. Units	
31		Peter RANDALL	Work		PR	DLT	100%	
32		Test bench	Work		TB	TO	100%	
33		Gina BRONWELL	Work		GB	DLT	100%	
34		Lenny FURY	Work		LF	DPE	100%	
35		Testing Department	Work		TD		100%	
36		Terry GORDON	Work		TG	DPE	100%	
37		Oscilloscope	Work		OS	TO	100%	

Name: Terry GORDON   Initials: TG   Max units: 100%   Previous

Costs
Std rate: € 0.00/h   Per use: € 0.   Hide Form View   Holidays 1
Ovt rate: € 0.00/h   Accrue at: Pror   ✓ Schedule   DPE
                                         Cost
                                         Work
Project | ID | Task Name | Work | | Notes | Start | Finish
                                         Objects

♦ In the list of forms, select the **Notes** option.

♦ In the top part of the screen, click each of the required resources and consult the notes that are associated with it.

♦ To return to the original view, use **Window - Remove Split**.

Filtering resources with notes

♦ On the **Formatting** toolbar, open the **Filter** list.

♦ Choose the **Resources With Attachments** option.

Filtering
resources for
a specific group

♦ Display the **Resource Sheet**.

♦ Open the **Filter** list and select the **Group** option.

♦ Enter the name of the group concerned.

You can use wildcards in this text box: a question mark (?) to indicate any character or an asterisk (*) to indicate a group of characters. You can use these wildcards only in text fields.

♦ Confirm by pressing Enter .

Printing
the resource list

♦ Display the **Resource Sheet**.

♦ Display the **Print Preview** by clicking the [button] tool button.

Project offers to print with a portrait orientation.

♦ To change the page orientation, click the **Page Setup** button, activate the **Page** tab then the **Landscape** option and click **OK**.

♦ Click the **Print** button and confirm with **OK**.

Introduction to effort-driven scheduling

Before you start assigning resources to your task list, it is important that you understand the principles of effort-driven scheduling.

♦ Microsoft Project 2000 reduces or increases the duration of a task according to the resources that you assign or withdraw, but it does not change the total work for the task. Remember that the total work for a task is different from the duration of a task. The total work for a task is the number of person-hours (in minutes, hours, days, weeks or months) that a work resource needs to complete a task. For example, suppose that a work resource needs 28 working hours to complete a task, but that the task has a duration of 2 days. This means that you must assign several resources to this task. In this case, two people could carry out the task in two days, by working on the task 7 hours a day.

♦ As you assign resources to a task, be aware that the total work for the task stays the same. On the other hand, Project changes the amount of work that is distributed amongst the resources assigned to this task.

♦ This process is called **effort-driven scheduling** and Microsoft Project 2000 uses it by default.

♦ However, Microsoft Project 2000 allows you to deactivate this process. This approach is useful, for example, when you want to increase the total work for a specific task as you assign resources to it.

♦ When the **Effort driven** option is set, Microsoft Project does not apply calculations that can change the duration of the task until you have made a first assignment of one or more resources to the task.

❏ *To deactivate effort-driven scheduling for all the new tasks that you create, use* ***Tools - Options - Schedule*** *tab and deactivate the* ***New tasks are effort driven*** *option.*

Assigning resources to one or more tasks

♦ Display the Gantt Chart.

♦ For each of the tasks concerned, check that the **Effort driven** option is set in the **Task Information** dialog box.

♦ Select the tasks to which you want to assign resources.

♦ Click the 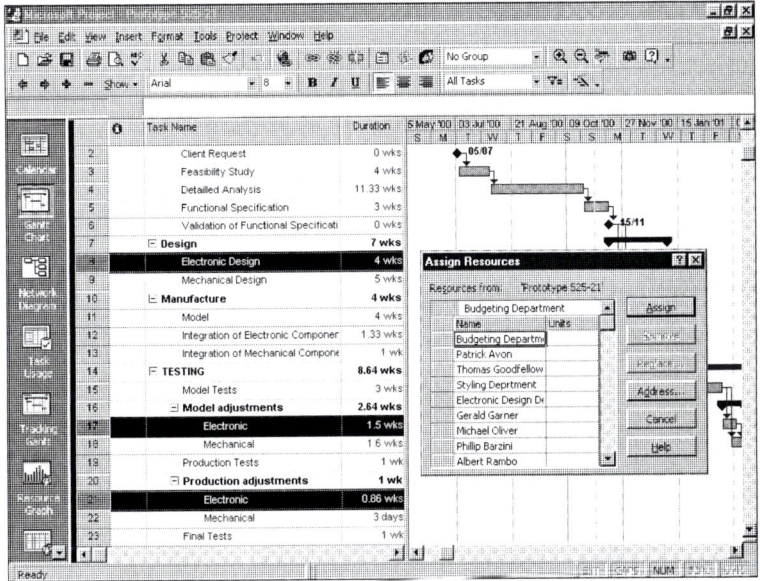 tool button.

The dialog box that appears shows all the resources you created.

Assigning a resource to work full-time

♦ In the **Assign Resources** dialog box, select the resources that you want to assign to work full-time.

♦ Click the **Assign** button.

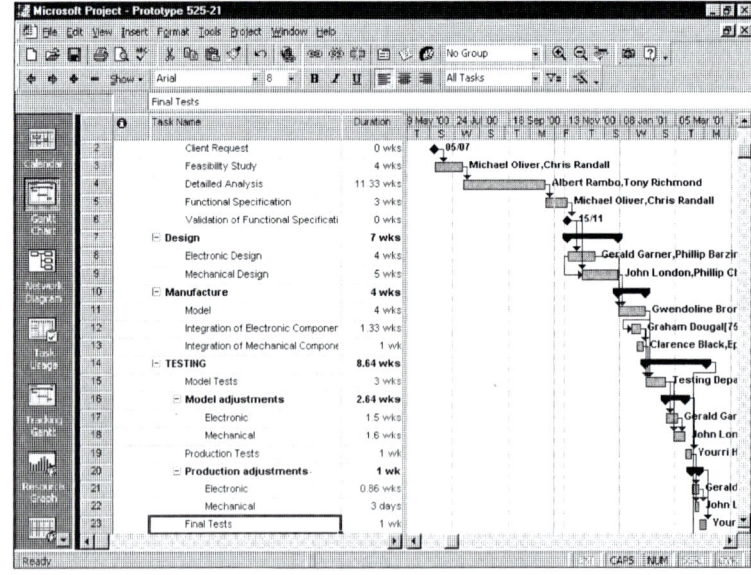

A *tick appears next to the resources that you have assigned to your selected tasks.*

The *value of 100% in the **Units** column indicates full-time assignment.*

♦ In this way, assign resources to all your other tasks, as required.

♦ When you have finished assigning resources, click **Close**.

The ***Resource Names** appear in the Gantt Chart and also in the final column of the Task Sheet.*

Assigning several units of the same resource

♦ Select the task(s) to which you want to assign the resource.

♦ Open the **Assign Resources** dialog box.

♦ Click in the **Units** cell for the resource concerned.

♦ Enter a number of units or a percentage greater than 100.

♦ Press Enter .

Assigning a resource to work part-time

♦ Select the task(s) to which you want to assign the resource.

♦ Open the **Assign Resources** dialog box.

♦ Click in the **Units** cell for the resource concerned.

♦ Enter a decimal fraction, to represent the part-time assignment, or a percentage less than 100.

♦ Press Enter .

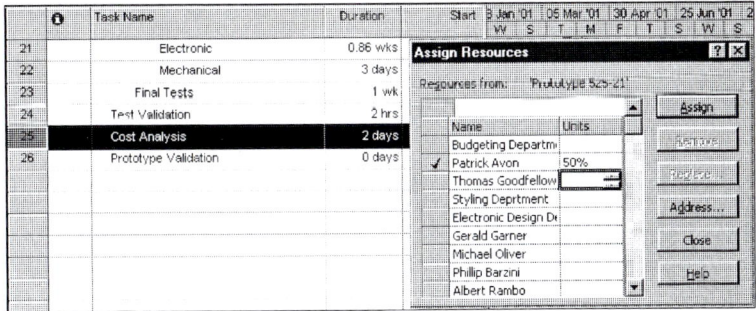

In this example, the resource has been assigned to work 50% of its time.

*When you assign a resource to a task for the first time, Microsoft Project does not vary the task duration, even if the **Effort driven** option is set for the task concerned.*

**Delaying
the work
of a resource
on a task**

♦ Access the **Resource Schedule** form for the task concerned.

♦ Select the required value in the **Delay** cell for the resource(s) concerned.

♦ Click the **OK** button that appears.

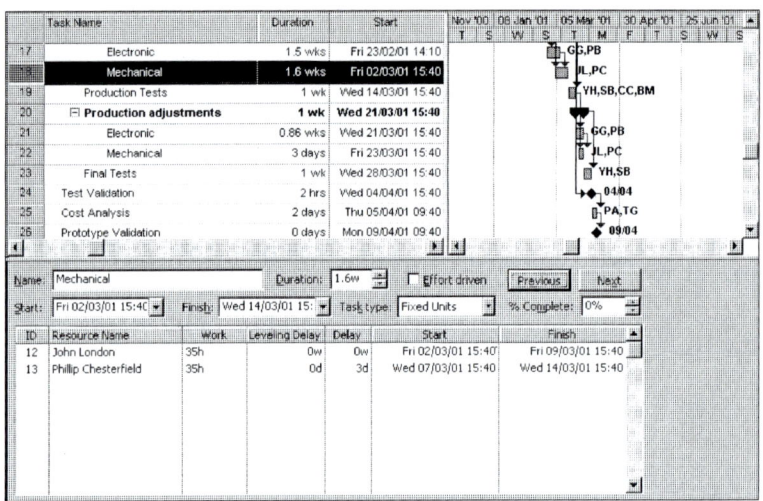

❑ If the **Effort driven** option is not active, the task duration increases and the next task is delayed.

**Defining
a work contour**

When you assign a resource to a task, Microsoft Project automatically allocates the same number of hours per time period, for the whole duration of the task. This represents an evenly distributed workload and is known as a flat work contour. However, you can specify a different work contour.

♦ **View**
Task Usage

*The **View** bar contains this button.*

♦ Locate the task for which you want to specify a work contour.

Choosing a predefined work contour

♦ Double-click the resource concerned.

♦ If necessary, activate the **General** tab.

♦ Open the **Work contour** list and choose the required contour.

♦ Click the **OK** button.

❏ *An icon appears in the indicators column, representing the contour that you have chosen:*

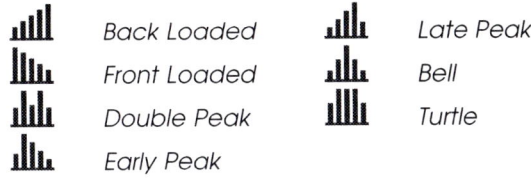

	Back Loaded		*Late Peak*
	Front Loaded		*Bell*
	Double Peak		*Turtle*
	Early Peak		

Customising a work contour

♦ Click the resource concerned.

♦ Click the ⬚ tool button to view the task concerned.

♦ For the days concerned, enter the specific hours that this resource must devote to this task.

		Task Name	Work	Details	02 Oct '00					
					S	M	T	W	T	F
1		⊟ Technical Specification	669.5 hrs	Work		7.7h	7.7h	8h	9.1h	7h
2		Client Request	0 hrs	Work						
3		⊟ Feasibility Study	140 hrs	Work						
		Michael Oliver	70 hrs	Work						
		Chris Randall	70 hrs	Work						
4		⊟ Detailed Analysis	350 hrs	Work						
		Albert Roberts	175 hrs	Work						
		Tony Richmon	175 hrs	Work						
5		⊟ Functional Specificatic	179.5 hrs	Work		7.7h	7.7h	8h	9.1h	7h
	📊	Michael Oliver	74.5 hrs	Work		0.7h	0.7h	1h	2.1h	0h
		Chris Randall	105 hrs	Work		7h	7h	7h	7h	7h
6		Validation of Function:	0 hrs	Work						
7		⊟ Design	630 hrs	Work						
8		⊟ Electronic Design	280 hrs	Work						
		Gerald Garner	140 hrs	Work						
		Phillip Barzini	140 hrs	Work						
9		⊟ Mechanical Design	350 hrs	Work						
		John London	175 hrs	Work						
		Phillip Chester	175 hrs	Work						
10		⊟ Manufacture	385 hrs	Work						
11		⊟ Model	280 hrs	Work						
		Gwendoline B:	140 hrs	Work						

In this example, Michael Oliver starts working on the functional specification on the 2nd October.

❏ The 📊 icon indicates that you have defined a custom work contour for this resource.

Displaying resource initials in the Gantt Chart

By default, the Gantt chart displays, the full names of the resources that you have assigned.

♦ Display the **Gantt Chart**.

♦ **Format**
Bar Styles

♦ If necessary, select the **Task** cell in the **Name** column.

♦ Activate the **Text** tab.

♦ Click the cell in which **Resource Names** appears.

♦ Open the list and choose **Resource Initials**.

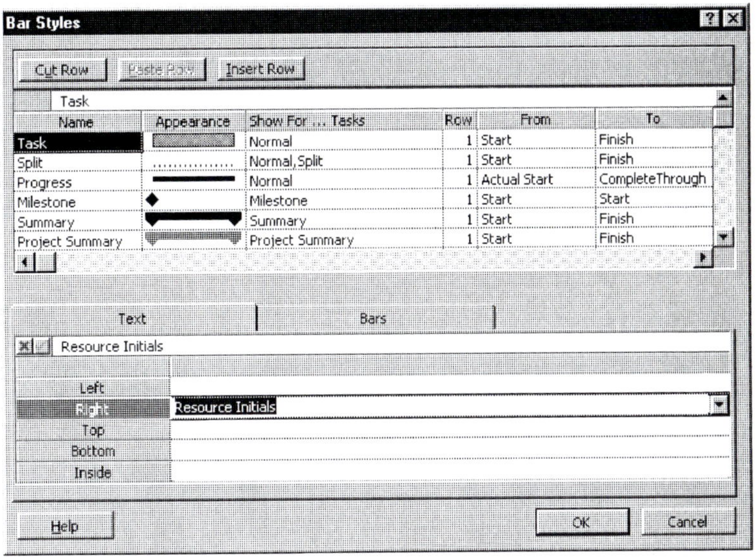

♦ Click the **OK** button.

The information relating to the number of assigned resource units disappears.

Printing resource assignments

♦ **View**
  Reports

♦ Double-click the **Assignments** button.

♦ Select either **Who Does What** or **Who Does What When**.

Printing the assignments of a specific resource

♦ **View**
  Reports

♦ Double-click the **Assignments** button and the **To-do List** button.

♦ Open the **Show tasks using** list and select the resource whose assignments you wish to print.

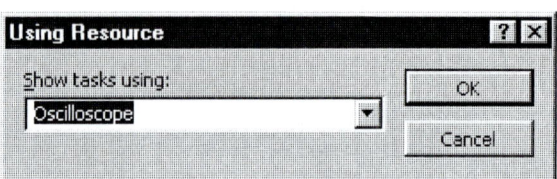

♦ Click the **OK** button.

*You can also filter the assignments of a resource. To do this, view the Task Sheet, open the **Filter** list and choose **Using Resource** or **Using Resource In Date Range**.*

. . . . *Personal notes* . . . .

Why modify resource assignments?

♦ Before you change a resource assignment, you must be clear as to why you want to make this change.

♦ You may want to modify a resource assignment because you made a mistake in your initial assignment, or perhaps because your plan has changed.

♦ For example, you have given a task a duration of 6 days, knowing you would assign 2 people to it.

Case 1: you assigned one resource but forgot the second. You made a mistake in the assignments, but this should not change the task duration.

Case 2: you assigned two resources. One of the project managers asks you to decrease the task duration. To do this, you add a third person, to do the work more quckly. In this case, your plans have changed, so adding the resource should alter the task duration.

Changing a resource assignment

♦ Double-click the task for which you want to modify the resource assignment.

♦ Activate the **Advanced** tab.

♦ If your modification must not affect the duration of the task, deactivate the **Effort driven** option.

♦ If your changes should affect the task duration, activate this option.

♦ Click the **OK** button.

♦ Modify the resource assignment as required.

Assigning an additional work resource

Without effort-driven scheduling

♦ Deactivate the **Effort driven** option for the task concerned.

♦ Assign the resource to the task, as for an initial assignment.

With effort-driven scheduling

♦ Double-click the task to which you want to assign the additional resource.

♦ Activate the **Advanced** tab and activate the **Effort driven** option, if necessary.

*When effort-driven scheduling is active, the option chosen in the **Task type** box may affect the recalculation of the task duration.*

♦ Ensure that the **Task type** is not **Fixed Duration** or the duration of the task will not change when you assign the additional resource.

♦ Click **OK** to validate your settings.

♦ Assign the resource to the task, as for an initial assignment.

Cancelling a resource assignment

♦ For each task concerned, activate or deactivate the **Effort driven** option in the **Task Information** dialog box (**Advanced** tab).

♦ Select the task(s) concerned.

♦ Open the **Assign Resources** dialog box.

♦ Select the resource that you want to cancel.

♦ Click the **Cancel** button.

**Replacing
a resource
with another**

♦ Select the task(s) concerned.

♦ Activate or deactivate the **Effort driven** option.

♦ Open the **Assign Resources** dialog box.

♦ Select the resource that you want to replace.

♦ Click the **Replace** button.

♦ Select the new resource.

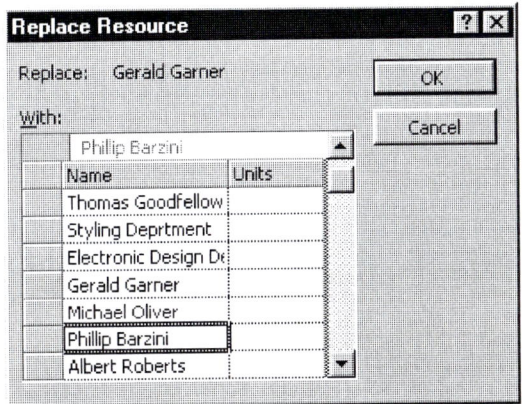

♦ Click the **OK** button.

**Changing
the number
of resource units
assigned**

With a change in the task duration

♦ Proceed as for an initial resource assignment.

Without changing the task duration

♦ Double-click the task concerned.

♦ Under the **Advanced** tab, deactivate the **Effort driven** option.

♦ Under the **Resources** tab, select the resource for which you want
to change the number of units assigned.

♦ Ensure that the **Task type** option is **Fixed Duration** and enter.

♦ Open the **Assign Resources** dialog box, select the resource that you want to replace and click the **Replace** button.

♦ In the **Replace Resource** dialog box, click in the **Units** cell for the resource concerned.

♦ Enter the new number of units, or the new percentage.

♦ Press Enter .

♦ Confirm by clicking **Close**.

. . . . *Personal notes* . . . .

Viewing the resource assignments

Using the Gantt Chart view

♦ Unless you specify otherwise, the Gantt Chart displays the resource names and the number of resource units assigned.

- The **Entry Table** also displays this information in its final column.

- The **Resource Work** form provides information concerning overtime hours.

- The **Resource Schedule** form shows any delays.

Resource usage

♦ **View**
Resource Usage

*The **View** bar contains this button.*

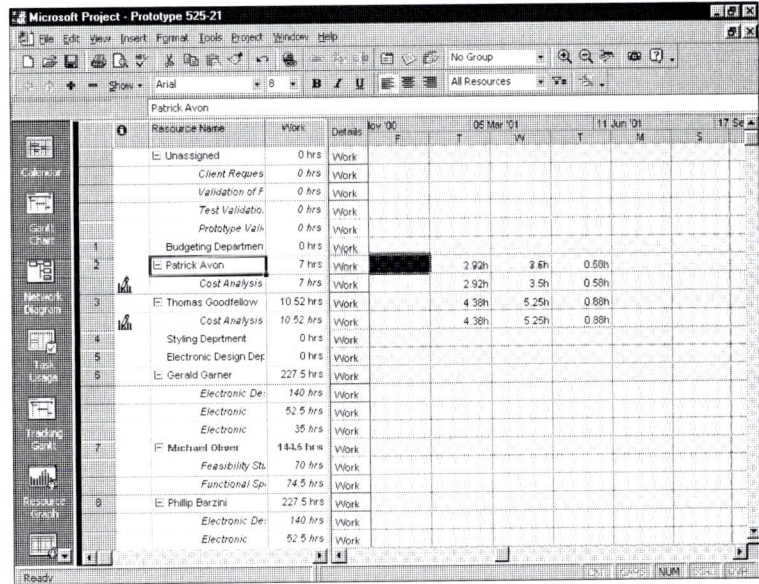

This view shows the resources of your project, together with the tasks that you have assigned to each of these resources.

*The left pane shows the **Usage** table, which contains the **Work** column.*

*The **Work** column shows the total number of hours assigned to the resource on the current project.*

The right pane contains a calendar with a default display in days. It lists the work hours per day, per resource (use the horizontal scroll bar to check this).

Customising the Resource Usage view

Changing the Timescale

♦ **Format**
Timescale

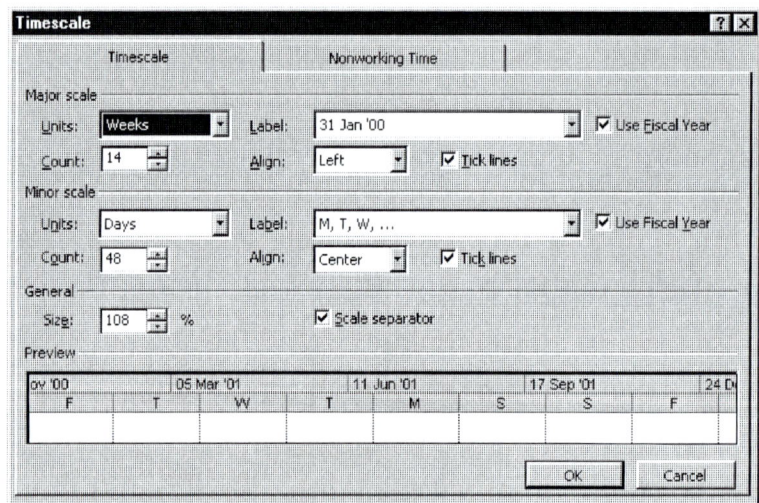

♦ Change these settings as required.

♦ Click the **OK** button.

Specifying what the calendar should display

♦ Right-click in the calendar part of the **Resource Usage** view.

Microsoft Project 2000 offers different types of information.

♦ At this level of your analysis, choose from the following options:

Work	indicates the amount of work scheduled for each of the resources.
Actual Work	indicates the amount of work that each of the resources has actually carried out.
Cumulative Work	shows the cumulative total for the resource for each work assignment.
Overallocation	indicates the amount of work overallocated to a given resource for a given assignment.
Cost	shows the scheduled cost of the resource for its assigned tasks.
Remaining Availability	indicates the amount of work you can still assign to a given resource.

Resource allocation

♦ View the **Resource Usage** or the **Resource Sheet**.

♦ **View**　　　
More Views

*The **View** bar contains this button.*

♦ Double-click the **Resource Allocation** option.

The window splits into two parts. The lower part of the window shows a Gantt Chart for the tasks to which you have assigned the resource that is selected in the upper part of the window.

♦ In the upper part of the window, click the resource that you want to study.

♦ To display the Gantt bar for one of the tasks for this resource, click the task concerned, then click the tool button.

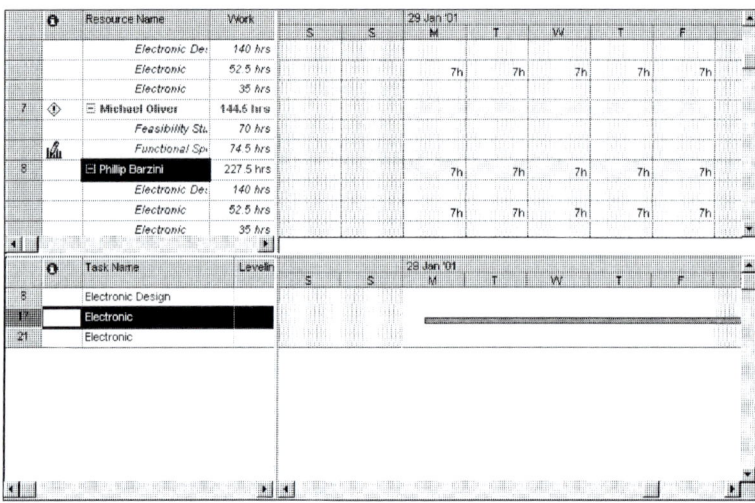

♦ To leave this view, use **Window - Remove Split**.

Task usage

♦ **View**
  Task Usage

*The **View** bar contains this button.*

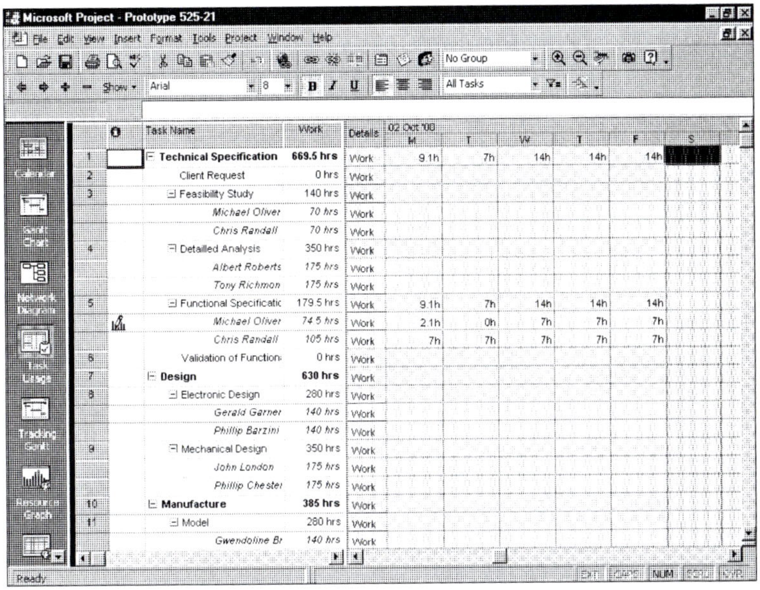

*This view shows the project's tasks and the resources assigned to them. The left pane shows the **Usage** table, which contains the **Work** column. This column shows the total hours assigned to the task. The right pane shows the daily calendar of scheduled time.*

❑ *If this view does not display the resource names for a given task, select the task concerned and click the*  *tool button.*

Authorising overtime work

♦ Select the task concerned.

♦ **Window Split**

♦ Right-click the form in the lower part of the screen.

♦ Choose the **Resource Work** option.

*The **Ovt. Work** column appears in the form.*

♦ Enter the overtime work according to the following rules:
<u>If you want the task duration to decrease</u>, enter only the number of overtime work hours.
<u>If you want the task duration to remain the same</u>, enter the number of overtime work hours <u>and</u> adjust the number of work hours. The task duration is calculated as follows:
Task duration = Work hours - Overtime work hours

♦ Confirm by clicking the **OK** button in the form.

*Project 2000 does not apply your changes while the form shows the **OK** button. When the **Previous** and **Next** buttons reappear in the form, you know that Project has accepted your changes.*

♦ To close the form, and return to the standard view, use **Window - Remove Split** or double-click the horizontal split bar.

Filtering tasks that have overtime assigned

♦ View the **Gantt Chart**.

♦ Open the **Filter** list.

♦ Choose the **Tasks/Assignments With Overtime** option.

Viewing the summary table for resources

♦ View the **Resource Usage** or the **Resource Sheet**.

♦ **View**
Table
Summary

*This table contains the **Peak** column, which shows the maximum number of units assigned from the resource at any given time.*

Studying overallocated resources

Definition

♦ A resource is overallocated when the work assigned to it exceeds its availability.

♦ Some overallocations (for example, 1 hour over two weeks) may be acceptable, but not all.

Detecting overallocated resources

♦ The **Resource Sheet** view, the **Resource Allocation** view and the **Resource Usage** view show overallocated resources in red.

♦ In the **Resource Allocation** view, a ◈ in the **Indicators** column signifies an overallocated resource.

Microsoft Project 2000

♦ To view only the overallocated resources, open the **Filter** list and choose the **Overallocated Resources** option.

♦ To print overallocated resources, select **View - Reports**, double-click **Assignments** then, double-click **Overallocated Resources**, and click **Print**, followed by **OK**.

♦ Close the **Reports** dialog box by clicking the **Close** button.

This report also lists the tasks to which you have assigned the resources.

Displaying overallocated work hours

♦ Display the **Resource Usage** view, using the **View** menu.

♦ Right-click in the calendar part of the view.

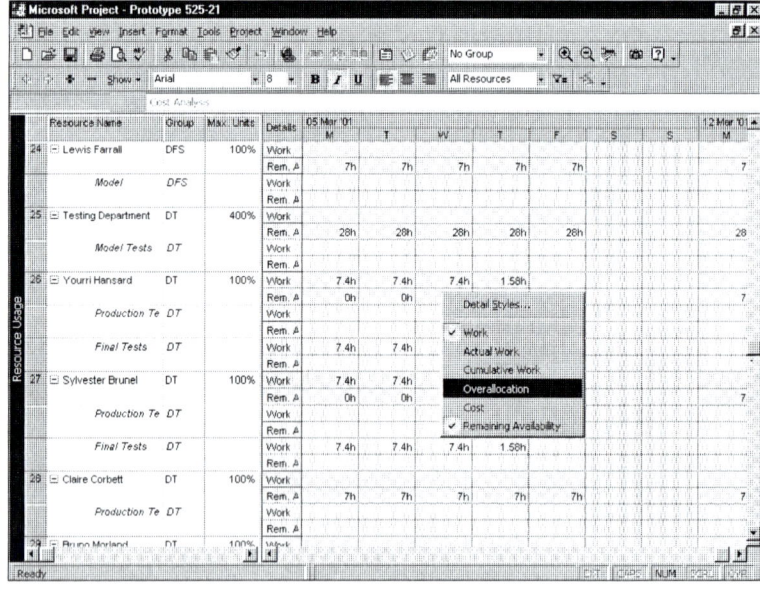

♦ Choose the **Overallocation** option.

♦ Drag over the time period that you want to examine.

Solving overallocation problems by levelling

The principle

♦ Microsoft Project 2000 delays or splits certain tasks so the assigned resources will no longer be overallocated.

Basic settings

♦ Access the resource levelling using **Tools - Resource Leveling**.

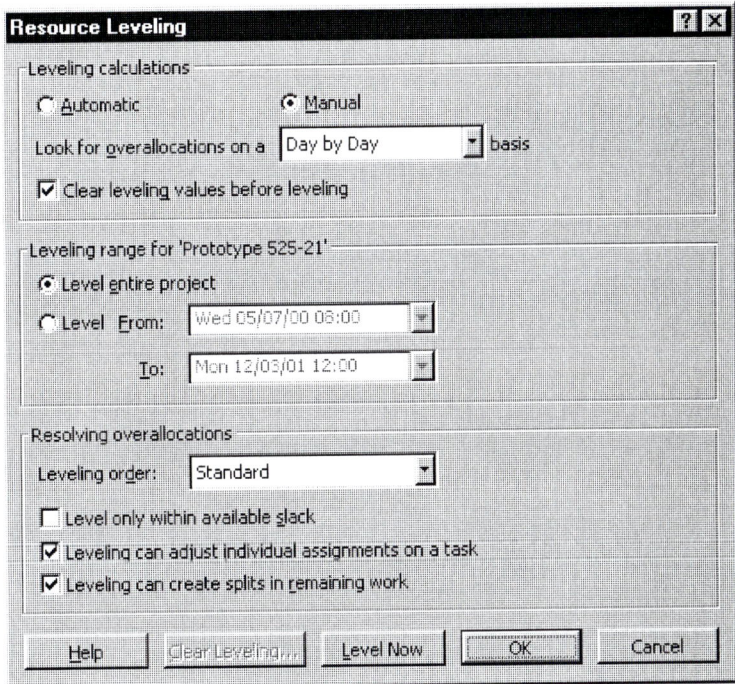

♦ Under **Leveling calculations**, choose either **Automatic** or **Manual**. If you choose **Automatic**, Project will attempt to solve overallocation problems as they arise. As this is not necessarily a useful approach, it is advisable to maintain **Manual** levelling.

♦ In the **Look for overallocations on a** list box, choose the period in which Project should look for overallocations before making its levelling calculations.

♦ Under **Leveling range for** choose to **Level entire project** or to level only the tasks from a specific time period, by choosing **Level** and specifying the time period using the **From** and **To** list boxes.

♦ Specify the **Leveling order** in which Project will delay the tasks:

Standard	Project determines the task to delay by examining the links with predecessors, slack, dates and priorities.
ID Only	Project starts by delaying the task with the highest ID number.
Priority, Standard	Project determines the task to delay by examining the priorities and then the links with predecessors, the slack and the dates.

♦ Activate, or deactivate these options: **Level only within available slack**, **Leveling can adjust individual assignments on a task** and/or **Leveling can create splits in remaining work**.

♦ Click **OK** or click **Level Now** to confirm and start the levelling.

Defining task priorities

♦ Select the tasks for which you want to assign the same priority level.

♦ On the **Standard** toolbar, click the tool button.

♦ Under the **General** tab, click the **Priority** box.

Multiple Task Information dialog box with tabs: General, Predecessors, Resources, Advanced, Notes. Fields: Name, Duration, Estimated, Percent complete, Priority, Dates (Start, Finish), Hide task bar, Roll up Gantt bar to summary. Buttons: Help, OK, Cancel.

♦ Indicate the importance of the selected tasks by entering a number between 0 and 1000 (the higher the number, the higher the priority assigned).

♦ Click the **OK** button.

*By default, nothing indicates the priorities defined. However, you can view these settings by using **Insert - Column** and inserting the **Priority** column into the table.*

Viewing the Leveling Gantt

♦ **View**
  More Views

♦ Double-click the **Leveling Gantt** option.

♦ If required, zoom the view using the **View - Zoom** command.

*This view displays the **Delay** table, which contains the **Leveling Delay** column.*

The Gantt Chart shows the delays using thin green lines.

❏ *To display task or delay information in a ScreenTip, point to the corresponding line.*

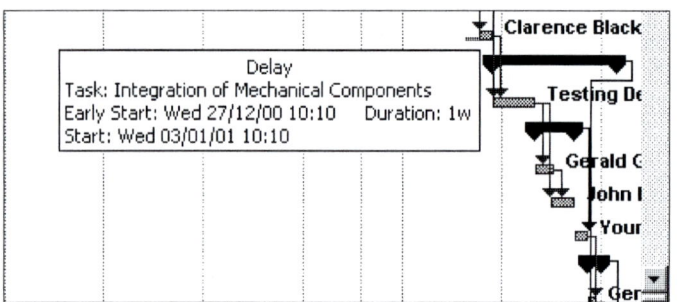

Clearing resource levelling

♦ **Tools**
  Resource Leveling

♦ Click the **Clear Leveling** button.

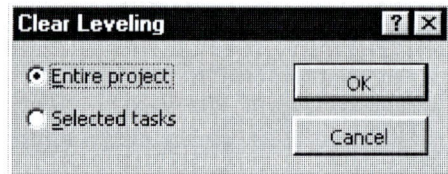

♦ Click **OK**.

Microsoft Project cancels all delays in the project.

Manually solving overallocation problems

♦ There are several ways of solving overallocation problems. You can:

– delay a task by entering a suitable value into the **Leveling Delay** field for the task (you can access this field by selecting **View - Table - More Tables - Delay**),

– break long tasks down into subtasks to assign resources more precisely,

– split tasks,

– subcontract certain tasks, so that you no longer have to apply resources to them,

– delay the work done by a resource using the **Delay** column of the **Resource Schedule** form,

– adjust the resource calendars by authorising overtime work to increase resource availability,

– assign new resources to reduce the duration of the tasks,

– replace resources by other resources that have more availability,

– optimise resource usage.

. . . . *Personal notes* . . . .

Introducing
project costs

♦ Costs are a key aspect in planning and controlling a project.

♦ Cost considerations can affect the speed with which you carry out tasks and the way in which you use resources.

♦ Comparing the costs at the end of a project with the costs you planned is one way of measuring the success of your project.

♦ Microsoft Project 2000 can show task costs and resource costs.

Entering
task costs

♦ View the Gantt Chart.

♦ **View**
   Table
   Cost

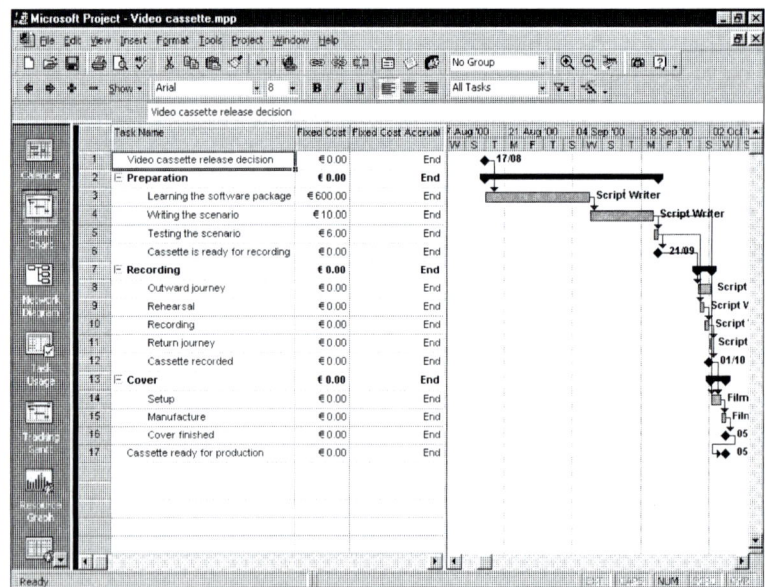

*The two basic fields concerning task costs are the **Fixed Cost** and **Fixed Cost Accrual** fields. Fixed costs are costs that stay the same irrespective of the task duration or of the work carried out.*

♦ Enter the task costs in the **Fixed Cost** column.

♦ In the **Fixed Cost Accrual** column, choose when you want the cost to be incurred to the task concerned. You can select **Start**, **Prorated** or **End**.

❏ *Project calculates the **Total Cost** field using the fixed costs for the task and the costs of the resources assigned to it.*

Entering costs for work resources

♦ Display the resource table using **View - Resource Sheet**.

♦ Enter the different costs of the work resources using the **Std. Rate**, **Ovt. Rate**, **Cost/Use** and **Accrue At** fields:

Std. Rate   the standard hourly cost for the resource,

Ovt. Rate   the hourly overtime cost for the resource,

Cost/Use   the fixed usage cost for each resource unit. Microsoft Project adds this cost each time you assign the resource unit to a task. This is a fixed cost irrespective of the length of time you use the resource.

Accrue At   This is the method that determines how costs accrue:

Start   costs are incurred when the task starts,

End   costs are incurred when there is zero work remaining,

Prorated   costs are incurred as the task progresses.

	Group	Max. Units	Std. Rate	Ovt. Rate	Cost/Use	Accrue At	Base Calendar
1	Training	100%	€12.28/hr	€15.60/hr	€0.00	Prorated	Standard
2	Video	100%	€0.00/hr	€0.00/hr	€0.00	Prorated	Standard
3	Film cutters	400%	€14.00/hr	€16.50/hr	€0.00	Prorated	Standard
4	Subcontractors	100%	€0.00/hr	€0.00/hr	€100.00	End	Standard
5	Fuel		€0.00		€0.00	Prorated	
6	Cover		€0.00		€0.00	Prorated	

By default, Microsoft Project assigns resource costs of zero. If your project uses standard rates, then you can specify them, under the **General** tab of the **Tools - Options** dialog box, in the **Default standard rate** box and the **Default overtime rate** box. These rates apply only to new resources that you create subsequently.

Entering costs for material resources

Entering a standard rate

♦ Display the resource table with the **View - Resource Sheet** command.

♦ Select the material type resource concerned.

♦ If necessary, complete the **Material Label** field.

♦ If necessary, insert the **Standard Rate** column into the resource table: select the column before which you are inserting the new column and use **Insert - Column**.

♦ Enter the rate in the **Standard Rate** column.

Entering a cost-per-use rate

♦ Display the resource table using **View - Resource Sheet**.

♦ Select the material-type resource to which you want to assign a cost per use. Microsoft Project will apply this cost only once, when you assign this resource to a given task.

♦ Enter the cost value in the **Cost/Use** field.

	Material Label	Initials	Group	Max. Units	Std. Rate	Ovt. Rate	Cost/Use	Accrue At
1		SE	Training	100%	€ 12.28/hr	€ 15.60/hr	€ 0.00	Prorated
2		FCR	Video	100%	€ 0.00/hr	€ 0.00/hr	€ 0.00	Prorated
3		FCU	Film cutters	400%	€ 14.00/hr	€ 16.50/hr	€ 0.00	Prorated
4		PS	Subcontractors	100%	€ 0.00/hr	€ 0.00/hr	€ 100.00	End
5	Litre	LPG	Fuel		€ 1.00		€ 0.00	Prorated
6		CM	Cover		€ 0.00		€ 50.00	Prorated

**Assigning
new cost rates
to resources**

*This technique helps you to plan future increases and decreases in
salaries.*

♦ Double-click the resource for which a future increase (or
decrease) in salary is planned.

♦ Activate the **Costs** tab.

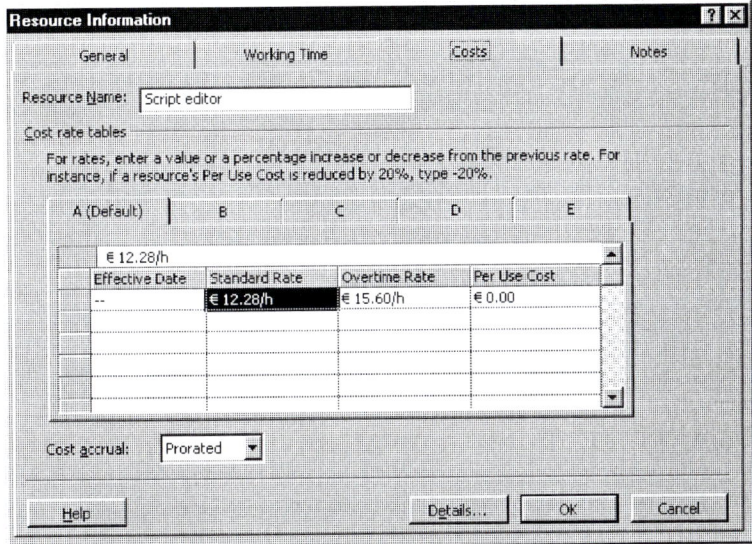

♦ Enter the **Effective Date** of the new rate.

The first row remains the same.

♦ Enter the new rates or enter percentage increases (or decreases).

*When you validate your entry, Microsoft Project automatically
calculates the new rate.*

Using several cost rate tables for a resource

You can define up to five different cost tables for each resource. For example, you could define one table for ordinary tasks and another table for special tasks.

Creating tables

♦ Double-click the resource concerned.

♦ Activate the **Costs** tab.

♦ Click the tab for the cost rate table on which you want to work: **A (Default)**, **B**, **C**, **D** or **E**.

♦ Enter the different costs in this table.

♦ Click the **OK** button.

❑ *To delete a value in one of the fields of a **Cost rate table**, replace the value by zero.*

Specifying the cost rate table for a resource assignment

*By default, Microsoft Project uses **Cost rate table A**.*

♦ **View**
   Resource Usage

♦ Double-click the assignment for which you want to specify a different cost rate table.

♦ Under the **General** tab, open the **Cost rate table** list and select the table you wish to use for this assignment.

Assignment Information

| General | Tracking | Notes |

Task: Design

Resource: Film cutter

Work: 30h   Units: 150%

Work contour: Flat

Start: Mon 02/10/00 08:30

Finish: Wed 04/10/00 13:30

Cost: € 400.00   Cost rate table: B

OK   Cancel

♦ Click the **OK** button.

Filtering tasks with costs exceeding a certain value

♦ Display the tasks.

♦ Open the **Filter** list.

♦ Select the **Cost Greater Than** filter.

♦ Enter the reference cost value.

♦ Click the **OK** button.

Printing the Cash Flow report

This report presents the following information:

– *costs per task and per week,*

– *total costs of all tasks per week,*

– *total costs per task (this corresponds to the **Total Cost** field in the task sheet),*

– *total budget cost.*

To calculate the task costs per week, Project divides the total cost of each task by its total duration and then multiplies the result by the duration of the task in each week.

♦ **View**
Reports

♦ Double-click the **Costs** button and the **Cash flow** button.

♦ Click the **Print** button and **OK**.

♦ Leave the **Reports** dialog box by clicking the **Close** button.

Viewing the cost accumulation of a resource

Using a graph

♦ **View**
Resource Graph

*The **View** bar contains this button.*

*By default, this graph shows the **Peak Units** for resource 1. This information is shown in calendar form.*

♦ Right-click in the right side of the screen.

♦ Choose the **Cumulative Cost** option.

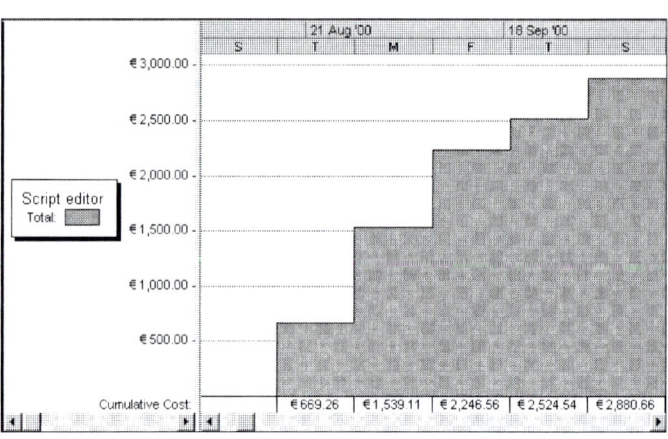

Using a custom cash flow report

♦ **View**
Reports

♦ Double-click the **Custom** button.

♦ Create your custom cash flow report:

In the **Custom Reports** dialog box choose **Cash Flow**.
Click the **Copy** button.
Enter the **Name** of the report.
Open the **Row** list and select the **Resources** option.
Open the **Filter** list and choose the **All Resources** option.

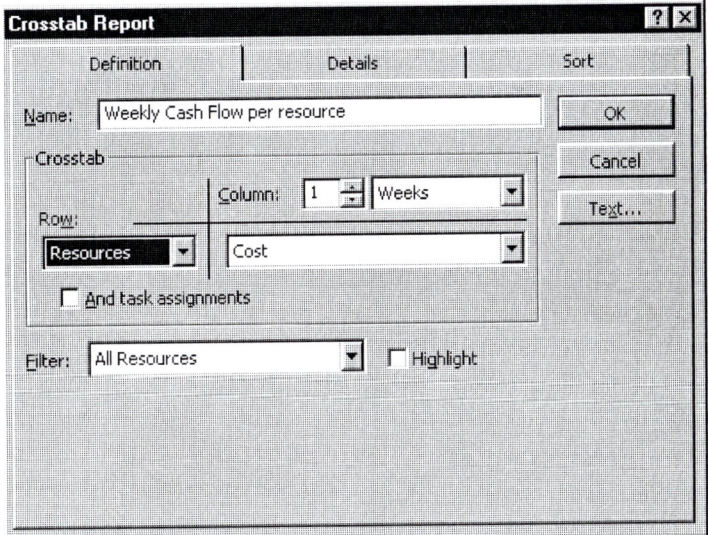

♦ Click the **OK** button.

♦ To view your custom cash flow report, select it in the **Custom Reports** dialog box and click either **Print** or **Preview**.

Microsoft Project 2000

187

Introducing Earned Value tables

Viewing the Earned Value table

♦ Display the project tasks, using **View - More Views - Task Sheet - Apply**.

You can use a different task view here if you wish, but this view makes better use of the available screen space.

♦ **View**
  Table
  More Tables

♦ Double-click the **Earned Value** option.

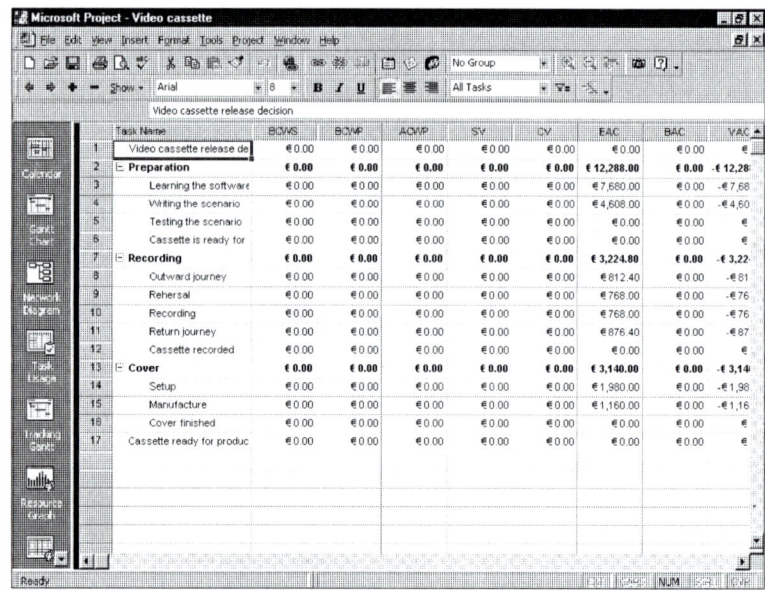

Printing the Earned Value table

♦ **View**
  Reports

♦ Double-click the **Costs** button and the **Earned Value** button.

Description of columns in the Earned Value table

♦ The **EAC** (Estimate At Completion) column contains the total cost of each task (you can, if you wish, compare it with the **Total** column of the weekly cash flow report).

♦ If you save the baseline for your project using **Tools - Tracking - Save Baseline - OK**, then Project copies the contents of the **EAC** column into the **BAC** (Budget At Completion) column, which corresponds to the baseline cost.

	Task Name	BCWS	BCWP	ACWP	SV	CV	EAC	BAC	VAC
1	Video cassette releas	€0.00	€0.00	€0.00	€0.00	€0.00	€0.00	€0.00	€0.00
2	⊟ Preparation	€1,512.00	€1,377.60	€125.90	-€134.40	€1,251.70	€6,444.00	€6,444.00	€0.00
3	Learning the soft	€1,512.00	€1,377.60	€125.90	-€134.40	€1,251.70	€1,680.00	€1,680.00	€0.00
4	Writing the scene	€0.00	€0.00	€0.00	€0.00	€0.00	€758.00	€758.00	€0.00
5	Tuning the scene	€0.00	€0.00	€0.00	€0.00	€0.00	€6.00	€6.00	€0.00
6	Cassette is reach	€0.00	€0.00	€0.00	€0.00	€0.00	€4,000.00	€4,000.00	€0.00

♦ The **BCWS** column shows the Budgeted Cost of Work Scheduled at a given date. This is the part of the budget that should have been used if the project had progressed according to the initial plan. BCWS = BAC x % of planned completion.

You should note that Project 2000 calculates according to elapsed durations and not according to worked durations.

♦ The **BCWP** column shows the Budgeted Cost of Work Performed.
BCWP = BAC x % actual completion.

BCWP is also known as "earned value".

♦ The **ACWP** column shows the Actual Cost of Work Performed. It represents the real costs of the tasks.

♦ The **SV** (earned value Schedule Variance) column shows, in cost terms, the difference between the current progress and the planned progress for the tasks.
SV = BCWP - BCWS

♦ The **CV** (earned value Cost Variance) column shows the variation with respect to the budget.
CV = ACWP - BCWP

♦ The **VAC** (Variance At Completion) column shows the difference between the budgeted at completion cost and the estimated at completion cost (VAC = BAC-EAC).

Changing the currency format for costs

♦ **Tools**
  Options

♦ If necessary, activate the **View** tab.

♦ Modify the **Currency options**.

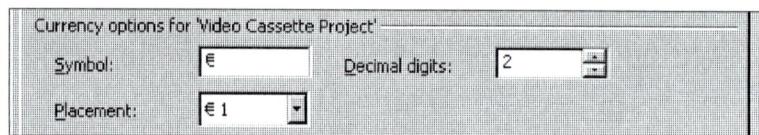

♦ Click the **OK** button.

. . . . *Personal notes* . . . .

Entering the task workload

You can indicate the workload for your tasks, without assigning specific resources to them.

♦ View the Gantt Chart.

♦ **View**
  Table
  Work

	Task Name	Work	Baseline	Variance	Actual	Remaining	% W. Comp.
1	Order 512	0 hrs	0 hrs	0 hrs	0 hrs	0 hrs	0%
2	Specification	4 hrs	0 hrs	4 hrs	1 hr	3 hrs	25%
3	Design	0 hrs	0 hrs	0 hrs	0 hrs	0 hrs	0%
4	Electronic preparation	0 hrs	0 hrs	0 hrs	0 hrs	0 hrs	0%
5	Mechanical preparation	0 hrs	0 hrs	0 hrs	0 hrs	0 hrs	0%
6	Electronic and mechanical tests	0 hrs	0 hrs	0 hrs	0 hrs	0 hrs	0%
7	Tests validated	0 hrs	0 hrs	0 hrs	0 hrs	0 hrs	0%
8	Mechanical sub-assembly	0 hrs	0 hrs	0 hrs	0 hrs	0 hrs	0%
9	Styling	0 hrs	0 hrs	0 hrs	0 hrs	0 hrs	0%
10	Final assembly	0 hrs	0 hrs	0 hrs	0 hrs	0 hrs	0%
11	Order finished	0 hrs	0 hrs	0 hrs	0 hrs	0 hrs	0%

*This table contains the following fields: the **ID** number, **Task Name**, **Work**, **Baseline** work, the **Variance** (between **Work** and **Baseline**), **Actual** work, **Remaining** work (between **Work** and **Actual**), and the **% W. Comp.** (the percentage of **Work** completed).*

♦ If the time unit in this table is unsuitable then use **Tools - Options Schedule** tab, open the **Work is entered in** list, choose the required unit and click **OK**.

♦ Enter the workload in the **Work** column.

Printing the task workload

♦ **View**
  Reports

♦ Double-click the **Workload** button and the **Task Usage** button.

♦ To print this report, click **Print** and then **OK**.

♦ To view this report on the screen, click anywhere in the table.

Microsoft Project 2000

Microsoft Project - Order 512								_ 🗗 🗙

◄ ► ▲ ▼ 🔍 🔲 ⊞　Page Setup...　　Print...　　Close　　Help

Task Usage as of Thu 09/11/00 10:14
Order 512

	24/06/00	03/07/00	10/07/00	17/07/00	24/07/00	31/07/00	07/08
Order 512							
Specification	1 wk						
Design		2.56 wks	2.56 wks	2.56 wks	2.56 wks	2.56 wks	2.5
Electronic preparation							
Mechanical preparation							
Electronic and mechanical tests							
Tests validated							
Mechanical sub-assembly							
Styling							
Final assembly							
Order finished							
Total	1 wk	2.56 wks	2.56 wks	2.56 wks	2.56 wks	2.56 wks	2.5

Page: 1 of 12　Size: 1 row by 12 columns　　　　　　　EXT　CAPS　**NUM**　SCRL　OVR

The status bar shows the total number of pages in the report.

. . . . *Personal notes* . . . .

Monitoring the progress of your project

♦ Before you can start tracking your project, you must define a baseline for it.

♦ A project that manages only tasks is easy to track: you compare only the planned dates with the actual dates, and the planned durations with the actual durations.

♦ With more sophisticated projects, tracking can become very complex (comparing items such as costs and numbers of hours worked).

♦ Tracking allows you to correct variations, to solve problems before they become critical and to enhance your professional knowledge and skills.

Saving the baseline

After you have carefully set up your plan but before your project starts, you must define a baseline so that you can track your project, by comparing the actual data with your planned data.

When you save the baseline, Microsoft Project 2000 saves many items of information, including the following:

Data item	*Saved as*
Duration	*Baseline duration*
Start	*Baseline start*
Finish	*Baseline finish*

You can resave your baseline as often as you like, to reflect important changes.

Microsoft Project does not allow you to track your project until you have saved a baseline at least once.

♦ **Tools**
 Tracking
 Save Baseline

♦ Make sure the **Save baseline** and **Entire project** options are active.

♦ Click the **OK** button.

❏ *To clear the baseline, select* **Tools - Tracking - Clear Baseline**, *activate the* **Clear baseline plan** *option and click* **OK***.*

Viewing the baseline table

♦ **View**
Table
More Tables

♦ Double-click the **Baseline** option.

Apart from the **Baseline Duration***,* **Baseline Start** *and* **Baseline Finish***, this table also shows* **Baseline Work** *and* **Baseline Cost***.*

Entering the current date of your project

By default, Project uses the current date of your computer as the "current project date" (Project uses this date in its task progress calculations). You can specify a different date if needed:

♦ **Project**
Project Information

♦ Enter the current date of your project in the **Current date** box.

♦ Click the **OK** button.

*The **Gantt Chart** shows the current date of your project as a vertical dotted line.*

The tasks to the left of this line should be completed (the past), the tasks through which this line passes should be in progress (the present) and the tasks to the right should not yet have started (the future).

❑ *Entering the **Current date** for your project in this way is only a temporary setting. If you close your file, Microsoft Project will still use the current date of your computer when you reopen it.*

Saving an interim plan

You can use this technique when your project is underway, after you have saved a baseline.

♦ **Tools**
  Tracking
  Save Baseline

♦ Activate the **Save interim plan** option.

♦ Specify the fields you wish to **Copy.**

♦ Specify the fields **Into** which Microsoft Project must copy.

♦ Click the **OK** button.

❑ *Microsoft Project can save up to 10 different interim plans.*

❑ *To clear an interim plan, use **Tools - Tracking - Clear Baseline**. Activate the **Clear interim plan** option, open the corresponding list, select the interim plan you want to clear, and click **OK**.*

Consulting the different plans

Microsoft Project does not offer a default view for this purpose. You must create a custom table.

♦ **View**
  Table
  More Tables

♦ Click the **New** button.

♦ Enter a **Name** for your table.

♦ Activate the **Show in menu** check box, if required.

♦ Insert the columns you require.

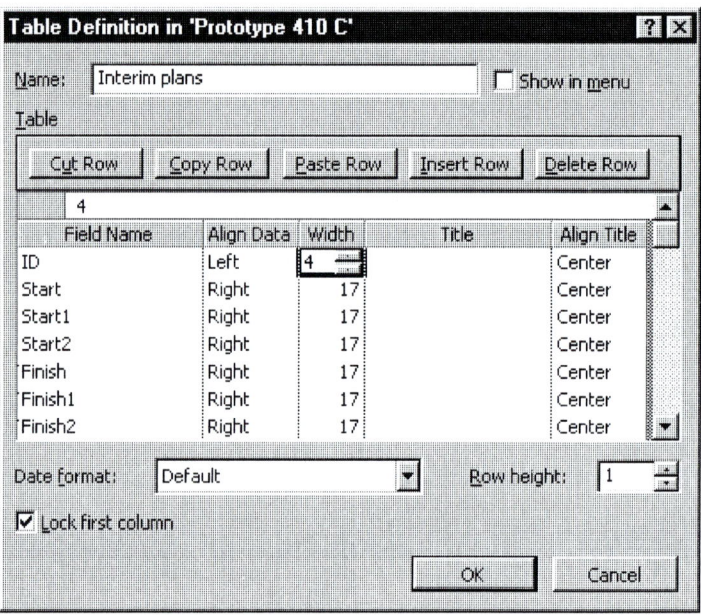

♦ Click **OK** and then click **Apply** to see your table.

**Displaying
the Tracking
toolbar**

♦ View
  Toolbars
  Tracking

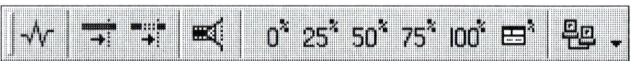

*The **Tracking** toolbar appears under the **Formatting** toolbar.*

Viewing Progress lines

For a given date, Project 2000 can construct a progress line, plotting the tasks that are underway.

♦ **Tools**
 Tracking
 Progress Lines

♦ Activate the **Dates and Intervals** tab, if necessary.

♦ To view the current progress line, activate the **Always display current progress line** check box, then activate the **At project status date** option or the **At current date** option.
If required, activate the **Display progress lines at recurring intervals** check box and choose the desired interval.
To display progress lines at specific dates, activate the **Display selected progress lines** option and enter your required dates in the **Progress Line Dates** column.

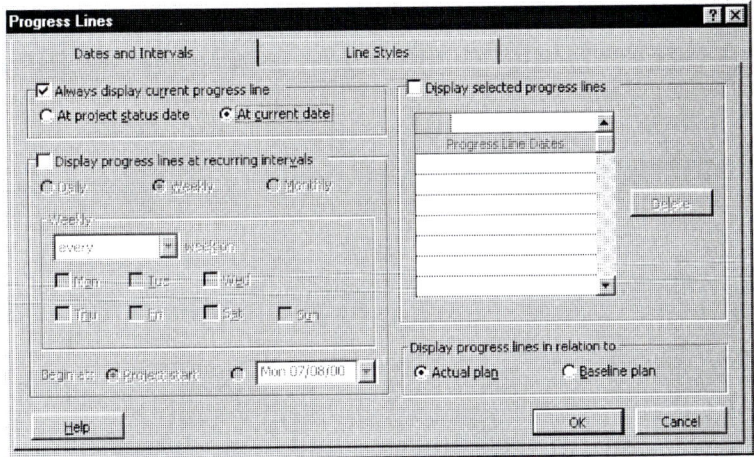

*Use the **Line Styles** options to customise the look of your progress lines.*

♦ Choose to **Display progress lines in relation to** either the **Actual plan** or the **Baseline plan**.

♦ Click the **OK** button.

		Task Name		July	January	July	January	July
			27/03 12/06 28/08	13/11 29/01 16/04	02/07 17/09	03/12 18/02 06/05	22/07 07/10 2
1	✓	Order 512	◆26/06				
2	✓	Specification	100%				
3	✓	Design	100%				
4	✓	Electronic preparation		100%			
5	✓	Mechanical preparation		100%			
6		Electronic and mechanical tests			49%		
7		Tests validated			◆01/07		
8		Mechanical sub-assembly			77%		
9		Styling			96%		
10		Final assembly				30%	
11		Order finished				◆16/10	

The peaks pointing to the left show tasks that are behind sche-dule and those that point to the right (there are none in this example) show tasks that are ahead of schedule.

♦ On the **Tracking** toolbar, click the 🔲 tool button.

♦ In the Gantt Chart, click where you want the progress line to appear.

❏ *A task is ahead of schedule when its actual start date is earlier than its planned start date.*

. . . . *Personal notes* . . . .

Updating task progress

Allowing Microsoft Project to update automatically

♦ **Tools**
Tracking
Update Project

♦ Retain the **Update work as complete through** option.

♦ Specify the date in the corresponding box, if necessary.

♦ Choose one of the following options:

Set 0% - 100% complete   Project calculates percentages of task completion.

Set 0% or 100% complete only   Project assigns 100% to completed tasks and 0% to all others, even those in progress.

♦ Indicate that Microsoft Project must update either the **Entire project**, or only **Selected tasks**.

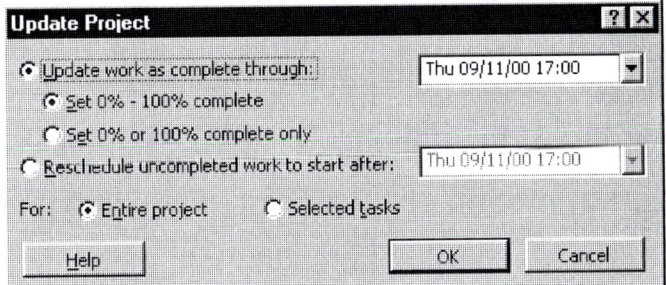

♦ Click the **OK** button.

In the Gantt Chart, the black lines in the middle of the task bars indicate the progress of the tasks concerned.

The ✔ icon shows that the task has been completed.

❏ You can also click the **Update as Scheduled** ⟶ tool button to let Project calculate the progress of tasks.

Microsoft Project 2000

Updating manually

♦ Select the task whose progress you want to update.

♦ **Tools**
  Tracking
  Update Tasks

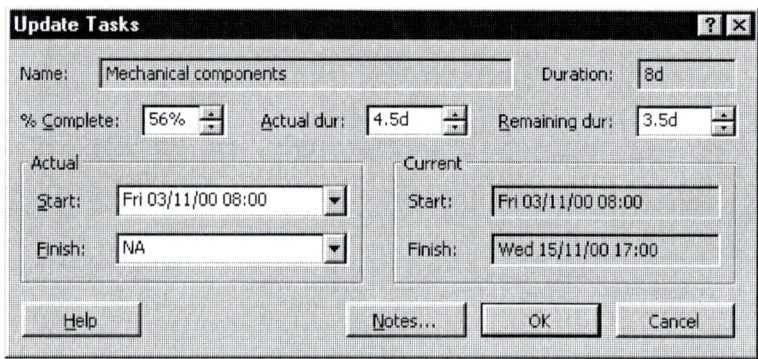

This dialog box allows you to update all task tracking informa-tion.

♦ Update your tasks according to their current progress.

Entering tracking information

♦ Select the task whose progress you want to update.

♦ **Tools**
  Tracking
  Update Tasks

For tasks that have been completed

♦ If the task was completed on schedule, then enter either **100** in the **% Complete** box, or **0** in the **Remaining dur** box.

♦ If the task took longer than planned, enter its actual duration in the **Actual dur** box.

*Project considers a task to be completed when its actual duration is <u>greater than or equal to</u> the planned duration. It also considers a task as completed if you give its **Actual Finish** date.*

♦ Click the **OK** button to confirm your settings.

For tasks that have not been completed

♦ To indicate that a task has not yet been completed, give either a **% Complete** value of between **0** and **100**, or a **Remaining dur** value greater than zero, or an **Actual dur** value less than the planned duration.

♦ If you fill in only one of these fields, Project calculates the other data in relation to the baseline. If this does not reflect the real situation, use several fields. Be careful: Project does not take the current date into account when making these calculations!

♦ Here are three examples for a task that has a planned duration of 5 days:
A - After 2.5 days, the task is proceeding according to schedule:

Information entered	Calculations made by Microsoft Project
% Complete: 50	Actual duration: 2.5d Remaining duration: 2.5d
Actual dur: 2.5d	% complete: 50 Remaining duration: 2.5d

B - After 3 days, only 50% of the task has been completed:

Information entered	Calculations made by Microsoft Project
% Complete: 50	Actual duration: 2.5d Remaining duration: 2.5d
Actual dur: 3d	% complete: 60 Remaining duration: 2d

To reflect reality, you must enter **% Complete: 50** and **Actual dur: 3d**.

This tells Project that the duration will be longer than scheduled. It will calculate a total duration of 6 days and a remaining duration of 3 days.

C - After 3 days, 4 days of work still remain:

Information entered	Calculations made by Microsoft Project
Actual dur: 3d	% complete: 60 Remaining duration: 2d
Remaining dur: 4d	% complete: 20 Actual duration: 1d

To reflect reality, you must enter **Actual dur: 3d** and **Remaining dur: 4d**.

Based on this data, Project calculates that the total duration will be 7 days, and that 43% of the task has been completed.

Setting an Outlook Reminder for a task

♦ You can ask Microsoft Project to remind you of the start or the finish of a task. To do this, go to the Gantt Chart.

♦ Select the task(s) for which you want to receive a reminder (to select several tasks, hold down Ctrl while you click each task).

♦ Display the **Workgroup** toolbar (**View - Toolbars - Workgroup**).

♦ Click the **Set Reminder** tool button ( ).

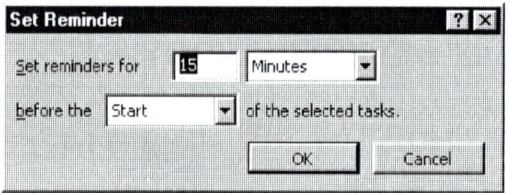

♦ Set the different options in the **Set Reminder** dialog box, and then click the **OK** button.

Adding tracking notes for a task

♦ Select the task for which you want to add tracking notes.

♦ **Tools**
  Tracking
  Update Tasks

♦ Click the **Notes** button.

♦ Enter and format your notes.

♦ Click the **OK** button twice.

Rescheduling slipped tasks

♦ Select the task(s) concerned.

♦ **Tools**
  Tracking
  Update Project

♦ Activate the **Reschedule uncompleted work to start after** option.

♦ If necessary, enter the required date in the corresponding box.

♦ Specify whether this rescheduling concerns the **Entire project** or just the **Selected tasks**.

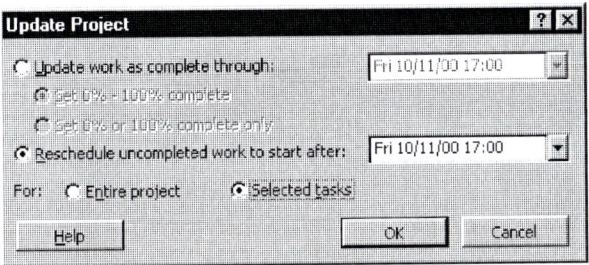

♦ Confirm with **OK**.

❏ *You can also use the **Reschedule Work** tool button (* *).*

**Viewing
the variance
between
your plan
and reality**

Using the Tracking Gantt view

♦ **View**
   Tracking Gantt

*The **View** bar contains this button.*

♦ If required, use **View - Zoom - Entire project - OK**.

The grey layers of the task bars show what is scheduled.

The blue layers (for non-critical tasks) or the red layers (for critical tasks) show the real situation.

This view also shows the completion percentages for the tasks.

Using the Variance table

♦ **View**
   Table
   Variance

	Start Var.	Finish Var.
1	0 days	0 days
2	**0 days**	**0 days**
3	0 days	0 days
4	0 days	0 days
5	**0 days**	**2.5 days**
6	0 days	0 days
7	0 days	2 days
8	2 days	2.5 days
9	**2.5 days**	**2.5 days**
10	**2.5 days**	**2.5 days**
11	2.5 days	2.5 days
12	2.5 days	2.5 days
13	2.5 days	2.5 days
14	2.5 days	2.5 days

*The final two columns of this table show the **Start Variance** and the **Finish Variance**.*

Project transfers variances from one task to the next according to their scheduling.

Using a custom table

♦ **View**
Table
More Tables

♦ To define your custom table, click the **New** button.

♦ Specify your table in the **Table Definition** dialog box.

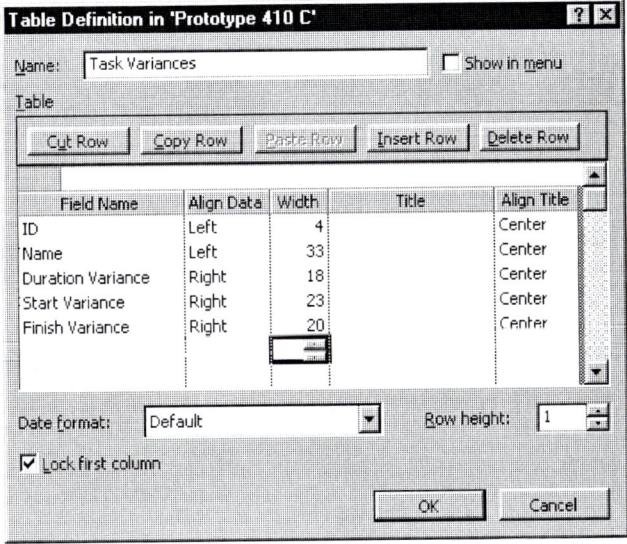

♦ Click **OK** then **Apply**.

♦ Use your new table as you would use any other table.

Viewing completed tasks

By applying a filter

♦ View the tasks of your project, then open the **Filter** list.

♦ Select the **Completed Tasks** filter.

By printing a report

♦ **View**
Reports

♦ Double-click the **Current Activities** button, followed by the **Completed Tasks** button.

♦ Click **Print** then **OK**.

This report shows rows of completed tasks, month by month.

Viewing the tasks in progress

On the screen

♦ Open the **Filter** list.

♦ Select the **In Progress Tasks** filter.

❏ *The **Incomplete Tasks** filter displays all tasks that have not yet been completed, whether they have been started or not.*

By printing a report

♦ **View**
Reports

♦ Double-click the **Current Activities** button then the **Tasks In Progress** button.

♦ Click **Print** then **OK**.

Viewing slipping tasks

Slipping tasks are tasks that have been delayed with respect to the baseline and that have not yet been completed.

On the screen

♦ Open the **Filter** list.

♦ Select the **Slipping Tasks** filter.

By printing a report

♦ **View**
Reports

♦ Double-click the **Current Activities** button, followed by the **Slipping Tasks** button.

♦ Click **Print** then **OK**.

. . . . *Personal notes* . . . .

Making it easier to view work carried out on a project

♦ View the Gantt Chart with the **Work** table.

♦ **Window**
Split

♦ Right-click the form that appears and choose the **Resource Work** form.

♦ In the Gantt Chart select the task concerned.

When you save the baseline, Microsoft Project copies the Resource Work field into the Baseline Work field.

Tracking the work of each assigned resource

For completed tasks

♦ Display the **Task Usage** view with the **Resource Work** form.

♦ Right-click in the (yellow) right pane of the **Task Usage** view, and choose the **Actual Work** option.

Enlarge the right pane by dragging the split bar, if necessary.

♦ Select the task concerned.

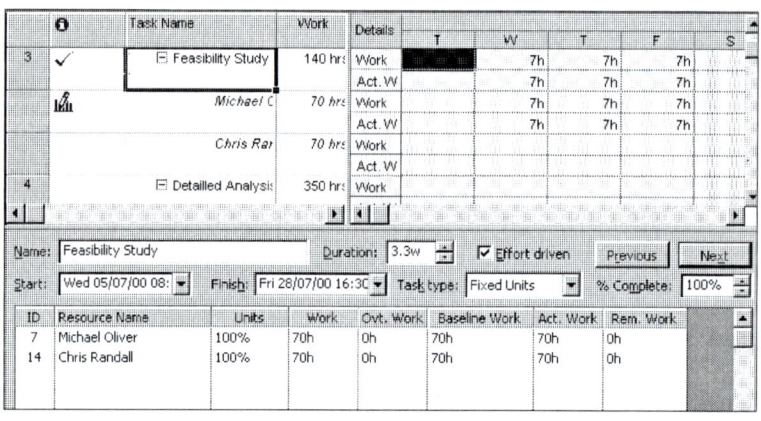

♦ If the **Act. Work** value is greater than the **Baseline Work** but the task's elapsed duration has not changed, specify how this work was carried out:

  – if you used overtime hours, fill in the **Work** and **Ovt. Work** field in the **Resource Work** form.

  – if the resource worked more hours but without doing overtime, those hours still have a cost: fill in the actual hours worked by the resource concerned, in the right pane of the **Task Usage** table.

♦ If necessary, click the **OK** button.

For tasks in progress

♦ Display the **Gantt Chart** view with the **Work** table and the **Resource Work** form.

♦ When you track a task for the first time, enter the **Actual Work** that the resource has carried out on the task.

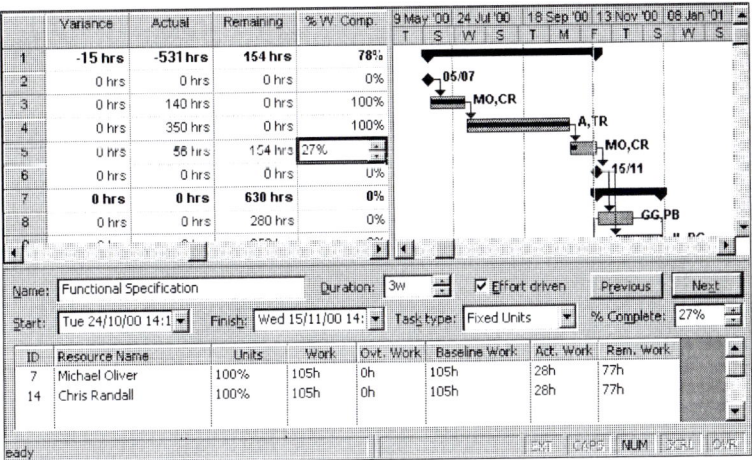

♦ A problem arises when you update the tracking information: resources report the work carried out since the last tracking. For example, you are told, "This week we worked X hours on this task".

♦ You may want to add this new value to the previous one, but there is a drawback. If you give a new progress percentage, then Project will instantly recalculate the actual work. How then can you find the previous actual work figure?

♦ To solve this problem in tracking updates, you should:

– dissociate the task update from the resource update,

– update the actual work on a daily basis.

Dissociating task update and resource update

♦ **Tools**
Options

♦ Activate the **Calculation** tab.

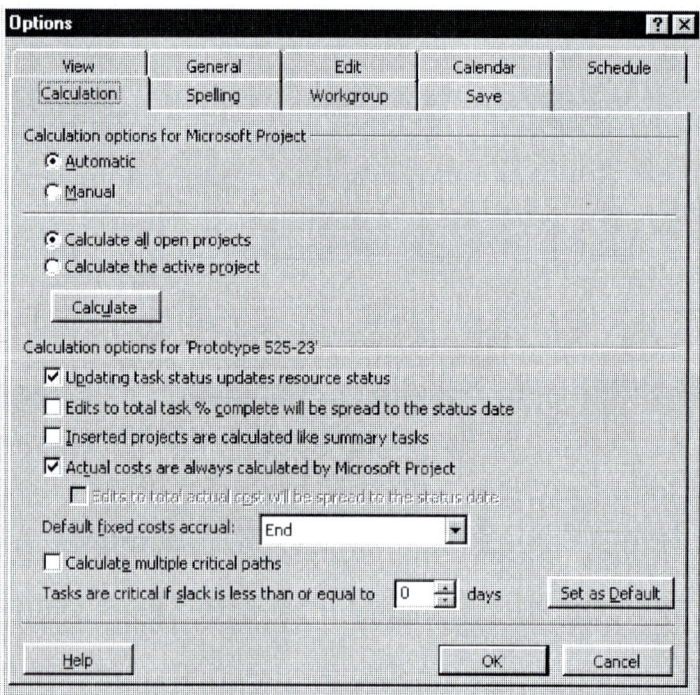

♦ Deactivate the **Updating task status updates resource status** check box.

♦ Click the **OK** button.

**Updating
actual work
on a daily basis**

♦ **View**
  Resource Usage

*The **View** bar contains this button.*

♦ **View**
  Table
  Work

♦ Enter the hours worked by the resource in the cells of the calendar pane.

**Displaying %
Work Complete
in the Tracking
Gantt**

♦ Display the **Tracking Gantt** view.

♦ **Format**
  Bar Styles

♦ In the **Name** column, click the **Critical** row.

♦ Activate the **Text** tab.

♦ Click the cell next to the **Left** row header, open the list in this cell and choose the *% **Work Complete*** option.

♦ Customise the non-critical bars in the same way.

♦ Click the **OK** button.

. . . . *Personal notes* . . . .

Tracking actual costs

By default, Project 2000 calculates actual costs and you cannot modify these values.

Deactivating the automatic calculation of actual costs

♦ **Tools**
 Options

♦ Activate the **Calculation** tab.

♦ Deactivate the **Actual costs are always calculated by Microsoft Project** check box.

♦ Activate the **Edits to total task % complete will be spread to the status date** check box, or deactivate it to spread cost modifications to the end of the actual task duration.

♦ Click the **OK** button.

Entering actual costs

♦ View the tasks.

♦ **View**
 Table
 Cost

♦ Enter the actual costs in the **Actual** field.

Defining the status date

*The status date of a project allows Project 2000 to calculate the values in the **Earned Value** table. If you do not specify this date, Project will calculate these values according to the current date.*

♦ **Project**
 Project Information

♦ Enter your required **Status date**.

♦ Click the **OK** button.

Viewing overbudget cost and work

On the screen

♦ Open the **Filter** list.

♦ Select the **Cost Overbudget** or **Work Overbudget** filter.

By printing a report

♦ **View**
Reports

♦ Double-click **Costs**.

♦ Choose **Overbudget Tasks** or **Overbudget Resources** then print.

Tracking overall work carried out on tasks

♦ Display the tasks.

♦ **View**
Table
Work

*When you save the baseline, Microsoft Project copies the **Work** field into the **Baseline Work** field.*

♦ Scroll the table horizontally to view the **% W. Comp.** column.

♦ Enter known information about the work actually carried out using the following rule:
for work that has been completed:

– if the actual work is greater than the scheduled work, enter this data in the **Actual** column.

– if it is less, enter it in the **Work** column.

214

**Description
of the methods**

*Members of a workgroup associated with a project can communicate with each other either using a traditional e-mail application such as Microsoft Outlook, or using **Microsoft Project Central**. In addition to an e-mail system, Project Central has features that help group members to exchange information on one or more projects.*

Features offered by the e-mail system

♦ Workgroup members can:

– receive task assignments

– accept or refuse task assignments.

– request or submit status reports.

– send and receive task updates.

– view only the tasks to which they have been assigned.

Features offered by Microsoft Project Central

Microsoft Project Central is a Microsoft Project add-on program that allows everyone involved in a project to contribute to the setting-up of the project plan. It offers different features according to whether you are a project manager or simply a member of the workgroup.

♦ Workgroup members can:

– consult the tasks of all their projects. They can view their tasks in a Gantt Chart. They can also group, sort and filter these tasks.

– consult information on the whole project and not only on the tasks to which they have been assigned (provided that the Project Central administrator has granted the necessary rights).

– create new tasks and send them to the project manager so that he/she can incorporate them into the project file.

– delegate tasks to other workgroup members.

♦ Project managers can:

– request and receive status reports, and if necessary, consolidate individual status reports into a project status report.

– automate project updates according to messages received from some or all members of the workgroup.

Usage constraints *Microsoft Project Central offers more features and flexibility than an e-mail workgroup system. However, both of these systems have constraints:*

Constraints with a workgroup e-mail system

♦ The project manager and the workgroup members must:

– have access to a network that can transport e-mail messages (have access to a LAN, for example).

– use a MAPI-compliant 32-bit e-mail client application (for example, Microsoft Outlook).

– install the WGsetup program on their computers (this program is available in the WGsetup folder of the Microsoft Project 2000 CD-ROM).

The project manager's computer, at least, must run Microsoft Project 2000.

Constraints with Microsoft Project Central

♦ To communicate with Microsoft Project Central, certain conditions must be met:

– At least the project manager's computer must run Microsoft Project 2000.

– Microsoft Project Central must be installed on a Web server that is connected to the Internet or to an intranet.

– Each workgroup member must have a Microsoft Project Central licence to access Microsoft Project Central.

– Each workgroup member must have a Web browser. This can be Microsoft Internet Explorer 4.01, or a later version, or the browser module that is supplied with Microsoft Project Central.

– If you use an intranet, each computer in the network must have a unique network identifier.

Types of e-mail message

♦ The project manager sends a **TeamAssign** message to a workgroup member to inform him/her of a task assignment. He/she can accept or refuse this assignment. If the member does not reply, then the assignment is considered as accepted.

♦ The project manager sends a **TeamUpdate** message to a workgroup member to inform the member of changes to a task to which he/she is assigned. The member can reply with a comments message.

♦ The project manager sends a **TeamStatus** message to a workgroup member to request information on a task's progress. The member then replies to give the task status. The project manager can then incorporate this information in the project plan, directly from the message.

Message exchange processes

The project manager sends TeamAssign, TeamUpdate, and Team Status messages to workgroup members in the same way, whatever the communication method that is used. On the other hand, the communication method affects how the project manager and the workgroup members reply to the messages that they receive.
The message exchange process differs according to whether you use the Microsoft Project Central or the e-mail message system.

With an e-mail message system

♦ The project manager sends TeamAssign or TeamUpdate messages to workgroup members from Microsoft Project 2000.

♦ The workgroup members reply by e-mail to the project manager's inbox.

♦ The project manager uses his/her e-mail message system to view and reply to messages from the workgroup members. The project manager can incorporate the contents of these messages directly into the project plan.

With Microsoft Project Central

♦ The project manager sends TeamAssign, TeamUpdate or Team-Status messages to workgroup members from Microsoft Project 2000.

♦ To receive these messages, the workgroup member opens a Microsoft Project Central session using a Web browser. He/she must reply to TeamStatus messages, while default assignments (TeamAssign messages) and updates (TeamUpdate messages) are accepted automatically. Despite this, he/she can still open Team-Assign and TeamUpdate messages to refuse assignments or send replies.

Workgroup members must check Microsoft Project Central regularly for new messages, unless the project manager asks Project to send automatic notifications to their inboxes each time it receives workgroup messages for them. In this case, the workgroup members must be connected by an e-mail system.

♦ The workgroup member can use Microsoft Project Central to send messages to the project manager, who can then enter the data concerned directly into the schedule.

♦ To receive messages and task updates from workgroup members, the project manager must also open a Microsoft Project Central session. The project manager can then update the project schedule automatically or manually.

**Activating
a default
communication
method**

E-mail message system (Email)

♦ To choose the default method of communicating with project resources, go into Microsoft Project 2000, select **Tools - Options**, and click the **Workgroup** tab.

♦ Open the **Default workgroup messages for** list box and choose the **Email** option, to communicate with workgroup members via your company's e-mail system.

*You can choose the **None** option if you do not use the Workgroup Messaging System in your project.*

♦ Click the **Set as Default** button to apply this setting to all future projects. Otherwise, it will apply only to the active project.

♦ Click the **OK** button.

Microsoft Project Central (Web)

♦ **Tools
Options
Workgroup** tab

♦ Open the **Default workgroup messages for** list box and choose the **Web** option.

♦ Click the **Set as Default** button to apply this setting to all future projects.

*A resource can use a communication method different from that defined for the project. In this case, open the **Project - Resource Information** dialog box and adjust the **Workgroup** value for each resource using another method.*

♦ Under **Web server settings for**, enter the **Microsoft Project Central Server URL**.

♦ To access Project Central, workgroup members can use one of two authentication methods. As project manager (and with the network administrator's approval), define the **Identification for Microsoft Project Central**, using one of these options:

– **Windows user account**: the user is authenticated automatically thanks to his/her Windows user account. This method offers better security for your project files and the user does not need to give a user name or password to access Project Central.

– **Microsoft Project user name**: the user is identified by a user name and a password (these are defined in Project Central by the administrator).

*Important note: the following operations concern only the **Windows user account** choice for **Identification for Microsoft Project Central Server**.*

♦ When you choose the **Windows user account** option, as project manager you can define your account: click the **Create Account** button, then click **OK** to close Microsoft Project's message that it has created your account on Project Central.

Project 2000 searches for your Windows user account automatically, by the user name that you entered when you started your computer. If it was able to create your account, then a message similar to the following appears:

If it was unable to create your account for whatever reason, the following message appears:

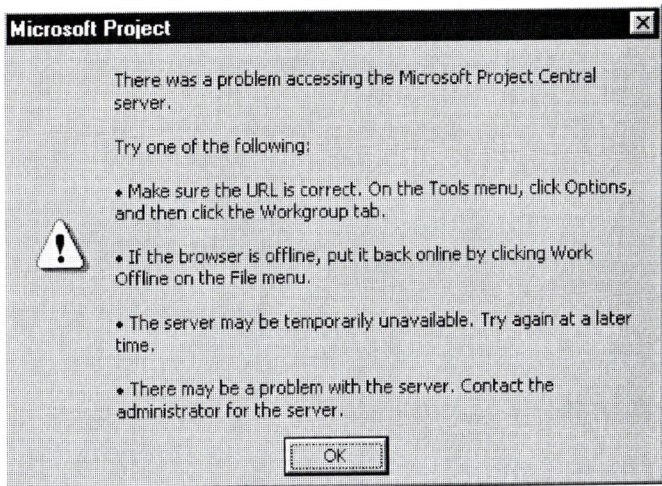

You can always create an account directly using the Project Central application (cf. Managing user accounts in Microsoft Project Central).

Microsoft Project creates your user account directly in Microsoft Project Central using the details of your Windows user account. By default, Microsoft Project Central grants you <u>Manager</u> rights, rather than Resource rights or Administrator rights.

♦ Activate the **Send hyperlink in E-mail note** option if, as project manager, you want Project 2000 to send automatic notification messages to workgroup members whenever Project Central receives new messages for them. If you do not activate this option, workgroup members will have to check Project Central regularly for new messages.

To use this feature, the workgroup members must be able to communicate with each other via an e-mail system and the resources to whom you send messages must have e-mail addresses.

♦ If necessary, click the **Set as Default** button to apply these settings to all future projects.

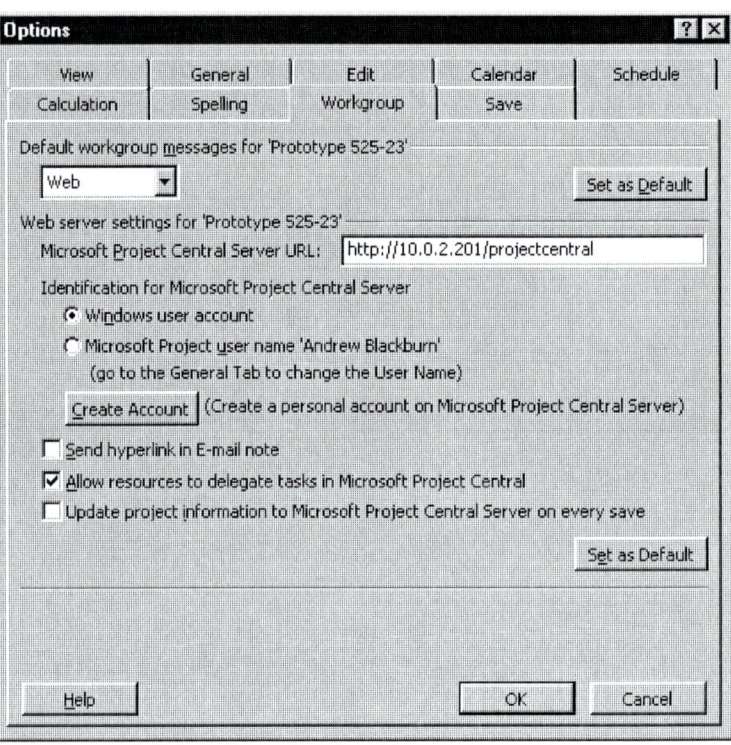

♦ Click **OK** to confirm your settings.

Activating a communication method for a resource

♦ Show the **Resource Sheet** of the project, select the resource concerned and click the 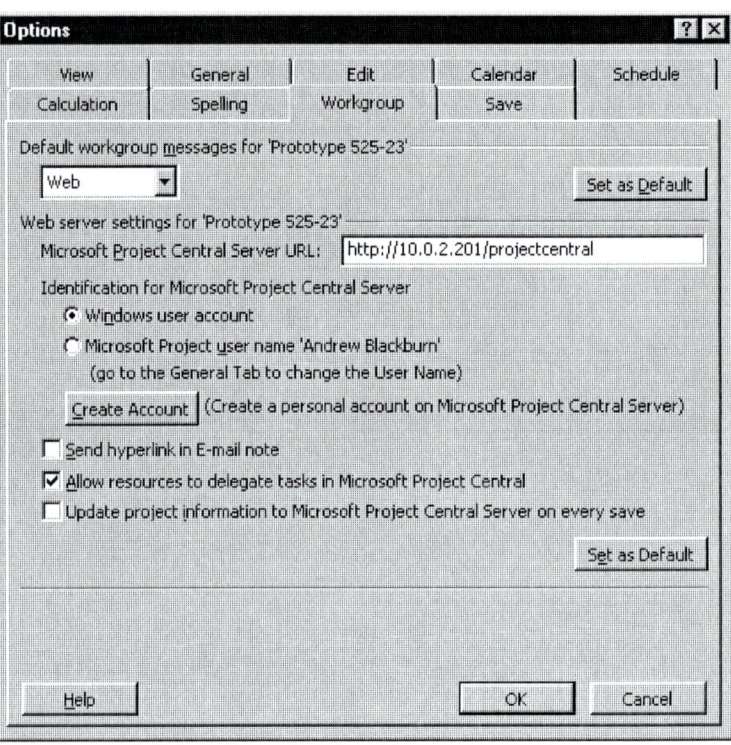 tool button to open the **Resource Information** dialog box.

♦ Click the **General** tab, open the **Workgroup** list and choose an option:

Default   the resource must use the communication method that you defined under the **Workgroup** tab of the **Tools - Options** dialog box.

None   if you do not use Workgroup Messaging in your project.

Email to communicate via your company's e-mail system.

Web to communicate via Microsoft Project Central.

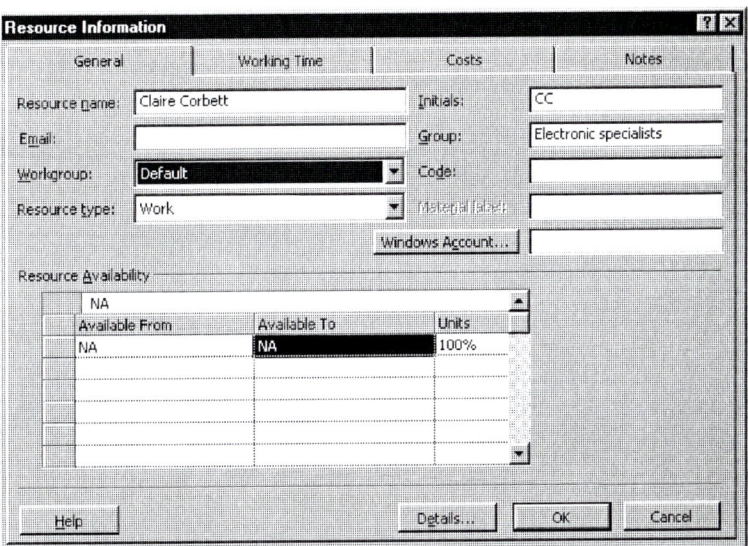

♦ Click the **OK** button.

❑ Microsoft Project applies the **Workgroup: Default** option to all new Work resources that you create.

❑ The **Workgroup** field of the **Resource Information** dialog box is not available for Material resources.

Microsoft Project 2000

Entering the e-mail address of a resource

♦ Display the Resource Sheet using **View - Resource Sheet**.

♦ Use the **Insert - Column** command and insert the **Email Address** field into the sheet. Click **OK**.

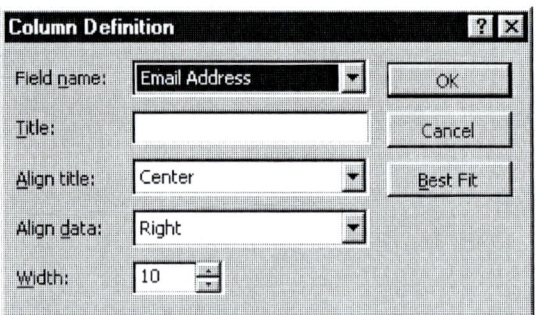

♦ Enter the **Email Address** of each work resource with whom you want to communicate by e-mail.

If the resource is located outside your organisation, then its e-mail address could have a format similar to the following: firstname.surname@supplier.suffix.

You can also enter or modify the e-mail address of a resource by selecting the resource concerned, choosing **Project - Resource Information** and completing the **Email** field under the **General** tab.

Sending an e-mail to a resource

Sending a note about a task

♦ Select the task(s) for which you want to make a comment.

The resources assigned to the selected tasks must be exclusively work resources and they must have e-mail addresses.

♦ **Tools**
Workgroup
Send Schedule Note

♦ In the **Address message to** frame, select the recipient category from the following options:

Project manager   to send the note to the project manager. To choose this option, the **Manager** field in **File - Properties - Summary** tab must be completed.

Resources   to send the note to all the work resources assigned to the whole project (if you choose **Entire project**) or only the resources assigned to the selected tasks (if you choose **Selected tasks**).

Contacts   to send the note to the designated contacts for the project task(s). To do this, make sure that the **Contact** field has been entered in the Gantt Chart entry sheet and that it contains the name of the person in charge of that task.

♦ To attach the whole project **File** or just a **Picture of selected tasks** to the note, tick the appropriate option in the **Attach** frame.

♦ Click **OK** to confirm.

Your computer's default mail application appears in a new window.

♦ Set up your message using this mail program (enter a **Subject** and the body of your message in the message box).

Microsoft Project 2000

If you use Microsoft Outlook 2000, you will see a window similar to the following:

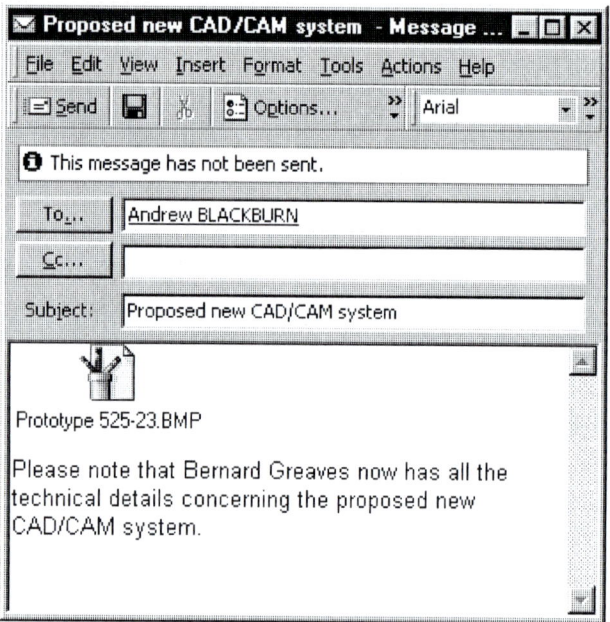

♦ Send your message, as you normally would.

*The message window closes as soon as you have sent your message. Microsoft Project 2000 does not indicate that you have sent a message. On the other hand, your mail application stores a trace of your message in its **Sent Items** folder.*

❑*If you send the complete project **File** with your message (the **Prototype 525.mmp** file, for example), the resource must have Project 2000 to open it. If you send just a **Picture of selected tasks**, you send a bitmap file that the resource will be able to view using standard Windows tools. Here is an example of such a file:*

ID	Task Name	Work	Baseline	'00 F	T	11 Dec '00 S	W	08 Jan '01 S	T	05 Feb ' M	F
9	Mechanical Design	350 hrs	350 hrs					Andrew Blackburn			

Sending a TeamAssign message to a resource

♦ View the tasks of your project and select the task concerned by the assignment.

♦ **Tools**
Workgroup
TeamAssign

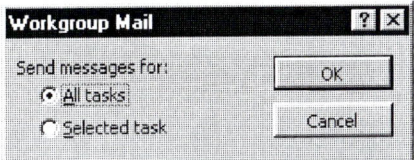

♦ In the **Workgroup Mail** dialog box, choose to **Send messages for All tasks** or for the **Selected task**, as required.

♦ Click the **OK** button.

*The **TeamAssign** dialog box appears.*

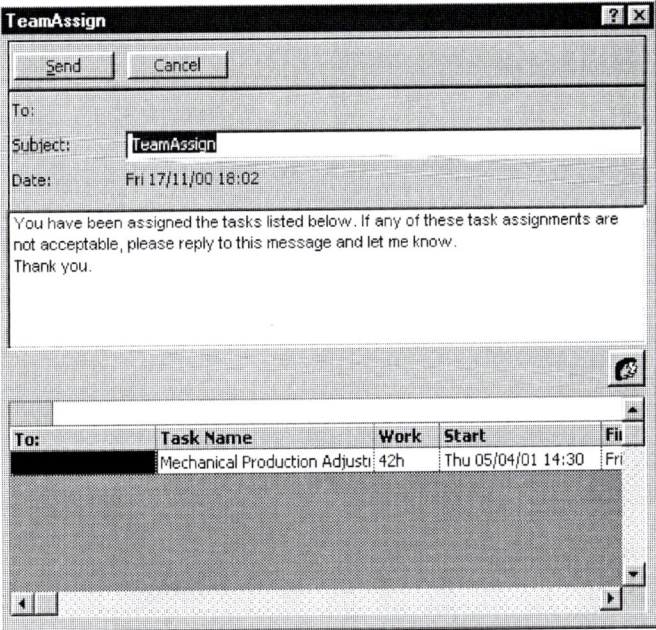

*This dialog box has two main frames. The upper frame contains the message itself, along with its **Subject**, its **Date** and its recipient (the **To** field: note that this field will be empty if you have not yet assigned a resource to the task concerned).*
The lower frame of this dialog box contains information on the task and the resource(s) that you are assigning to it.

♦ If necessary, modify the **Subject** and/or the message itself.

♦ You can enter or modify the resource name in the **To** field of the lower frame of the **TeamAssign** dialog box, using the button.

*If you click this button, the **Resource Assignment** dialog box appears.*

♦ To send your message, click the **Send** button of the **TeamAssign** dialog box, or choose to **Cancel** your message.

❑ *The Entry Sheet of the **Gantt Chart** shows the* *icon in the Indicators column, to the left of the **Task Name** for which you sent your **TeamAssign** message. This icon will remain until all the resources concerned have replied to this message.*

Sending a TeamStatus message to a resource

♦ Display the tasks.

♦ Update the project (**Tools - Tracking - Update Project - OK**).

♦ Select the task concerned by the status request.

♦ **Tools**
  Workgroup
  TeamStatus

♦ In the **Workgroup Mail** dialog box, choose to **Send messages for All tasks** or for the **Selected task**, as required.

♦ Click the **OK** button.

Microsoft Project 2000

*The **TeamStatus** dialog box appears.*

This dialog box has two main frames. The upper frame contains
the message itself, along with its **Subject**, its **Date** and its recipient. The lower frame of this dialog box contains information on
the task and the resource(s) that are assigned to it.

♦ If necessary, modify the **Subject** and/or the message itself.

♦ To send your message, click the **Send** button of the **TeamStatus**
dialog box, or choose to **Cancel** your message.

❏ *The Entry Sheet of the Gantt Chart shows the ⬛ icon in the Indicators column, to the left of the **Task Name** for which you sent
your **TeamStatus** message. This icon will remain until all the resources concerned have replied to this message.*

Sending a TeamUpdate message to a resource

*The project manager sends a **TeamUpdate** message by e-mail, or via Microsoft Project Central, to inform resources of changes that have been made to tasks to which they are assigned (for example, this may be to tell them that the start or finish date, or the assignment itself has been changed). You can send this notification message only to resources that have previously replied, accepting the task assignment concerned.*

♦ As project manager, select the task concerned and make the changes that you require.

*The Entry Sheet of the **Gantt Chart** shows the icon in the Indicators column, to the left of the **Task Name** for the task that you modified. This is to remind you to send a **TeamUpdate** message to the resources concerned.*

♦ **Tools**
Workgroup
TeamUpdate

*The **TeamUpdate** dialog box appears.*

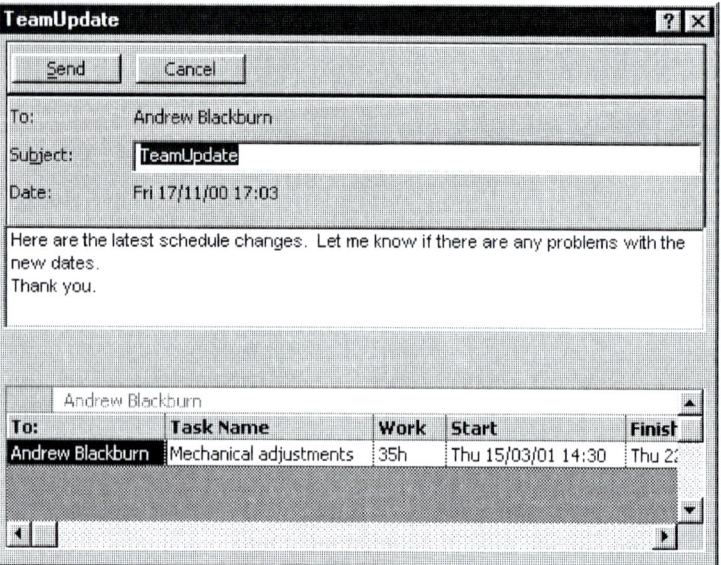

♦ If necessary, modify the **Subject** and/or the message itself.

♦ To send your message, click the **Send** button of the **Team-Update** dialog box or choose to **Cancel** your message.

As soon as you send this message, the icon disappears from the Indicators column to the left of the Task Name.

❏ *The **Update Needed** filter allows you to display only those tasks that you have modified and for which you must send a **Team-Update** message to the workgroup members concerned.*

Replying to an e-mail using Microsoft Outlook

Accepting/refusing a task assignment (TeamAssign)

♦ As a resource, go into the Microsoft Outlook application and open the **TeamAssign** message.

The mail application of the resource receives this message, made up of a header and an attached file called MSPJ.MXM. Before you can reply to such messages, you must have installed the WGsetup program (see the "Usage Constraints" section in the "How to communicate" chapter).

♦ Click the **Reply** button to reply to the message, or click the **Close** button if you do not want to reply to the message.

If you do not reply to this message then Microsoft Project will consider that you accept the assignment by default.

Microsoft Project 2000

◆ When you reply to this message, you can accept or refuse the assignment. To do this, double-click the **Accept?** header to activate **Yes** or **No**.

◆ If you wish, you can add a note in the **Message** frame.

◆ Click **Send** or **Close**.

❏ *If you accept a task assignment that was sent to you by Microsoft Project, Microsoft Outlook 2000 will add this task into your* ***Tasks*** *folder.*

Providing progress status information on a task (TeamStatus)

◆ As a resource, go into the Microsoft Outlook application and open the **TeamStatus** message.

The mail application of the resource receives this message, which Microsoft Project generates as a header, and an attached file of the type MSPJ.MXM. Before you can reply to such messages, you must have installed the WGsetup program (see the "Usage Constraints" section in the "How to communicate" chapter).

♦ To postpone your reply, click the **Save and Send Later** button.

♦ If you do not want to reply to the message, click **Close**.

♦ To reply to the message at once, click the **Reply** button.

*When you click the **Reply** button, it changes to a **Send** button.*

♦ Before you send your reply, modify as necessary the information in the lower frame of this dialog box. In addition, you can add a note in the **Message** frame if you wish.

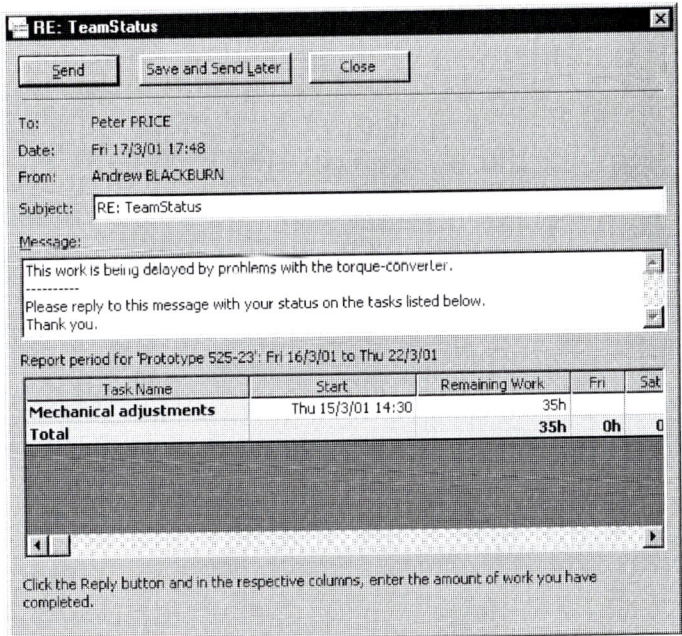

♦ Click the **Send** button to send your reply at once or click the **Save and Send Later** button if you prefer to reply later.

Dealing with a reply from a resource using Microsoft Outlook

*When resources have replied to **TeamStatus** and **TeamAssign** messages received from the project manager, the project manager can update the tasks concerned from the e-mail application.*

Updating task assignments with Microsoft Outlook (TeamAssign)

♦ As project manager, go into Microsoft Outlook and open the message that you have received from the resource. The subject of this message is **RE: TeamAssign**.

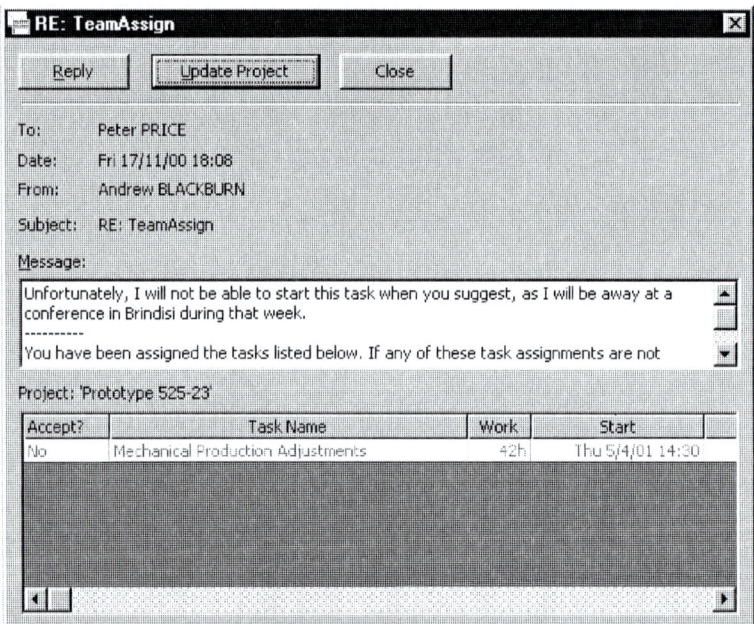

♦ To ask the resource for further details on this message, click **Reply** and prepare and send your message as you would normally do.

This action will not affect the task concerned in your project.

♦ To confirm the assignment, or to cancel it, according to the resource's reply, click the **Update Project** button.

If it is not already running, Project 2000 will start up automatically and will open the project concerned.

*In the Entry Table of the **Gantt Chart**, the* 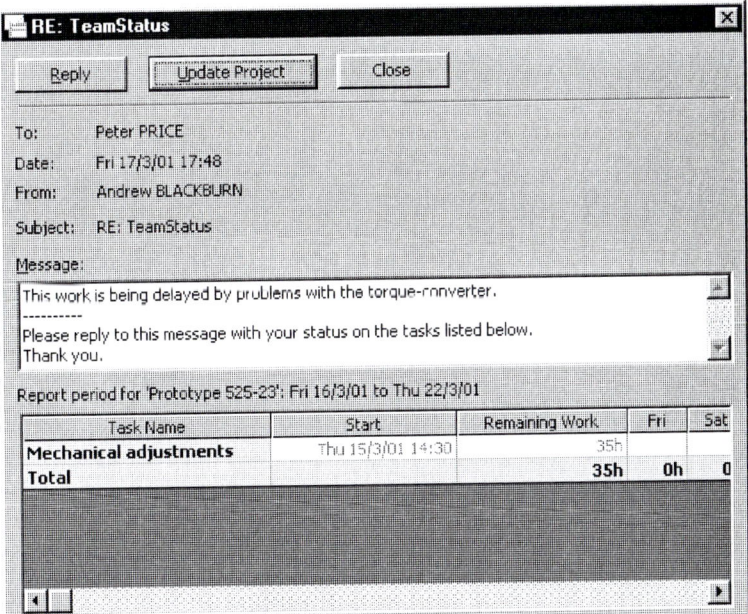 *icon that indicates that you are awaiting a **TeamAssign** reply for the task concerned, will no longer appear (provided that you are not still waiting for a **TeamStatus** reply from another resource for this task).*

♦ In Project 2000, click the ![tool] tool button, if you want to modify the resource assignment according to the response that you received.

Updating task status with Microsoft Outlook (TeamStatus)

♦ As project manager, go into Microsoft Outlook, and open the message that you have received from the resource. The subject of this message is **RE: TeamStatus**.

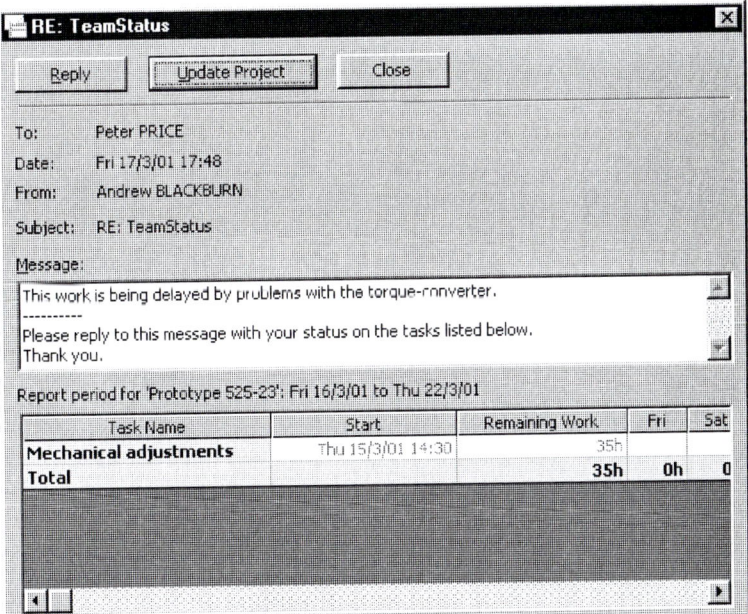

♦ You can ask the resource for further details on this message by clicking the **Reply** button, then preparing and sending your message as you would normally do.

This action will not affect the task concerned in your project.

♦ To adjust the task status in your project, click the **Update Project** button.

If it is not already running, Project 2000 will start up automatically and open the project concerned. Project will then use the transmitted data to update the corresponding fields in your project.

❑ *In the Entry Table of the Gantt Chart, the* *icon that indicates that you are awaiting a* **TeamStatus** *response for the task concerned will no longer appear (provided that you are not still waiting for a* **TeamStatus** *reply from another resource for this task).*

. . . . *Personal notes* . . . .

Introducing Microsoft Project Central

♦ Microsoft Project Central allows you to define the information that specific users may access. Four main elements of Microsoft Project Central make this possible:

– The Microsoft Project Central administrator defines the **Views**. By defining fields and filters, the administrator organises and controls the project information that is available on-line.

– Each **User** is assigned to a Microsoft Project Central category. This assignment determines the views, the projects and the project information to which the user has access. For example, a user may be able to see all the tasks to which resources have been assigned, or only those tasks to which certain resources have been assigned, or only those tasks to which he/she has been assigned.

– Project Central **Categories** associate users, projects and views. When you associate a user with a category, then that user can access certain projects, possibly using specific views.

– The **Update method** allows you to define how Microsoft Project Central must update projects.

Setting up a Windows account in Microsoft Project 2000

*You must have an account to connect to Project Central. If you choose **Windows user account** as the identification method, then when the project manager first sends a message to a workgroup member, Microsoft Project Central will automatically create an account for the user, with **Resource** rights by default. However, to enable Project Central to do this, the project manager must first set up an account for each workgroup member in the Project 2000 application.*
*Consequently, when you define the identification method as **Windows user account**, you must set up Windows accounts for each of your resources.*

♦ Show the **Resource Sheet**.

♦ Use the **Insert - Column** command and insert the **Windows User Account** field.

♦ For each resource that must connect to Project Central using his/her **Windows user account**, give the name of this account in the following format: Domain name\User name, then enter.

❏ *You can also define a Windows user account for a resource under the **General** tab of the **Resource Information** dialog box, by clicking the **Windows Account** button. Microsoft Project then searches the network for the Windows user account.*

❏ *If Project finds the appropriate account, then click **Yes**. Otherwise display more names and make your choice.*

Accessing Microsoft Project Central

You can open Microsoft Project Central either with Project 2000 or with a Web browser (the examples in this chapter were created using Microsoft Internet Explorer 5).

♦ To connect to Project Central from Project 2000, select the **Tools - Workgroup - TeamInbox** command.

*The **Welcome to Microsoft Project Central** page opens automatically in your browser, provided that Project Central is able to identify your Windows user account. You must have previously defined this account on the Project Central server.*

*However, for workgroup members who identify themselves using a Microsoft Project user name, rather than a Windows user account, Project Central displays the following dialog box, so they can enter their **User Name** and **Password**:*

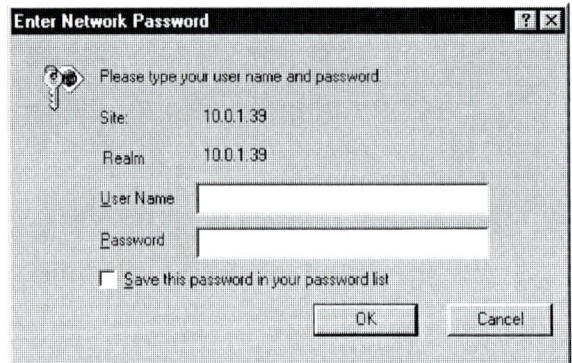

♦ To access Microsoft Project Central from your Web browser, open your Web browser, and in the address box, enter the URL address of your Project Central server.

Description of the Microsoft Project Central screen

*This screen offers different options according to your user category (**Manager**, **Administrator**, or **Resource**). For example, as a **Manager** or a **Resource** you will not have access to the **Admin** page, which is reserved for **Administrators**.*

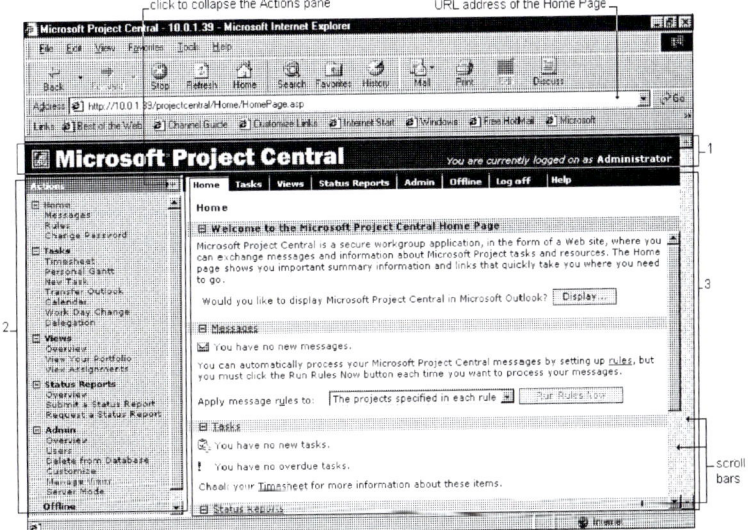

The Project Central screen comprises three main areas:

1 -   The page header that indicates the name of the application (Microsoft Project Central) and your user name.

2 -   The Actions pane that lists all the actions you can carry out, grouped by type of action.

*3 -   The work area. The menu bar at the top allows you to open the different pages of this screen. The **Home Page** appears by default. The number of pages offered will vary according to your user category (Manager, Administrator, or Resource).*

♦ To view different parts of the screen, use the horizontal and vertical scroll bars as necessary.

♦ You can access the different Actions pages (**Home**, **Tasks**, **Views**, **Status Reports**, **Admin**, **Offline**, **Log off**, or **Help**) in two ways:

    – either click the corresponding tab in the work area,

    – or click the corresponding link in the Actions pane.

In addition, the Home Page provides links to other pages, such as the Tasks page.

♦ To access specific parts of each page, click the corresponding menu in the work area menu bar. Alternatively, point to the corresponding menu, and choose one of the options that appear.

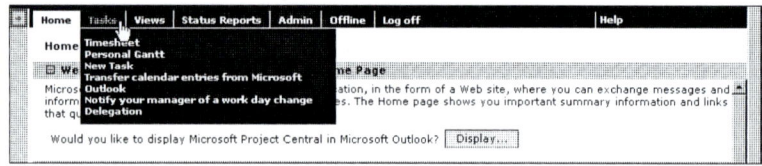

*You can access most of the Microsoft Project Central screen pages using the options in the **Actions** frame.*

♦ Each Project Central page provides information and links to the other pages:

Home	**Information on** the numbers of new tasks or messages received.
	Links to messages, rules, tasks in a timesheet, status reports, your portfolio or assignments and Project Central administration, to customise this application.
Tasks	**Information on** tasks in a timesheet.
	Links to Gantt charts.

Views	**An overview of** how to customise the views.
	Links to your portfolio or assignments.
Status Reports	**Links to** the different status report actions.
Admin (reserved for administrators)	**An overview of** administrative actions.
	Links to managing user accounts, deleting database elements, customising Project Central features, the server setup.
Offline	**Information on** working offline.
	Links to logging off the network.
Log off	Closes the session.
	Links to opening a new session (if you use Windows user account identification, log on again in Project 2000 or your browser).
Help	Project Central online help.

Managing user accounts in Project Central

*With Windows user account identification, when the project manager sends a message to a workgroup member, then Project Central automatically creates a user account for the workgroup member, provided that this account does not already exist, and that you fill in the Windows user account field correctly. However, if the Microsoft Project Central administrator wants to define status reports or message rules for a specific group member before they receive messages, then the administrator must create the accounts in Project Central manually. Only **Administrators** can manage user accounts in Project Central.*

Creating a Project Central account

♦ To create a Project Central user, you must log on to Microsoft Project Central with an account that has Administrator rights.

*Project Central creates the **Administrator** user account automatically when you install this application on the server.*

♦ Point to the **Admin** menu and choose the **Users** option.

The list of users appears in a table.

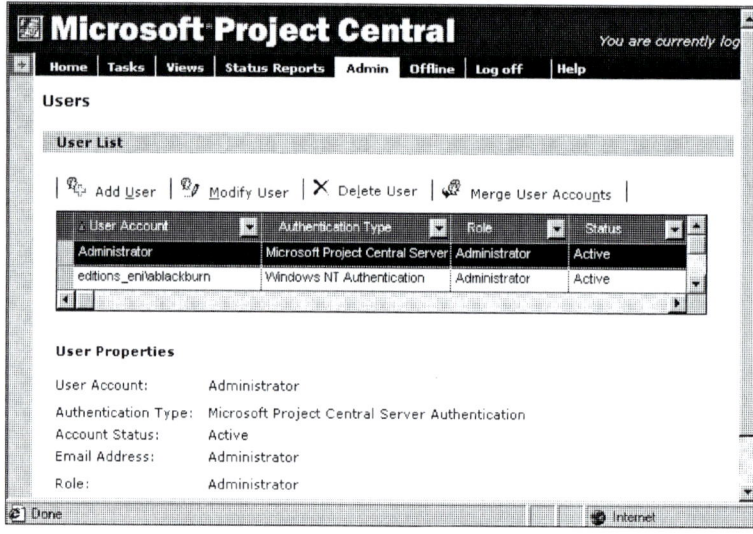

♦ Click the **Add User** button.

♦ Use the vertical scroll bar to display the following entry fields:

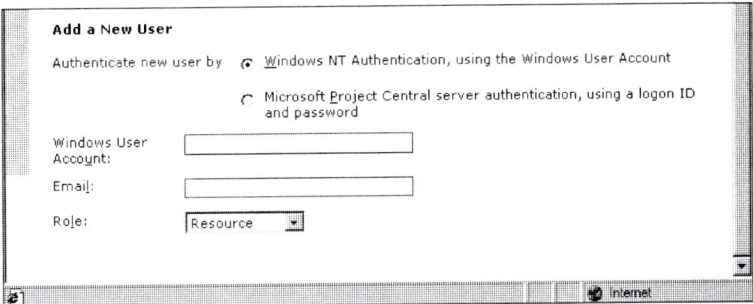

♦ Choose how your new user must be authenticated, from the following list of options:

  – **Windows NT Authentication, using the Windows User Account**: choose this option if you chose **Windows user account** as the identification method in Microsoft Project 2000.

  – **Microsoft Project Central server authentication, using a logon ID and password**: choose this option if you want the user to enter a user name and a password when he/she logs on.

♦ Fill in the boxes to define the new user (the boxes differ according to the chosen option). If you chose **Windows NT Authentication, using the Windows User Account**, specify the **Windows User Account**. On the other hand, if you chose **Microsoft Project Central server authentication, using a logon ID and password**, specify the **User Account** and **Password**.

♦ Whatever authentication method you choose, you must specify the **Email** and you must choose the **Role** from a drop down list: **Resource**, **Manager**, or **Administrator**.

*Project Central provides several user categories, each of which has specific default access rights to information. When you choose the **Role** of the new user, you automatically assign it to a category.*

*You can change a user's access rights by going into the **View** menu and specifying the data that users from each of these categories are allowed to access. This book does not give details of the procedure.*

♦ To confirm your new user account, click the **Save Changes** button at the top of the page. Alternatively, you can cancel this new account by clicking **Cancel**.

*If you choose to **Save Changes**, Microsoft Project Central notifies you when it has completed the update. In this case, click **OK**.*

Modifying a Project Central account

♦ Show the **Users** table, with the **Users** option from the **Admin** menu.

♦ Click the row of the **User Account** that you want to modify.

♦ Click the **Modify User** button.

♦ Use the vertical scroll bar to display the user entry fields and make the required modifications.

♦ Click the **Save Changes** button at the top of the page to confirm your changes, or click **Cancel** if you do not want to save them.

Deleting a Project Central account

♦ Show the **Users** table, with the **Users** option from the **Admin** menu.

♦ Click the row of the **User Account** that you want to delete.

♦ Click the **Delete User** button.

The following warning appears:

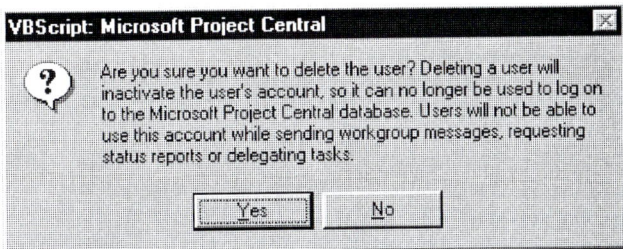

Note that Microsoft Project Central does not really delete the user account. It merely deactivates it.

♦ Click **Yes** to deactivate the user or **No** to leave the user active.

Sending a message to Project Central

*As project manager, when you have chosen the Web identification method and set the **Windows Account**, **Workgroup** and **Email** fields in the **Resource Information** dialog box for each workgroup member, then you can send messages to these workgroup members from Project 2000 to Project Central, via the Web. You can send a message via the Web, in the way described in the "Sending an e-mail to a resource" section.*

Sending a TeamAssign message

♦ View the **Gantt Chart**.

♦ Select the task concerned then use the **Tools - Workgroup - TeamAssign** command.

Microsoft Project 2000

♦ In the **Workgroup Mail** dialog box, choose to **Send messages for All tasks** or for the **Selected task**, as required. Then click the **OK** button.

♦ In the **TeamAssign** dialog box, specify the **To** field, modify the message as necessary and click the **Send** button.

To troubleshoot message transmission errors, see the "Using the Microsoft Project Central Spooler" section below.

Sending a TeamStatus message

♦ View the **Gantt Chart**.

♦ Select the task concerned then use the **Tools - Workgroup - TeamStatus** command.

♦ In the **Workgroup Mail** dialog box, choose to **Send messages for All tasks** or for the **Selected task**, as required. Then click the **OK** button.

♦ In the **TeamStatus** dialog box, modify the message as necessary and click the **Send** button.

Using the Project Central Spooler

Project 2000 uses the Project Central Spooler to forward messages from the Project 2000 workgroup to Project Central. If the message has been forwarded correctly, the Project Central Spooler displays the [icon] icon to the right of the status bar. When a problem occurs, the [icon] icon appears instead.

♦ To view a message transmission problem, double-click the icon to the right of the status bar.

```
■ Microsoft Project Central Spooler                                [×]
  File  Edit  Actions  Help
Microsoft Project Central Spooler Error
A web server error has occurred : (0x8C040018)
Message Type : TeamStatus
Resource : Andrew Blackburn
Project File : Prototype 525-23.mpp
Microsoft Project Central Spooler Server : http://10.0.1.39/projectcentral
```

If a problem occurs with the message transmission, the Spooler displays the type of error that occurred, the resource to whom you tried to send the message, the Project file from which you sent the message, and the server associated with this workgroup message.

♦ When you have solved the problem, you can resend your message(s) by opening the **Actions** menu in the **Microsoft Project Central Spooler** window and choosing the **Resubmit Messages** option.

♦ To cancel (roll back) all your messages, use the **Actions - Rollback Project** command.

♦ To close the **Microsoft Project Central Spooler** window, use **File - Exit**.

Managing messages for a resource in Project Central

To view and reply to messages from the project manager, the resource must activate Microsoft Project Central.

♦ On the resource machine, go into the Web browser, give the URL address of the server on which Project Central is installed, and enter.

*If the resource is identified by his/her Windows user account, the Microsoft Project Central Home page appears automatically. Otherwise, the resource must enter his/her **User Name** and **Password** (cf. "Accessing Microsoft Project Central").*

Microsoft Project 2000

247

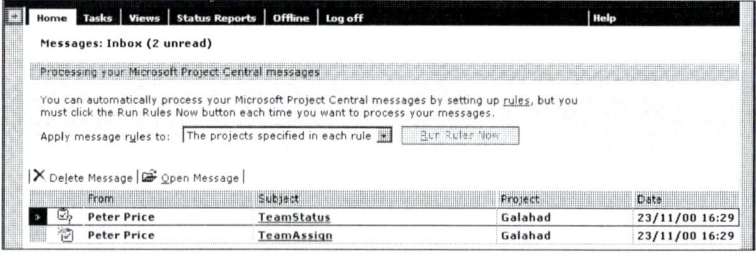

If you are a resource, you cannot access the **Admin** *menu. Microsoft Project Central indicates the number of messages that it has received for you (2 messages in this example).*

♦ In the work area of the **Home** page, click the **Messages** link or the **Microsoft Project Central Inbox** link.

The messages appear in a table that has five columns. The messages that you have not yet read appear in bold characters.

As a workgroup member working on a project, you can receive TeamAssign, TeamStatus and TeamUpdate messages, in addition to task delegation messages that inform you of new task assignments that other resources have delegated to you.

As project manager, you can receive replies to TeamAssign messages, replies to TeamStatus messages, or other messages from workgroup members that contain information that you can integrate into your project.

Opening a message

♦ Select the message that you want to consult by clicking the grey square to the far left of the message. Then click the **Open Message** button.

When you select a message, the square turns black and a small grey arrow appears in it.

❏ *You can also open a message by clicking its **Subject**.*

❏ *To delete a message, select it and click **Delete Message**.*

Accepting/refusing a task assignment (TeamAssign)

♦ Open the **TeamAssign** message.

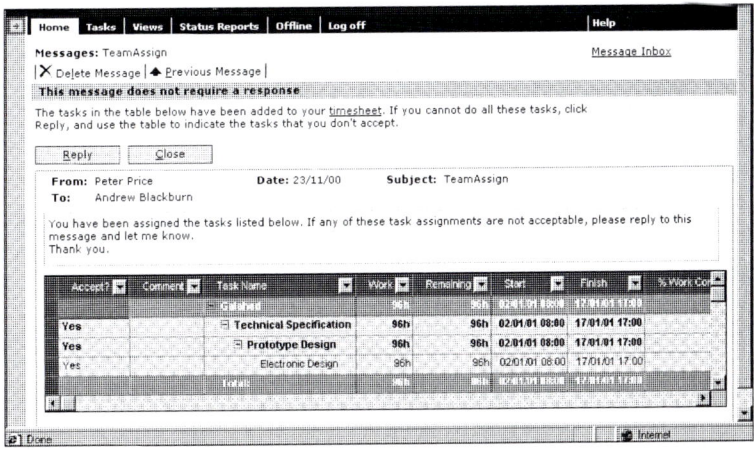

Microsoft Project 2000

This is an assignment request that the project manager has sent.

♦ Click the **Reply** button to reply to the message, or click the **Close** button if you do not want to reply to the message.

♦ When you reply to this message, you can leave the **Yes** field in the **Accept?** column to accept the task or click **Yes** and choose **No** in the drop-down list to refuse it.

♦ If you wish, you can add a note in the **Original Message** box.

♦ To send your reply, click the **Send** button. Otherwise, click the **Close** button if you want to reply later.

When you reply to a message it disappears from the message list.

When you accept a task it is automatically entered into the tasks list.

When the project manager reads your reply to this assignment request, he/she can update the project accordingly.

Providing progress status information on a task (TeamStatus)

♦ Open the **TeamStatus** message.

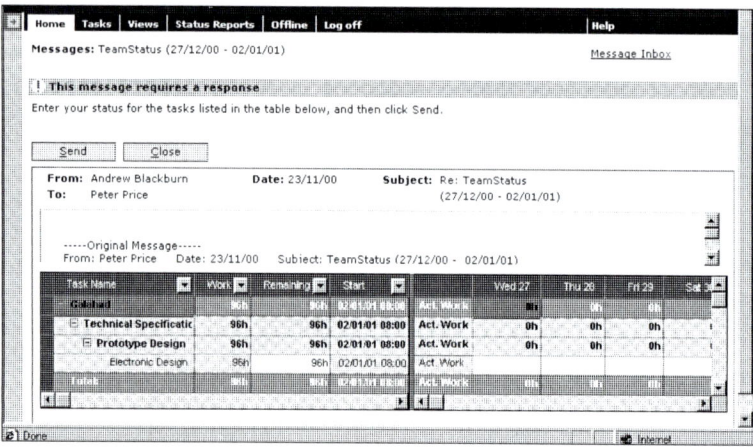

Note that Microsoft Project Central reminds you that this type of message requires a response.

♦ Before you send your reply, you might like to modify the information in the lower frame of this screen. You can add a note in the **Original Message** box if you wish.

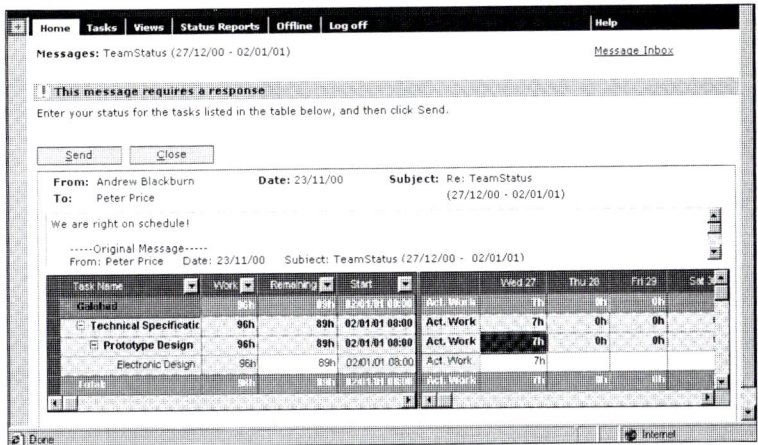

♦ Click the **Send** button to send your reply at once, or click the **Close** button, if you prefer to reply later.

When you reply to a message it disappears from the message list.

Updating tasks in Project Central

As a resource

As a resource, you can use the Timesheet to work directly on the tasks that the project manager has assigned to you.

♦ Log on to the Microsoft Project Central application, as a resource.

♦ Open the **Tasks** menu and choose the **Timesheet** option. If you are in the **Home** page, you can click the **Timesheet** link.

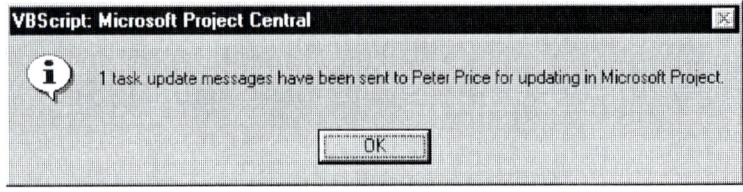

By default, the **View Options** tab is active. The upper part of this screen allows you to define the display options and the lower part shows task information. This task information includes start and finish dates, completed work, remaining work and the name of the project concerned.

This task information is automatically grouped by project name.

♦ To update the task progress, click in the **Act. Work** cell for the date concerned and enter the required number of hours.

♦ To save your changes without advising the project manager, click the **Save Changes** button.

♦ To inform the project manager of the changes that you have made to the Timesheet, click the **Send Update** button.

Microsoft Project Central then tells you how many messages it has sent:

♦ To filter or to sort the tasks that appear in the Timesheet, click the **Filter and Grouping** tab of the **Tasks** screen, then specify your settings using the options and lists provided.

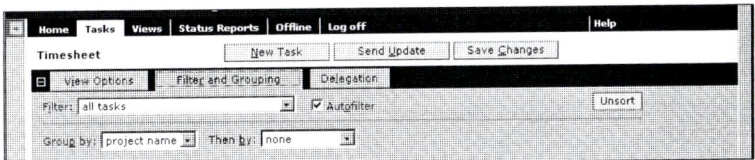

*The **Filter** list contains the filters that you could apply to the tasks. By default, Project Central shows **all tasks**.*
*The **Group by** list box and the **Then by** list box allow you to indicate one or two grouping criteria.*

❑ *The **New Task** button that appears at the top of this page allows the workgroup member to create a new task in a project of his/her choice.*

❑ *Point to the indicators in the left hand column of this table, to view the information associated with them in a ScreenTip.*

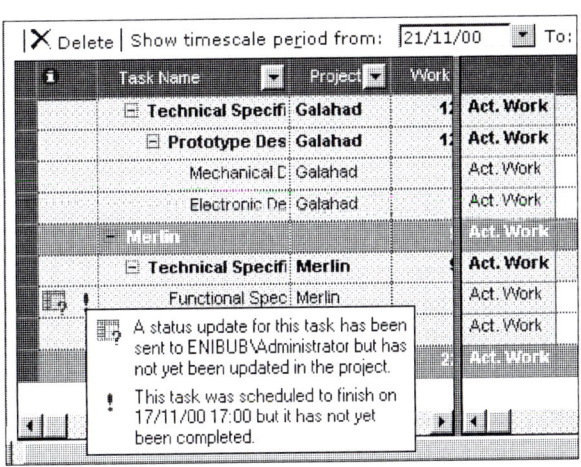

As project manager

When a resource either accepts or refuses a task assignment, or provides information concerning the progress that has been made with a task, the project manager must process the messages from the resource concerned to update the project.

♦ As project manager, go into the Microsoft Project application and open the project that must be updated.

♦ Select the **Tools - Workgroup - TeamInbox** menu option and open the **Home** page of Project Central.

♦ In the **Home** page, click the **Messages** link to view the list of messages that you have received.

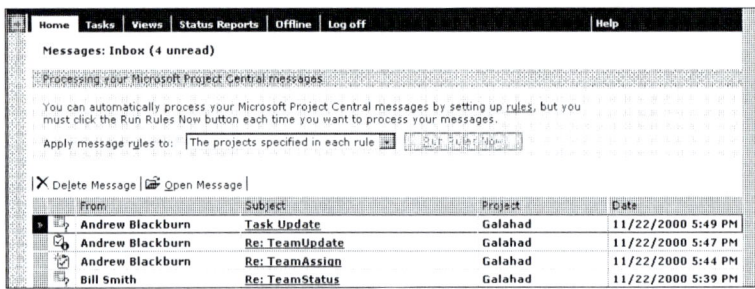

♦ Click the **Task Update** subject, to open the corresponding message.

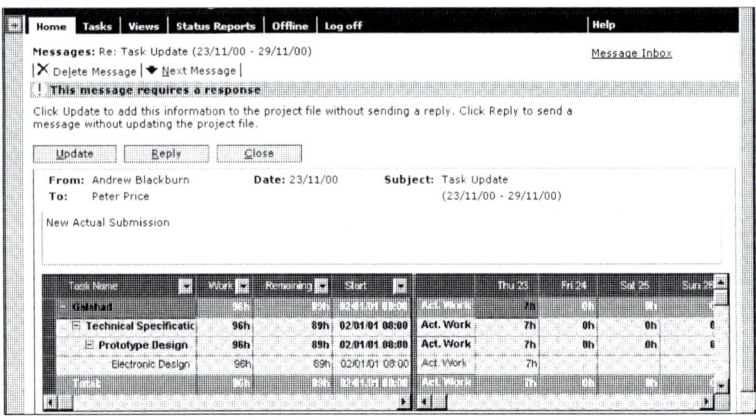

♦ Click the **Update** button, to update your project without replying to the resource that initiated the task update.

After updating your project, Microsoft Project Central asks you whether or not you wish to delete the message from your inbox.

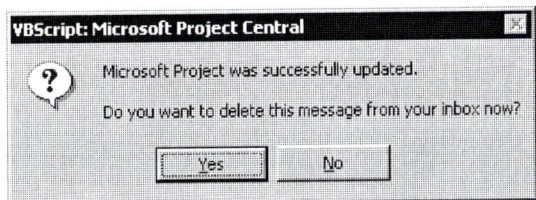

Delegating a task using Project Central

A workgroup member can delegate tasks to another workgroup member using the Project Central application. However, in order to allow this, the project manager and the Project Central administrator must first apply a number of settings.

Enabling task delegation for a project

♦ As project manager, go into the Project 2000 application and open the project in which you want to allow task delegation. Choose the **Tools - Options** menu option, click the **Workgroup** tab and check that the **Allow resources to delegate tasks in Microsoft Project Central** option is active.

♦ As Administrator, log on to the Project Central application.

♦ Select the **Admin - Customize** command and click the **Task Delegation Settings** link.

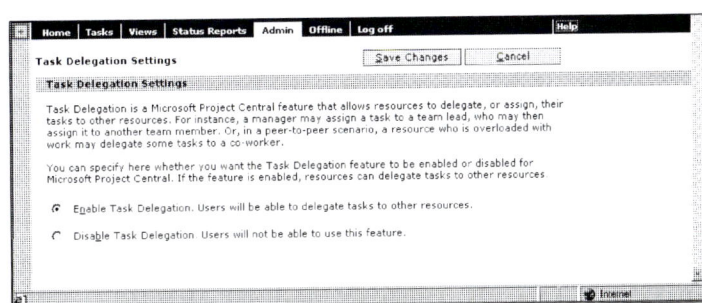

♦ Activate **Enable Task Delegation. Users will be able to delegate tasks to other resources.**

♦ Click the **Save Changes** button.

Delegating a task

When the project manager and the Microsoft Project Central administrator have applied the necessary settings, a workgroup member will be able to delegate a task to another workgroup member, provided that:

– the task is not 100% complete,

– the task has not already been delegated,

– the task does not have actual figures entered and the task is not awaiting update by the project manager.

♦ As the resource that would like to delegate a task, log on to Microsoft Project Central and choose the **Tasks - Delegation** menu option.

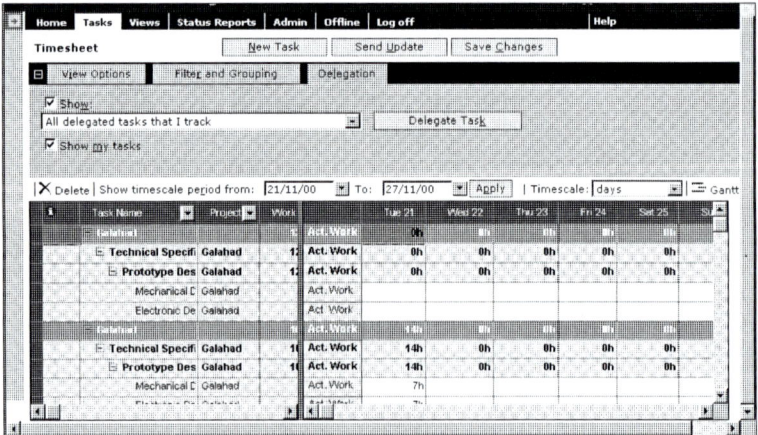

♦ Click the task that you want to delegate to another resource and click the **Delegate Task** button.

*Microsoft Project Central then launches a **Delegate task** wizard, which follows two steps.*

♦ In the first of these steps, you must answer the question **Who do you want to delegate this task to?**: select the resource concerned in the corresponding list box, or choose to **Create a new resource**, if necessary.

♦ If you want to **assume the lead role** for this task, then activate the **Yes** option in response to this question. In this case you will receive, for your approval, notification of the actual figures that the resource submits. When you have done this you must submit these updates to the project manager.

♦ If you want to **track this task** after you have delegated it, then activate the **Yes** option in response to this question. In this case, a copy of this task will appear in your Timesheet. You will not be able to modify it but you will be able to track the updates that the new resource makes.

♦ If you want to send any remarks to the new resource, you can enter them in the **Comments** box.

♦ Click the **Next** button to move on to step 2.

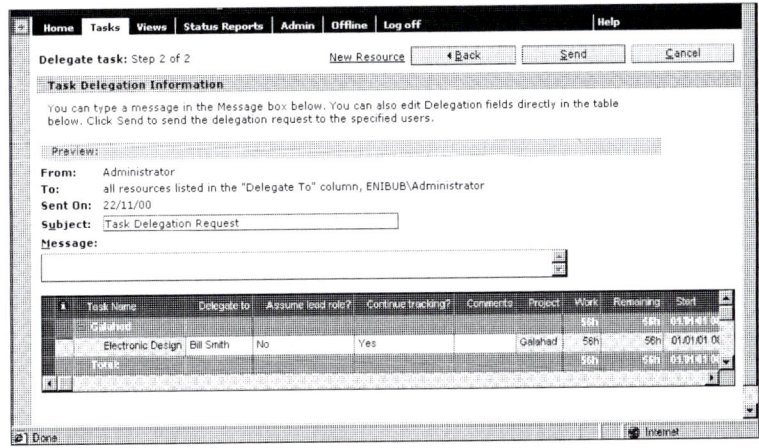

*By default, the **Subject** of your message is **Task Delegation Request**.*

♦ To modify the **Subject** of your message, select the contents of the **Subject** box and enter your new text.

♦ If you wish, you can enter a **Message** to accompany your delegation request.

♦ To return to step 1, click the **Back** button. To send your request to the workgroup members that are listed in the **Delegate to** column, click the **Send** button.

When you have sent your request, Microsoft Project Central reports back to you, confirming the names of the project manager(s) and the resource(s) to whom it has sent your request.

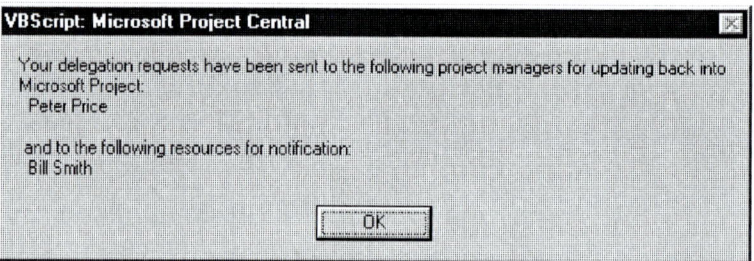

The project manager then receives a Task Delegation Request message stating that a resource to whom he/she assigned a task would like to delegate this task to another resource. The project manager must read and process this message before he/she deals with any other messages that may be in his/her inbox. The project manager can choose to accept or to refuse this delegation request. If the project manager accepts the request, then the new resource assignment will replace the former one.

On the other hand, if the project manager refuses the request then the assignment will remain unchanged. In this case the resource that wanted to delegate the task receives a message stating that the project manager has not accepted the request. In addition, the task is removed from the task list of the resource to whom the task would have been delegated and remains only in the task list of the original resource.

❏ *If a task that you selected cannot be delegated, then Microsoft Project Central displays the message below. In this case, click **OK**, solve the problem and restart the delegation procedure.*

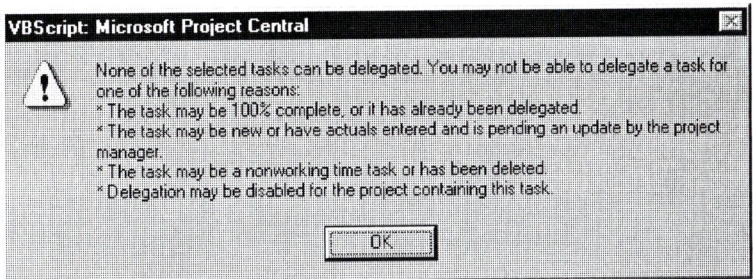

❏ *In the Tasks table the delegated tasks that you chose to track, or for which you chose to assume the lead role, appear in a different colour (in yellow). In addition, if you point to the* *icon that appears to the left of the **Task Name**, then information concerning the delegation appears in a ScreenTip.*

. . . . *Personal notes* . . . .

TASK FIELDS

C = Calculated field, E = Enter field, N = Null

Actual Cost (C-E)	Costs incurred for work already performed by all resources on a task.
Actual Duration (C-E)	Actual working time for a task so far.
Actual Finish (C-E)	Actual task finish date and time.
Actual Overtime Cost (C)	Actual costs incurred for overtime work by all assigned resources.
Actual Overtime Work (C)	Actual overtime work by all resources assigned to a task.
Actual Start (C or E)	The date and time that a task actually began.
Actual Work	Actual work done by the resources assigned to a task.
ACWP (C)	Actual cost of work.
Assignment (C)	Indicates an assignment row.
Assignment Delay (N)	Amount of time a resource is to wait before starting work on an assignment.
Assignment Units (N)	Percentage or number representing the assigned resource allocation.
BAC (C-E)	Budget at completion.
Baseline Cost (C-E)	Total planned cost for a task. See also BAC.
Baseline Duration (C-E)	Original span of time planned to complete a task.
Baseline Finish (C-E)	Planned completion date for a task at the time a baseline was saved.
Baseline Start (C-E)	Planned start date for a task at the time you saved a baseline.
Baseline Work (C-E)	Originally planned amount of work by all resources assigned to a task.
BCWP (C)	Budgeted cost of work planned, also known as earned value.
BCWS (C)	Budgeted cost of work scheduled.
Confirmed (C)	Indicates if resources assigned to a task have accepted or rejected the task assignment in response to a TeamAssign message.
Constraint Date (E)	Specific date associated with certain constraint types.
Constraint Type (E)	Type of constraint which can apply for scheduling a task.
Contact (E)	Name of an individual responsible for a task.
Cost (C-E)	Total planned, or projected, cost for a task. This can also be referred to as estimate at completion (EAC).
Cost Rate Table (N)	Options for cost rate tables to use for resources assigned to a task.
Cost Variance (C)	Difference between the baseline cost and total cost for a task. Also referred to as variance at completion (VAC).

Cost 1-10 (E)	Custom task cost information entered in the project.
Created (C)	Date and time at which a task was added to the project.
Critical (C)	Task is on the critical path.
CV (C)	Earned value cost variance, i.e. the difference between planned and actual costs of a task at the status date or today's date.
Date1-10 (E)	Specialised task date information entered and stored separately in a project.
Dead line	Target date for task completion.
Duration (C-E)	Total span of active working time for a task.
Duration Variance (C)	Difference between the baseline duration of a task and the total duration (current estimate) of a task.
Duration1-10 (E)	Specialised task duration information entered and stored separately in a project.
EAC (C-E)	Estimate at completion i.e. total planned, or projected, cost for a task.
Early Finish (C)	Earliest date that a task can possibly finish.
Early Start (C)	Earliest date that a task can possibly start.
Effort Driven (E)	Scheduling for the task is effort driven. Total task work remains at its current value, regardless of how many resources are assigned to the task.
Estimated	Indicates whether or not a task duration is an estimate.
Finish (C-E)	Planned task completion date and time.
Finish Variance (C)	Difference between the baseline finish date of a task and its current finish date.
Finish1-10 (E)	Specific task finish date information entered and stored separately in a project.
Fixed Cost (E)	Task expense not associated with a resource cost.
Fixed Cost Accrual (E)	How and when fixed costs are to be charged, or accrued, to the cost of a task.
Flag1-20 (E)	Marking of a task for further action or identification of some kind.
Free Slack (C)	Amount of time that a task can be delayed without delaying any successor tasks. Also known as free float.
Hide Bar (E)	Indicates if the Gantt bars and Calendar bars for a task are hidden.
Hyperlink (E)	Name, or hyperlink representation, for a hyperlink associated with a task.
Hyperlink Address (E)	Address for a hyperlink associated with a task.
Hyperlink Href (E)	Combination, or concatenation, of the Hyperlink Address and Hyperlink SubAddress fields associated with a task.
Hyperlink SubAddress (E)	Specific location in a document within a hyperlink associated with a task.

ID (C)	Identification number automatically assigned to each task as it is added to the project.
Indicators (C)	Icons showing different types of information about a task.
Late Finish (C)	Latest date at which a task can finish without delaying the finish of the project.
Late Start (C)	Latest date at which a task can start without delaying the finish of the project.
Level Assignments (E)	Indicates whether or not the levelling function can delay and split individual assignments in order to resolve overallocations.
Leveling Can Split (E)	Indicates whether or not the resource levelling function can split remaining work on this task.
Leveling Delay (C-E)	Amount of time that a task is to be delayed from its early start date as a result of resource levelling.
Linked Fields (C)	OLE links to the task.
Marked (E)	Indicates if a task is marked for further action or identification of some kind.
Milestone (C-E)	Milestone tasks.
Name (E)	Name of a task.
Notes (E)	Notes about a task.
Number1-20 (E)	Custom numeric task-related information entered in the project.
Objects (C)	Number of objects attached to a task.
Outline Code 1-10	The alphanumerical code you define to represent a hierarchical task structure.
Outline Level (C)	Number indicating the level of the task in the project outline hierarchy.
Outline Number (C)	Number of the task in the structure of an outline.
Overallocated (C)	Assigned resources on a task cannot execute the task within normal working capacity.
Overtime Cost (C)	Total overtime cost for a task.
Overtime Work (C)	Amount of overtime planned to be used by all resources assigned to a task.
% Complete (C-E)	Current status of a task, expressed as the percentage completion of the task.
% Work Complete (C-E)	Current status of a task, expressed as the percentage of the work completed on a task.
Predecessors (E)	ID numbers for predecessors.
Preleveled Finish (C)	Finish date of a task prior to resource levelling.
Preleveled Start (C)	Start date of a task prior to resource levelling.
Priority (E)	Options for the level of importance to be assigned to a task.
Project (C)	Name of the project from which a task originated.
Regular Work (C)	Total amount of normal working hours planned for all resources assigned to a task.

Remaining Cost (C)	Remaining planned expense of a task.
Remaining Duration (C-E)	Amount of time required to complete the unfinished portion of a task.
Remaining Overtime Cost (C)	Remaining planned overtime expense for a task.
Remaining Overtime Work (C)	Remaining overtime planned by all assigned resources to complete a task.
Remaining Work (C-E)	Amount of time, or person-hours, still required by a resource to complete all assigned tasks.
Resource Group (C)	List of resource groups to which the resources assigned to a task belong.
Resource Initials (C)	Abbreviations of the names of resources assigned to a task.
Resource Names (E)	Names of all resources assigned to a task.
Response Pending (C)	Indicates if an answer has been received from all TeamAssign messages sent to the resources assigned to a task.
Resume (C-E)	Date that the remaining portion of a task should resume, following entry of a new value in the % Complete field.
Rollup (E)	For subtasks: information on the subtask Gantt bars will be rolled up to the summary task bar. For summary tasks: Summary task bar displays rolled up bars.
Start (C-E)	Planned start date and time.
Start Variance (C)	Time difference between baseline start date and currently planned start date for a task.
Start 1-10 (E)	Specific task start date information entered and stored separately in the project.
Stop (C-E)	End date for the actual portion of a task.
Subproject File (E)	Name of a project inserted into the active project file.
Subproject Read Only (E)	Indicates if the subproject of this task is a read-only project.
Successors (E)	ID numbers for successor tasks.
Summary (C)	Summary tasks.
SV (C)	Earned value schedule variance i.e. the difference in cost between current progress and the baseline plan of the task up to the status date or today's date.
Task calendar	Lists all calendars available to be applied to a task.
TeamStatus Pending	Indicates if an answer has been received in response to a TeamStatus message sent to a resource about assigned tasks.
Text 1-30 (E)	Custom text task information.
Total Slack (C)	Amount of time a task can be delayed without delaying the project finish date. Also known as total float.
Type (E)	Choices which control the effect that editing work, assignment units or duration has on the calculations of the other two fields.

Unique ID (C)	Number automatically designated by Microsoft Project when a new task is created.
Unique ID Predecessors (E)	Unique ID numbers for the predecessor tasks.
Unique ID Successors (E)	Unique ID numbers for successor tasks.
Update Needed (C)	Indicates if a TeamUpdate message should be sent to the assigned resources.
VAC (C)	Variance at completion, i.e. the difference between the baseline cost and total cost for a task.
WBS (C-E)	Work breakdown structure code.
Work (C-E)	Total amount of work planned to be performed on a task by all assigned resources.
Work Contour (N)	Determines how work for an assignment is to be distributed across the duration of the assignment.
Work Variance (C)	Difference between baseline work and the currently planned work for a task.

RESOURCE FIELDS

Accrue At (E)	Options for how and when resource standard and overtime costs are to be charged, or accrued, to the cost of a task.
Actual Cost (C)	Sum of costs incurred for the work already performed by a resource for all assigned tasks.
Actual Finish (N)	Actual completion date and time of an assignment.
Actual Overtime Cost (C)	Actual costs incurred for overtime work performed by a resource for all assigned tasks.
Actual Overtime Work (C)	Actual amount of overtime work performed by a resource for all assignments.
Actual Start (N)	Actual assignment start date and time.
Actual Work (C)	Actual amount of work done by a resource for all assignments.
ACWP (C)	Actual cost of work performed for all of a resource's assignments.
Assignment (C)	The Assignment field indicates if a row is an assignment row.
Assignment Delay (N)	Amount of time a resource is to wait before starting work on an assignment.
Assignment Units (N)	Percentage or number representing the amount of a resource's capacity assigned to each of the resource's tasks.
Available From (E)	First date at which a resource is available for work.
Available To (E)	Last date at which a resource will be available for work.
Base Calendar (E)	Indicates which is the base calendar for a resource calendar.

BAC (C-E)	Budget at completion, i.e. total planned cost for a resource for all assigned tasks.
Baseline Cost (C-E)	Total planned cost for a resource for all assigned tasks (see also BAC).
Baseline Finish (N)	Planned completion date for a task or assignment.
Baseline Start (N)	Planned start date for a task or assignment.
Baseline Work (C-E)	Originally planned amount of work for all assignments assigned to a resource.
BCWP (C)	Budgeted cost of work performed.
BCWS (C)	Budgeted cost of work planned.
Can Level (E)	Enables levelling of a resource.
Code (E)	Code, abbreviation, or number to be entered as part of a resource's information.
Confirmed (C)	Indicates whether or not a resource has accepted all task assignments in response to your TeamAssign messages.
Cost (C)	Total planned cost for a resource for all assigned tasks.
Cost Per Use (E)	Cost which accrues each time a resource is used.
Cost Rate Table (N)	Cost rate table options to use for a resource on an assignment.
Cost Variance (C)	Difference between the baseline cost and total cost for a resource.
Cost1-10 (E)	Custom resource cost information entered in the project.
CV (C)	Earned value cost variance, i.e. the difference between planned and actual costs for the resource to achieve the current level of completion up to the status date or today's date.
Date1-10 (E)	Custom fields showing specialised resource date information entered and stored separately in a project.
Duration1-10 (E)	Any specialised resource duration information entered and stored separately in a project.
EAC (C)	Estimate at completion. The Cost field shows the total planned cost for a resource for all assigned tasks.
Email Address (E)	E-mail address of a resource.
Finish (C)	Planned completion date and time for a resource to complete work on all assigned tasks.
Finish 1-10 (E)	Specific custom resource finish date information entered and stored separately in a project.
Flag1-20 (E)	Marking of a resource for further action or identification of some kind.
Group (E)	Name of the group to which a resource belongs.
Hyperlink (E)	Name or hyperlink representation, for a resource.
Hyperlink Address (E)	Address for a hyperlink associated with a resource.

Microsoft Project 2000

Hyperlink Href (E)	Combination, or concatenation, of the Hyperlink Address and Hyperlink SubAddress fields associated with a resource.
Hyperlink SubAddress (E)	Specific location in a document within a hyperlink associated with a resource.
ID (C)	Identification number automatically assigned to each resource by Microsoft Project.
Indicators (C)	Icons showing different types of information about a resource.
Initials (E)	Abbreviation for a resource name.
Leveling Delay (N)	Amount of time an assignment is to be delayed from the planned start date as a result of resource levelling.
Linked Fields (C)	Indicates OLE links to the resource.
Material Label	The unit of measurement entered for a materiel resource.
Max Units (E)	Maximum percentage or number of units of capacity for which a resource is available to accomplish any tasks.
Name (E)	Name of a resource.
Notes (E)	Notes which can be entered concerning a resource.
Number1-20 (E)	Custom numeric resource information entered in the project.
Objects (C)	Number of objects associated with a resource.
Outline code 1-10	The alphanumerical code you define to represent a hierarchical resource structure.
Overallocated (C)	Resource is assigned to do work on all assigned tasks above normal work capacity.
Overtime Cost (C)	Total overtime cost for a resource on all assigned tasks.
Overtime Rate (E)	Overtime pay rate for work performed by a resource.
Overtime Work (C)	Amount of overtime working for all tasks assigned to a resource.
Peak (C)	Maximum percentage or number of units for which a resource is assigned for all tasks.
% Work Complete (C)	Current status of all tasks assigned to a resource.
Phonetics (C-E)	Used only in the Japanese version of Microsoft Project.
Project (C)	Name of the project from which a resource originated.
Regular Work (C)	Normal working hours for all assignments.
Remaining Cost (C)	Remaining planned expense which will be incurred in completing the remaining work assigned to a resource.
Remaining Overtime Cost (C)	Remaining planned overtime expense of a resource.
Remaining Overtime Work (C)	Remaining amount of overtime required by a resource to complete all assigned tasks.
Remaining Work (C)	Amount of working time still required by a resource to complete all assigned tasks.
Response Pending (C)	Indicates if an answer has been received from all TeamAssign messages sent to a resource concerning assigned tasks.

Standard Rate (E)	Wage rate for normal working hours for a resource.
Start (C)	Planned start date and time for an assigned resource to begin working on all assigned tasks.
Start1-10 (E)	Custom fields for any specific resource start date information entered and stored separately in the project.
SV (C)	Earned value schedule variance i.e. cost variations between current progress and the baseline plan of all the resource's assigned tasks up to the status date or today's date.
Task Summary Name (N)	Names of the summary tasks for the task associated with a resource assignment.
TeamStatus Pending (C)	Indicates if an answer has been received in response to a TeamStatus message sent to a resource concerning assigned tasks.
Text1-30 (E)	Custom text information entered in the project regarding resources.
Unique ID (C)	Number automatically designated by Microsoft Project when a new resource is added.
Update Needed (C)	Indicates if a TeamUpdate message should be sent to a resource because of changes to any of the resource's assigned tasks.
VAC (C)	Difference between baseline cost and total cost for a resource.
Windows User Account	The windows user name entered for a work resource.
Work (C)	Total amount of work planned for a resource on all assigned tasks.
Work Contour (N)	Resource assignment contour shape for a resource's assignment.
Work Variance (C)	Difference between total baseline work and currently planned work.
Workgroup (C-E)	Workgroup messaging method for project resources.

ASSIGNMENT FIELDS

Actual Cost (C-E)	Actual costs incurred for work completed by a resource on a task.
Actual Finish (C-E)	Actual assignment completion date and time.
Actual Overtime Cost (C-E)	Actual costs of completed overtime work by a resource on a task.
Actual Overtime Work (C-E)	Actual amount of overtime work completed by a resource on an assigned task.
Actual Start (C-E)	Actual start date and time for an assignment.
Actual Work (C-E)	Actual amount of work completed by a resource on a task.
ACWP (C)	Actual cost of work performed by a resource on a task, up to the project status date or today's date.

Assignment (C)	Indicates an assignment row.
Assignment Delay (C-E)	Amount of time a resource is to wait after the task start date before starting work on an assignment.
Assignment Units (C-E)	Percentage or number of resource units assigned to a task.
BAC (C-E)	Budget at completion i.e. total planned cost for work to be performed by a resource on a task.
Baseline Cost (C-E)	Total planned cost for work to be performed by a resource on a task.
Baseline Finish (C-E)	Planned completion date for an assignment at the time the baseline was saved.
Baseline Start (C-E)	Planned start date for an assignment at the time the baseline was saved.
Baseline Work (C-E)	Originally planned amount of work time to be performed by a resource on a task.
BCWP (C)	Budgeted cost of work performed.
BCWS (C)	Budgeted cost of work planned i.e. costs of an assignment up to the status date or today's date.
Confirmed (C-E)	Accepted or rejection of the task assignment by the resource in response to a TeamAssign message.
Cost (C)	Total planned, or projected, cost for a resource assignment.
Cost Rate Table (E)	Cost rate table options for the resource on an assignment.
Cost Variance (C)	Difference between baseline cost and total cost for a resource assignment on a task.
Cost1-10 (E)	Custom assignment cost information entered in a project.
Critical	Indicates whether the assignment's task is a critical task.
CV (C)	Earned value cost variance shows the difference between planned and actual costs of achievement of the current level of completion.
Date1-10 (E)	Specialised assignment date information entered and stored separately in a project.
Duration1-10 (E)	Custom showing any specialised assignment duration information you want to enter and store separately in your project.
EAC (C)	Total planned, or projected, cost for a resource assignment.
Finish (C-E)	Planned finish date and time for completion work on a task.
Finish Variance (C)	Difference between a resource baseline finish date and currently planned finish date.
Finish1-10 (E)	Specific assignment finish date information entered and stored separately in a project.
Flag1-20 (E)	Marking of an assignment further action or identification of some kind.
Hyperlink (E)	Name or hyperlink representation, associated with an assignment.

Hyperlink Address (E)	Address for a hyperlink associated with an assignment.
Hyperlink Href (E)	Combination, or concatenation, of the Hyperlink Address and Hyperlink SubAddress fields associated with an assignment.
Hyperlink SubAddress (E)	Specific location in a document within a hyperlink associated with an assignment.
Indicators (C)	Icons that showing different types of information about an assignment.
Leveling Delay (C-E)	Amount of delay from the planned start date as a result of re-source levelling for an assignment.
Linked Fields (C)	OLE links to the assignment.
Notes (E)	Notes entered concerning an assignment.
Notes (E) -20 (E)	Custom numeric information entered in the project regarding assignments.
Outline Level (C)	Number that indicating the level of the assignment in project outline hierarchy.
Overallocated (C)	Assignment of a resource above normal working capacity.
Overtime Cost (C)	Total overtime cost for a resource assignment.
Overtime Work (E)	Amount of overtime to be performed by a resource on a task.
Peak (C)	Maximum percentage or number of resource assignment units.
% Work Complete (C-E)	Current status of an assignment, expressed as the percentage of completion.
Priority (C)	Level of importance given to a task, indicating the potential for delaying or splitting an assignment during levelling.
Project (C)	Name of the project from which an assignment originates.
Regular Work (C-E)	Total planned normal working hours by a resource assigned to a task.
Remaining Cost (C)	Remaining planned expense of an assignment.
Remaining Overtime Cost (C)	Remaining planned overtime costs for an assignment.
Remaining Overtime Work (C-E)	Amount of overtime remaining on an assignment.
Remaining Work (C-E)	Amount of working time, still required by a resource to complete an assignment.
Resource Group (C)	Name of the group to which the resource for an assignment belongs.
Resource ID (C)	Identification number assigned to each resource by Microsoft Project.
Resource Initials (C)	Abbreviations of the names of the resources to which an assignment belongs.
Resource Names (C)	Name of the resource to which an assignment belongs.
Response Pending (C-E)	Indicates if an answer has been received from a TeamAssign message sent to a resource assigned to a task.

Start (C-E)	Planned start date and time for an assigned resource to begin working on a task.
Start Variance (C)	Difference between an assignment's baseline start date and its currently planned start date.
Start1-10 (E)	Customised specific assignment start date information entered and stored separately in the project.
SV (C)	Earned value schedule variance i.e. the difference between current progress and baseline costs for the assignment up to the status date or today's date.
Task ID (C)	Number assigned by Microsoft Project to each task as it is added to the project.
Task Name (C)	Name of the task to which an assignment belongs.
Task Summary Name (C)	Name of the summary task for the task associated with the assignment.
TeamStatus Pending (C-E)	Indicates if a status message has been received in response to a TeamStatus message sent to a resource assigned to a task.
Text1-30 (E)	Custom text information entered in the project regarding assignments.
Type	Indicates whether the resource type for this assignment's resource is work or material.
Unique ID (C)	Number automatically designated by Microsoft Project whenever a new assignment is created.
Update Needed (C)	Indicates if a TeamUpdate message should be sent to the resource assigned to a task.
VAC (C)	Variance at completion i.e. the difference between baseline cost and total actual cost for a resource assignment.
Work (C-E)	Total amount of work planned for a resource on a task.
Work Contour (E)	Options for the contour shape for an assignment.
Work Variance (C)	Difference between baseline work and currently planned work for an assignment.

Shortcut keys

File

`Ctrl` **N** or `F11`	New
`Ctrl` **O**	Open
`Ctrl` **P**	Print
`Ctrl` **S**	Save
`F12`	Save As
`Ctrl` `F4`	Close
`Alt` `F4`	Exit

Edit

`Ctrl` **C**	Copy
`Ctrl` **X**	Cut
`Ctrl` **V**	Paste
`Del`	Delete
`Ctrl` **D**	Fill Down
`Ctrl` **F**	Find
`Ctrl` **G** or `F5`	Go To
`Ctrl` `F2`	Link Tasks
`Ctrl` `⇧ Shift` `F2`	Unlink Tasks
`Ctrl` **Z**	Undo
`Ctrl` **H**	Replace
`Ctrl` `Del`	Clear Contents

Insert

`Ins`	New Task/New Resource
`⇧ Shift` `F2`	Task/Resource Information
`Ctrl` **K**	Insert Hyperlink

Window

`⇧ Shift` `F11`	New Window

Planning functions

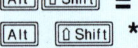

Promote
Demote
Mask subordinate tasks
View subordinate tasks
View all tasks

Opening

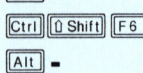

The application **Control** menu
On-line help
Menu bar
Next window
Next sheet
Previous window
Project System menu

Repeating an operation

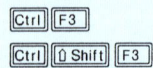

Same filter
Same sort

Calculating

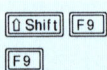

The active project
All open projects

Viewing

All tasks/resources
Column definition dialog box

Using the project window

`Ctrl` `F10`
`Ctrl` `F7`
`⇧ Shift` `F11`

Maximising
Moving
New Window

Restoring

`⇧ Shift` `F3`
`Ctrl` `F5`

Sort in numerical order
Project window

Timescale keys

`Ctrl` `/`
`Ctrl` `⇧ Shift` `*`

Viewing a smaller timescale
Viewing a larger timescale

Various keys

`Alt` `F5`
`F7`
`F1`
`Ctrl` `F9`
`Ctrl` `Del`

Go to the next overallocation
Check spelling
Open Help
Activate/deactivate automatic calculation
Delete the contents of a cell

Standard toolbar

1... ..25

1	New	13	Link Tasks
2	Open	14	Unlink Tasks
3	Save	15	Split Task
4	Print	16	Task/Resource Information
5	Print Preview	17	Resource Notes
6	Spelling	18	Assign Group by Resources
7	Cut	19	Group By
8	Copy	20	Zoom In
9	Paste	21	Zoom Out
10	Format Painter	22	Go To Selected Task
11	Undo	23	Copy Picture
12	Insert Hyperlink	24	Microsoft Project Help

Formatting toolbar

1... ...16

1	Outdent	9	Italic
2	Indent	10	Underline
3	Show Subtasks	11	Align Left
4	Hide Subtasks	12	Centre
5	Show	13	Align Right
6	Font	14	Filter
7	Font Size	15	AutoFilter
8	Bold	16	Gantt Chart Wizard

Tracking toolbar

1... ...11

1	Project Statistics	7	50% Complete
2	Update as Scheduled	8	75% Complete
3	Reschedule Work	9	100% Complete
4	Add Progress Line	10	Update Tasks
5	0% Complete	11	Workgroup Toolbar
6	25% Complete		

Web toolbar

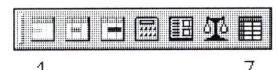

1...   ...10

1	Back	6	Search the Web
2	Forward	7	Favorites
3	Stop Current Jump	8	Go
4	Refresh Current Page	9	Show Only Web Toolbar
5	Start Page	10	Address

PERT Analysis toolbar

1...   ...7

1	Optimistic Gantt	5	PERT Entry Form
2	Expected Gantt	6	Set PERT Weights
3	Pessimistic Gantt	7	PERT Entry Sheet
4	Calculate PERT		

H

HEADERS AND FOOTERS *See PAGE SETUP*

HOURS *See CALENDAR*

HTML FORMAT *See WEB, FILES*

I

L

LEGENDS *See PAGE SETUP*

LEVELLING *See RESOURCES*

M

P

See also WORK

S

T

See also PROJECT CENTRAL

W

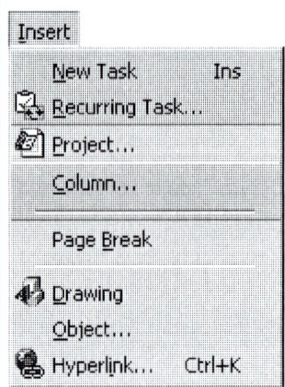

Ⅴiew

Calendar
Diagramme de Gantt
✓ Gantt Chart
Network Diagram
Réseau PERT
Task Usage
Tracking Gantt
Utilisation des tâches

Resource Graph
Resource Sheet
Resource Usage
Tableau des ressources
Utilisation des ressources

More Views...
Table: Work ▶

Reports...

Toolbars ▶
✓ View Bar

Header and Footer...
Zoom...

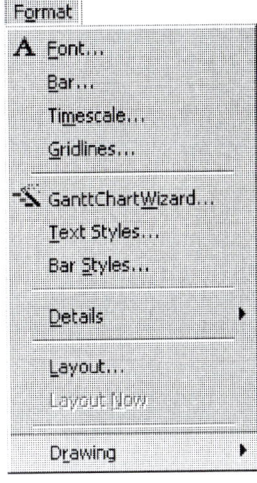

Format

A Font...
Bar...
Timescale...
Gridlines...

GanttChartWizard...
Text Styles...
Bar Styles...

Details ▶

Layout...
Layout Now

Drawing ▶

Project

Sort ▶
Filtered for: All Tasks ▶
Group by: No Group ▶
Outline ▶
WBS ▶

Task Information... Shift+F2
Task Notes...

Project Information...

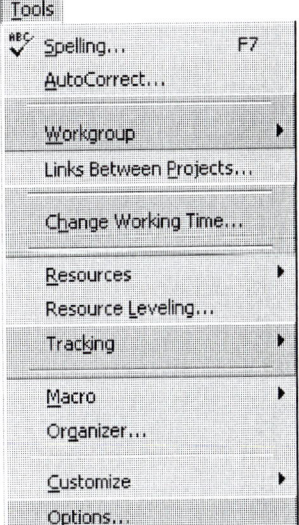

Tools

ᴬᴮᶜ Spelling... F7
AutoCorrect...

Workgroup ▶
Links Between Projects...

Change Working Time...

Resources ▶
Resource Leveling...
Tracking ▶

Macro ▶
Organizer...

Customize ▶
Options...

▲ Quick Reference Guide ▲ Practical Guide ▲ Microsoft® Approved
▲ User Manual ▲ Training CD-ROM Publication

VISIT OUR WEB SITE http://www.eni-publishing.com

Ask for
our free brochure

**For more information
on our new titles
please complete
this card and return**

Name: ....

....

Company: ....

Address: ....

....

Postcode: ....

Town: ....

Phone: ....

E-mail: ....

ENI Publishing LTD

500 Chiswick High Road

London W4 5RG